Global Business Management
Foundations

Leslie P. Willcocks

Steve Brookes
Publishing

3rd edition

A 'Steve Brookes Publishing' book

www.stevebrookes.com

Layout Design:
Stephanie Lester

Cover Design:
Cliff Hayes
www.hayesdesign.co.uk

Copy editor:
Bronwyn Robertson
www.theartsva.com

Author:
Leslie P. Willcocks

This 3rd edition published in 2016 by:
Steve Brookes Publishing
60 Loxley Road
Stratford-upon-Avon
Warwickshire CV37 7DR
United Kingdom
Tel: +44(0)1789 267124
Email: sales@stevebrookes.com

A CIP catalogue record for this book is available from the British Library

ISBN 978-0-956414-53-3

Printed and bound in Malta by Latitude Press Ltd.

Contents

Introduction

CHAPTER 1
Globalization and Trade:
Is It Really a Flat World?

CHAPTER 2
Political, Economic and Legal Environments:
Diversity or Growing Uniformity?

CHAPTER 3
Cultural Social and Ethical Challenges: Towards CSR

CHAPTER 4
Strategy in Global Context: One Size Fits All?

CHAPTER 5
International Competitive Strategy: Debating Approaches

CHAPTER 6
Market Entry and Evolution: Commitment Versus Risk

CHAPTER 7

International Marketing and R&D Strategy: 'Seeing the Business Through the Customers' Eyes'

CHAPTER 8

Structuring and Integrating the International Business

CHAPTER 9
Global Sourcing of Production and Services

CHAPTER 10
Global Information Systems Management

CHAPTER 11
International Dimensions of Human Resources Management

A Guide to Further Reading

References

Introduction

Welcome to the third edition of this book. If business was the same everywhere, we could all get on with providing products or services and, through gaining competitive advantage, make profits. But despite the flattening effects of globalization, international business demonstrates huge diversity and complexity. To understand business context, threats, and opportunities, you need to consider the drivers and nature of globalization, and the political, economic, social, technological, and legal differences that regions and countries exhibit. Then you need to work within the frameworks of multi-lateral organizations and regional economic blocs.

Then, as a manager faced with this complexity and diversity, you need to devise strategies that work internationally, in different parts of the globe, plan entry strategies for new markets, and decide who you need to establish alliances with, and how your strategy is to evolve. You then need to work at the detail of managing. Specifically designing structure and organization, devising sourcing and supply chain arrangements, establishing information systems that perform globally, and distinctive arrangements for managing international human resources.

As a student, you will find understanding and analyzing international business and making managerial judgements full of fresh challenges, and you will also find that the study of this subject area not only provides insights, but also gives you the analytical equipment and knowledge to actually begin to perform in a business that operates globally.

This book is designed as an introduction to the subject, and is based on teaching undergraduate and masters degree courses at the London School of Economics and Political Science, and running executive programmes around the globe over many years. The specific objectives of this book are:

- To give a research-based grounding in the context of international business including the globalizing trends, formal and informal institutions, political, economic, social, technological, and legal issues and the resultant diversity found in international business.

- To prepare readers to be able to discuss cultural, ethical, and social issues for international business and suggest policies on corporate social responsibility.

- To provide an introduction to and develop understanding of international trade and investment, multilateral organizations and regional integration, and the global financial system.

- To establish understanding of and illustrate how firms develop international business, and marketing, and R&D strategies, enter markets and alliances, and evolve on the global stage.

- To give insight through frameworks, studies, and examples of how businesses manage organization structure and architecture, sourcing and the supply chain, information systems and human resources, in different parts of the globe, globally, regionally and domestically.

- To give insight into the contexts of international business, and be able to work within these contexts to make judgements on strategizing and managing operations in the global economy.

The book is structured into two parts. Part One provides an introduction to the global business environment and covers trends towards globalization, and the formal and informal institutions of countries. In particular it focuses on international political, economic, legal, cultural, and social diversity. It also gives you an overview of why international trade takes place, why firms invest abroad, and how the global financial system and the cross-border institutions like the IMF, World Bank and regional economic blocs operate and impact upon business. This first part provides the context of international business. Part Two gives insight into how to analyze that context to arrive at competitive international strategies, enter markets and evolve. It then concentrates on major operational areas of an international business, namely designing the organization, global sourcing and supply chain management, establishing global information systems and managing human resources.

This book grew out of the many requests from students and practitioners for a book based on the courses I have been running over several years. I would like to thank them all for their encouragement and inspiration. My LSE students are a real tonic because they bring bright new brains to subjects that I think I know inside out, only to discover from them new information, new theories, new twists, and other ways of looking at the evidence. This indeed is a marvel of both collective intelligence and also of the cultural diversity we get at the university. I would like to thank the executives too, for their wonderful illustrative stories, the hard-won knowledge they bring to bear on issues, and their kindness and openness when it comes to research access, despite their intensely busy globalized work patterns.

Over the years I have published quite a few books and each time three things seem to be true. The first is that business change is accelerating and bringing with it ever more turbulence and uncertainty. As one example close to home, in June 2016 my own country, the United Kingdom, voted in a national election to leave the European Union. My country steps into an unknown future. The need for managing in a global context has never been more urgent. Secondly, the books have been getting published faster and faster. Thirdly, as evidence for the reality behind the ideas in this book, the process involves more and more people from different countries around the globe.

I would like to thank Steve Brookes and Stephanie Lester (from SB Publishing) for all their encouragement and support in getting this third edition together, and publishing again in a remarkably short time.

I would also like to thank my beloved wife, Damaris, who makes all things possible.

'No man is an island, entire of itself. Each is a piece of the continent, a part of the main'

John Donne, Meditation xvii

'The current state of the world is one of semi-globalization.... distance still matters'

Pankaj Ghemawat, 2007

CHAPTER 1
Globalization and Trade: Is It Really a Flat World?

1.1 Introduction

Globalization can be defined as the shift towards a more integrated and interdependent world economy. In other words, the world is moving away from self-contained national economies, toward an interdependent, integrated global system. A major part of this is increased international trade and foreign direct investment. International trade occurs when a firm exports goods or services to consumers in another country. Foreign direct investment (FDI) occurs when a firm invests resources in business activities outside its home country. What does all this mean? In his 2003 book *The World is Flat* Thomas Friedman gives the example of his Dell notebook. He found it had been designed in Austin Texas, USA and Taiwan. Dell uses 30 key components in the notebook, and these are sourced from over 20 countries around the world, with the factories owned by local firms but also in many cases foreign multinationals – defined here as firms that engage in foreign direct investments and operate in multiple foreign countries. And this is just the start of the notebook's global journey!

What does all this mean for you and me? Consider my own day. I wake up in the UK in a bed made by Sweden's Ikea, get dressed in a shirt made in India, and American Levi's jeans that were produced in China. After putting on my Taiwanese-made trainers, and drinking an Italian-style cappuccino, I drive to work in my Japanese Honda that was manufactured in the UK. On the way to a client headquartered in the Netherlands, but with operations in the UK, I talked to my friend on a Nokia cell phone designed in Finland, about getting together later for Spanish-style tapas and Corona beer from Mexico. As you can see, my day has already been filled with the effects of globalization. But there are others. As examples only, is my job safe? Are there new job prospects? Where is the next technological change going to come from? Is globalization adversely affecting my environment?

From a business perspective, you can think of globalization in terms of the globalization of markets and the globalization of production. The globalization of markets refers to the merging of historically distinct and separate national markets into one huge global marketplace. As trade barriers between countries fall, companies like Ikea, Sony, and Coca-Cola are able to sell their products to a global market where consumers are more and more alike. But the globalization of markets does not mean that consumers are the same everywhere. Important differences between markets do exist. National markets are still very relevant, challenging companies to develop different marketing strategies and operating procedures. The second facet of globalization - the globalization of production - refers to the sourcing of goods and services from locations around the globe to take advantage of national differences in the cost and quality of factors of production like land, labour, and capital. Companies hope that, by sourcing and producing their products in the optimal location, they will be able to better compete against their rivals. Boeing, for example, outsourced about 65 percent of its 787 aircraft manufacture to foreign companies. Boeing believes that this strategy allows it to use the best suppliers in the world, an advantage that will help to win market share over its rival Airbus Industries. Even healthcare is globalized. For example, US and Canadian hospitals now routinely send X-rays via the internet to be read in India, and some insurance companies even recommend having certain medical operations conducted in foreign countries.

This chapter introduces you to globalization and international trade, the trends towards globalization and its main drivers. We explore the major debates for and against globalization, and whether firms wishing to operate internationally can work on the basis of the assumption that the world is flat, or something else. We look at the implications of globalization for firms wanting to extend themselves further globally. We also explore theories of international trade and assess the role of governments and national institutions in supporting or acting as barriers to international trade.

1.2 What Is Globalization?

What is globalization and what are the challenges it raises for business organizations worldwide? Some identify globalization with the accelerated spread of communication and transportation technology. Others identify globalization with the rising power of multinational enterprises (MNEs) and increased inequality in the world. Some experience it as increased competition for jobs, especially for low skilled workers. Others emphasize how globalization is a force eliminating differences amongst distinctive cultures and identities, while still others argue this is exaggerated and the world is still defined by national boundaries, and others see the world moving rapidly towards a homogenous plain without national boundaries. Defining globalization has big implications; how it is explained to the public influences how the idea is received. According to Peter Dicken this general "wooliness" when describing globalization, has led to "heated and polarized argument across the entire political and ideological spectrum" (Dicken, 2007).

However, there are some general characteristics that most can agree upon. Globalization is recognized as a complex set of processes influencing the world economy. Globalization involves increasing amounts of cross border trade, with traditional distances between nations lessening, due to advances in transportation and telecommunications technology. Globalization does involve the rise of MNEs and has seen the globalizing of markets and production that has resulted in increased competition for jobs and between nations. Globalization has also seen some erosion of differences amongst distinctive national cultures and identities, but, as we shall see below and in chapter 4 when we look at Ghemawat's CAGE framework, the extent may be exaggerated. Firms that treat all markets the same, and offer the same products/services everywhere invariably learn the limits of this approach.

Globalization has also seen the development of international bodies to try to deal with all this increased interconnectedness. There are now international governing bodies such as the GATT (The General Agreement on Tariffs and Trade) and the WTO (World Trade Organization), which hold the key to many economic decisions affecting the world and have power over nations akin to a political body or national government. These governing bodies symbolize the interconnectedness of the world just as the United Nations did after the end of World War Two. The International Monetary Fund (IMF) and the World Bank were created in 1944. The goal of the International Monetary Fund is to maintain order in the international monetary system, and as we will see in chapter 2, the International Monetary Fund is a significant player in the global economy. The World Bank promotes economic development by making loans to cash-strapped nations wishing to make significant infrastructure improvements like building dams or roads. These international organizations influence, and sometimes decide the fate of, businesses and communities wishing to collaborate with or limit their access with other countries.

1.3 Trends Toward Globalization

Globalization is hardly new. People have been trading internationally for several thousands of years. However, the last 150 years have seen an intensification of globalization, and what Jones (2004) depicts as two waves arising in each case from a combination of long-term trends and pendulum swings. He sees the first wave of globalization as starting in 1880 and rising to a high in 1929 then declining and disintegrating from 1930 to 1980. He sees a second wave starting in post World War II and rising from 1950 to beyond 2010. We will focus on the current wave of globalization that has evolved since World War II.

In the 1950s and 1960s barriers to trade and capital movements were pervasive, even amongst developed countries. Meanwhile developing countries tended to nurture and protect domestic industries, while China and the USSR sought to develop self-sufficiently. In the 1970s and 1980s globalization as international trade remained largely a matter for developed economies in the *Triad* of North America, Western Europe, and Japan.

However, globalization accelerated dramatically in the 1990s. An emerging economy is one that has only recently established institutional frameworks that facilitate international trade and investment. Typically they have low or middle level incomes amongst their population, and above average economic growth compared to other nations. Emerging economies joined much more in global trade, particularly the largest in terms of population, namely Brazil, Russia, India, and China – the so-called BRIC countries. In the 1990s world output grew by 23 percent over the decade, global trade expanded by 80 percent and the total flow of FDI increased fivefold. Gross Domestic Product (GDP) is the sum of value added by resident firms, households and governments operating in an economy.

In the first decade of the 21st century world GDP, cross border trade and per capita GDP all soared to new, unprecedented levels, with half of the world's GDP growth coming from emerging economies (4.6 percent annual growth 1997-2007). Developed economies averaged 2 percent annual growth in the same period. All this before the 2008/9 global economic crisis with global output, trade, and investment plummeting, and unemployment rising. From mid-2009 there was renewed confidence after massive government intervention in developing economies, but economic recovery has been slow in developed economies, while some emerging economies have rebounded faster. Overall second wave theorized by Jones (2004) has become less steep from 2010-12 as globalization has slowed down.

What has been driving globalization? Two macro factors are important: first, the decline in trade and investment barriers since World War II and second, technological change, specifically dramatic improvements in communication, information processing, and transportation technologies. At the end of World War II, many advanced nations committed to removing barriers that prevented the free flow of goods, services, and capital between countries. They formalized the process through the General Agreement on Tariffs and Trade, or GATT. Since 1950, average tariffs have fallen significantly and in recent years have been as low as 4 percent. Foreign direct investment (FDI) has also been rising as countries have increasingly opened their market to firms. We have seen how the global economy has changed massively over the last 30 years. Hill (2011) suggests that four trends have been particularly important:

- *Changes in world output and world trade.* In the 1960s, the USA dominated the world economy and world trade picture. US multinational companies were powerful, and because of the Cold War, a significant portion of the world was off limits to the Western companies. Today, this picture has changed. In 2008, the USA accounted for only about 20 percent of world economic activity. Other developed countries saw their share of global economic activity decline over time as well. Developing nations saw just the opposite trend – their share of world output is rising, and by 2020, it is expected that they will account for more than 60 percent of world economic activity. Countries like China, Thailand, and Indonesia have emerged as global economic players. Most experts expect that similar trends will continue. Countries like the USA, the UK, Germany, and Japan that were among the first to industrialize, will continue to see their standings in world exports and world output slip, while developing nations like China, India, South Korea, and Thailand see their economies and role in global trade and investment increase. Despite its decline, the USA is still the world's largest exporter. However, China has emerged to challenge the USA for this position.

- *Foreign direct investment.* In the 1960s, the USA accounted for over 66 percent of worldwide foreign direct investment flows. The UK was a distant second with just 10 percent of worldwide investment flows. Today, investments by developing nations are on the rise, while the stock, or total cumulative value, of foreign investments by rich industrial countries is falling. Developing nations like China have also become important destinations for foreign direct investment flows. The share of total stock of foreign direct investment by the world's six most important sources - USA, UK, Japan, Germany, France, Netherlands, and developing countries - has changed significantly from 1980 to 2007. In particular, USA had noticeably declined (from 38 to 18 percent), and the world's developing countries had moved from under 1 to 15 percent. Increased growth in cross-border flows of foreign direct investment is very noticeable in the official figures, reaching an all-time high in 2007. One can also note the rising importance of developing nations as destinations for FDI. These two trends reflect the internationalization of company operations.

- *Types of companies.* The global economy has also shifted in terms of the type of companies that are involved. A multinational enterprise is any business that has productive activities in two or more countries. Since the 1960s, two important trends have emerged. First, an increase in the number of non-US multinationals. Multinational firms from France, Germany, Britain, and Japan have become more important, and there has been a notable decline in the role of US firms. Firms from developing countries such as China and South Korea have also emerged as important players. Think of South Korea's Samsung and Hong Kong's Hutchison Whampoa. The second trend is the growth in the number of mini-multinationals. China's Lenovo for example, acquired IBM's PC division in 2004, in an effort to become a global player in the PC industry, and moved its headquarters to the USA as part of its strategy. Traditionally, global markets have been the venue for large firms, but today, thanks to advances in technology like the internet, international sales can account for a significant share of revenues for small companies too.

- *Change in world order.* The collapse of Russian communism has brought about new opportunities in Eastern Europe, and China's economic development and enormous population presents huge opportunities for companies. Mexico and Latin America have also emerged both as new markets, and as source and production locations. India has been predicted to be a major global player in the near future. From an international business perspective the growth of these markets creates new opportunities for foreign firms, but the growth is also an interesting competitive threat. China and India for example, are now home to a number of companies that either are or could become significant players in their global industries.

1.4 The Globalization Debates

What will the global economy look like in the 21st century? The world is moving toward a more global economic system but this interdependency creates new types of risk. For example, recall the global impacts of the financial crisis that swept through South East Asia in the late 1990s, and the more recent financial crisis that began in the United States in 2008, and then affected economies across the globe. Proponents of globalization, such as Bhagwati (2004), focus on the benefits of globalization, but some people worry that the shift toward a more integrated and interdependent global economy is not necessarily a good thing. Critics worry for example, that globalization will cause job losses, damage the environment, and create cultural imperialism. Supporters however, argue that globalization means lower prices, more economic growth, and more jobs. Anti-globalization protesters who fear that globalization is forever changing the world in a negative way now turn up at almost every major meeting of global institutions like the WTO and IMF. Four major areas of debate recur.

- *Jobs and income.* How do critics and supporters view globalization and jobs and income? Critics of globalization worry that jobs are being lost to low-wage nations. They argue that falling trade barriers are allowing companies to move manufacturing jobs to countries where wage rates are low. For example, clothing manufacturing has increasingly shifted away from the USA where workers might earn $9 per hour to countries like Honduras where wages are less than 50 cents per hour. Critics believe that this leads to falling wages and living standards in the USA. Supporters, however, claim that free trade will prompt countries to specialize in what they can produce most efficiently, and to import everything else. They argue that the whole economy will be better off as a result. In other words, if you can buy an imported shirt that was made for pennies in Honduras, you will have more money to spend on products the USA can produce efficiently like computers and software.

- *Labour policies and the environment.* How do globalization's supporters and critics view globalization, labour policies and the environment? Protesters fear that free trade encourages firms from advanced nations, where there are costly environmental standards, to move manufacturing facilities offshore to less developed countries with lax environmental and labour regulations. However, advocates of globalization claim that environmental regulation and stricter labour standards go hand in hand with economic progress, so foreign direct investment actually encourages countries to raise their standards. Some studies support this claim with the exception of carbon dioxide emissions, which appear to rise along with income levels. Advocates of globalization argue that by tying free trade agreements to the implementation of tougher environmental and labour laws, economic growth and globalization can occur together with a decrease in environmental pollution.

- *Shifts in economic power.* A further concern raised by critics of globalization is the worry that economic power is shifting away from national governments and towards supranational organizations like the WTO and the European Union (EU). However, globalization's supporters argue that the power of these organizations is limited to that granted by their members. They also point out that the organizations are designed to promote the collective interests of members, and they will not gain support for policies that do not achieve this goal.

- *Wealth distribution.* Critics of globalization worry that the gap between rich and poor is growing and that the benefits of globalization have not been shared equally. While supporters of globalization concede the gap between rich and poor has become wider, they also contend that it has more to do with the policies countries have followed than with globalization. For example, many countries have chosen to pursue totalitarian regimes, or have failed to contain population growth, and many countries have huge debt loads that are stagnating economic growth.

1.5 Does Distance Still Matter?

Still another debate has been over the degree of globalization, its impacts and its implications for international business. Friedman (2007) believes globalization is accelerating and is flattening the world so that every nation will eventually be part of the global marketplace and production process. Dicken (2007) calls this a 'hyper globalist view'. Friedman takes a technological stance on globalization believing it to be shaped considerably by technological advances, cheap computer access, and the easy assimilation and transportation of knowledge over the World Wide Web. Before computer access was a worldwide phenomenon geographical distance played a big impact on how firms conducted business. Without the ability to communicate easily and freely with other countries, a sweatshop in Hanoi, to take one example, would be rather tricky to co-ordinate from say France. Without the internet, video conferencing, where companies thousands of miles apart can communicate in real time, would not be possible. Moreover outsourcing would be harder as there would be no reliable, efficient way of collaborating with other departments in the same office or in a different country.

Friedman argues that *ten flatteners* have shaped globalization and have caused increased homogeneity in the world. These include the fall of the Berlin Wall representing economic liberalization, the development of internet protocols, workflow and open source software, the increased use of outsourcing and offshoring, the development of global supply chains, the increased use of specialized firms to carry out internal functions, the development of search engines, and latterly of wireless, digital, mobile, personal, and virtual technologies. From this perspective, technological capacity and connectedness define the parameters of globalization and this is only set to continue as the age of the personal technology relationship is gaining momentum, where people not content with established information-sharing bodies, take matters into their own hands with blogs, review sites, and establishing their own media channels. Everyone essentially becomes in control of their own personal networking and spread of influence.

However, Friedman may not provide the only valid argument for defining globalization. Although to hyper-globalists globalization literally means the free co-operation and connection with nations all over the world, to people like Ghemawat (2001) and Dicken (2007), flattening is a gross overstatement and creates a general misconception about the extent of globalization's reach. In his influential article *Distance Still Matters*, Ghemawat argues that companies in their pursuit of the benefits from globalization, consistently 'overestimate the attractiveness of foreign markets'. Ghemawat argues that the true amount of trade and investment between countries is influenced largely by geographical and cultural differences. He cites that countries 5,000 miles apart only perform 20 percent of the trade they would otherwise do if they were 1,000 miles apart, and furthermore trade is ten times more likely to take place if a country was a former colony of another – which, Ghemawat argues, significantly lowers the cultural barriers to trade.

These figures taken together explain a key point in Ghemawat's argument, which is that 'distance still matters and companies must explicitly and thoroughly account for it when they make decisions about global expansion'. Arguing against Friedman's flattening argument, Ghemawat elaborates that global communications and technologies have been argued to be 'shrinking the world, running it into a small and relatively homogenous place. But when it comes to business, that's not only an incorrect assumption but also a dangerous one'.

The cultural difference between countries is still wide and complex, and although outsourcing and foreign direct investment have recently grown between nations, it is evident, as we shall see in chapter 3, that cultural differences still prove challenging. In support of Ghemawat's statement, Dicken (2007) argues that quantitative and aggregative evidence suggests that the world economy was 'more open and more integrated in the half century prior to the First World War, than it is today'. Ghemawat also supports this empirical based analysis stating that cultural differences in religious beliefs, language, social norms, and behaviours have a huge impact in the risk involved in trading and the likelihood of succeeding. Therefore, according to these theorists, globalization cannot be characterized as flattening the world. As Dicken puts it: 'there are undoubtedly globalizing forces at work, but we do not have a fully *globalized* world'.

Dicken explains that part of the problem with defining globalization is understanding that aggregative and quantitative analysis though valid, are not the only story we should take on board when thinking about the world economy today. The economy today he goes on to suggest, constitutes a deep and complex integration that cannot be captured in the statistics of trade and foreign direct investment (FDI). Instead globalization is: 'a supercomplex series of multicentric, multiscalar, multitemporal, multiform and multicausal processes'. This explanation, in contrast to Friedman's linear model of technological progress, is more dynamic and circulatory in design. To summarize, it would seem that globalization includes fluctuating levels of trade and FDI, economic growth of emerging markets, growing Transnational Corporations (TNCs), outsourcing and labour force migration, as well as technological innovations that have facilitated these movements.

In his article *Distance Still Matters,* Ghemawat complements this view by suggesting that companies often overestimate the ease with which their business can move abroad. The cultural, administrative, and geographical distance between nations presents a fundamental challenge to firms facing the globalization of the world economy today. Ghemawat uses the example of Rupert Murdoch's venture in Asia with Star Television network, which assumed that the Asian audiences would be enthusiastic about English language programmes and films. Furthermore, Murdoch's underestimating of the administrative differences between Asia and the USA led him into political calamity as he claimed live on television that freedom to watch what one wanted was a threat to Asian 'totalitarian regimes everywhere'. This led to the blocking of Star TV from Chinese television, which is a huge market for Murdoch. Coca-Cola also had problems in the Peruvian market when they attempted to replace Inca Kola, the national beverage, with their own US branded Cola. The Peruvian people held mass demonstrations against Coco-Cola until their Inca Cola was returned to the shelves. Being sensitive to national differences is not just a consideration; in international business it may well be an imperative to survival – something we explore in detail in later chapters.

1.6 What Does Globalization Mean For Firms?

Let's take stock of the point we have reached. All this means that managing an international business, or any firm that engages in international trade or investment, will be different from managing a domestic business. In particular, firms operating internationally will find that countries and cultures differ – a subject we will explore in much more detail in chapters 2 and 3. It will emerge from those chapters that the range of problems faced by managers is greater and more complex, not least because government intervention in markets creates limitations for companies, as does the way the global trading system operates and the existence of international institutions (see below and chapter 2). At the same time firms can work with the forces for globalization and improve their global performance. Such forces include:

- *Low barriers to trade and investment.* These mean that firms can see the world as their market, rather than a single country. Low trade and investment barriers also mean that firms can locate production facilities in the optimal location, wherever in the world that might be. Production and sales now take place in multiple markets creating interdependency between countries for goods and services.

- *Technological change.* Major advances in communication, information processing, and transportation technology have made what had been possibilities into tangible realities. The cost of global communication has fallen, for example, because advances in telecommunications and information processing help firms coordinate and control global organizations at a fraction of what it might have cost even a decade ago. The microprocessor that facilitates high-power, low-cost computing is perhaps the most important of these developments. Dell for example, takes advantage of these innovations to control its globally dispersed production system. When a customer submits an order via the company's website, it's immediately transmitted to the suppliers of the various components, wherever they are located in the world. Suppliers have real time access to Dell's order flows, and can then adjust their production accordingly. Dell uses inexpensive airfreight to transport its products to meet demand as needed. The company maintains a customer service operation in India where English-speaking personnel handle calls from the USA. Indeed, the internet has made it possible for even small companies to play a role in the global economy. Yet, less than twenty years ago, this technology did not even exist. Growth in internet usage has gone from fewer than one million users in 1990 to more than two billion users in 2012.

- *Transportation improvements.* Improvements in transportation such as containerization and the development of super freighters have also facilitated the growth of globalization. The time it takes people and products to get from one place to another has shrunk, as has the cost. Ecuador has been able to capitalize on falling transportation costs to become a global supplier of roses.

There is evidence that there are huge global shifts in the ways in which we do business, and overall the strongest companies are international but are also, as we shall see in chapter 7, strategically sensitive to localising their products or service when operating in different markets. For example, Google search engine found this to be a winning combination in their expansion into China. Here, despite an initial backlash, Google pursued a local strategy for their Chinese market using a Chinese name for their search engine and customizing their web page to fit the tastes of Chinese internet users who tend to spend longer on a given page and read the left hand side of the screen first. However, global linkages and interdependencies, and working in foreign markets also mean global risks. As a symbol of the risks of globalization for a firm, Google also ran into subsequent problems with the Chinese government on a number of issues.

1.7 International Trade Theory: From Free Trade to Factor Endowments

Free trade refers to a situation where a government does not attempt to influence through quotas or duties what its citizens can buy from another country or what they can produce and sell to another country. Economists have debated the merits of free trade for centuries. You probably do not need trade theories to explain some patterns of trade – it is easy to see why Saudi Arabia exports oil and Brazil exports coffee. But other patterns are harder to explain. Why Switzerland exports watches and pharmaceuticals, or why Japan exports consumer electronics. Why is India a major outsourcing destination for IT services, but has no sizeable domestic market in this area? And why does Ford assemble cars made for the American market in Mexico, while BMW and Nissan manufacture cars for Americans in the USA? You can think of your own trading puzzles!

We need to understand such patterns of trade and the factors that influence them. So let us look at the several theories of trade, and also at the important role of national governments in influencing modern patterns of international trade. A little historical background is useful here, since three quite old theories still influence modern day thinking – for better or worse. The first of these is mercantilism.

The main idea behind the mercantilist philosophy, which was around in the mid-16th century, was that the accumulation of gold and sliver were essential to the wealth and power of a nation. It was in the best interests of a country to try to maximize its holdings of gold and silver by encouraging exports and discouraging imports. To achieve this, imports were limited through tariffs and quotas, while exports were maximized through government subsidies. A key flaw in the philosophy, however, was that it was a zero-sum game. A country could only achieve its goal of maximizing a trade surplus at the expense of another nation. If one country successfully exported more than it imported, and consequently increased its holdings of gold and silver, another country would fail to achieve a trade surplus and would become relatively weaker. The more modern version of mercantilism is protectionism, where a country actively protects its domestic firms from imports while promoting exports, for example China in 2008-13 keeping the exchange rate of the renminbi low.

A second influential set of ideas came from Adam Smith who argued, in his *The Wealth of Nations (1776),* that trade without government intervention could be beneficial to countries if each country produced and exported those products in which it was most efficient, or in his words, had an absolute advantage. Smith argued that if countries specialized in the production of goods in which they had an absolute advantage, firstly each country could produce more, and secondly they could then trade these goods for the goods produced by other countries. The result would be a win-win game rather than the zero-sum gain under protectionism. Note however, that such absolute advantage is a rare occurrence. What happens, for example, if one nation has an absolute advantage in the production of all products? Or a nation cannot establish an absolute advantage in any product or service?

Ricardo developed the theory of trade further by arguing for comparative advantage. It actually still makes sense for a country to specialize in the production of those goods that it produces most efficiently and to buy goods that it produces relatively less efficiently from other countries, even if this means buying goods from other countries that it has an absolute advantage in, i.e. could produce more efficiently itself. The key issue here is ***opportunity cost***. Peng and Meyer (2011) usefully point out how practical this idea of ***comparative advantage*** is by the example of a student. Assume she studies a degree to become a business manager. Firstly, while studying she does not make sweaters, food or software but buys these from others in order to focus on getting the best degree possible. Assume, however she has to drive a taxi to make some money to pay for studies, and becomes an excellent taxi driver. Once she gets her degree her salary may be say $100,000 with high prospects, while the best she can earn as a taxi driver might be $50,000. Therefore she hires taxis, even though she may have an absolute advantage in that skill, because the opportunity cost of driving taxis and being a business manager, instead of focusing on just the latter, are very big indeed. Both she and taxi drivers gain from this application of the theory of comparative advantage.

A key idea in all this is productivity. Smith looked at absolute productivity differences between countries, while Ricardo looked at relative productivity differences. Ohlin (1933) extended Ricardo's work by suggesting that a country's comparative advantage is a result of differences in ***national factor endowments***. The Heckscher-Ohlin theory argues that countries will export goods that make intensive use of factors of production like land, labour, and capital that are locally abundant. At the same time, countries will import goods that make intensive use of factors that are locally scarce. For example, a country like China with abundant low-cost labour will produce and export products that are labour intensive like textiles, while the UK, which lacks abundant low cost labour, imports textiles from China. Another example (and many can be cited) is Brazil, which, with its abundant resources of land, water, and weather, has become an agricultural powerhouse. One example here is its production of half the world's exports in sugar-based ethanol – which has been mandated as an additive to gasoline used in cars since the 1970s.

OK, enough history. These trade theories paint a static picture of the world, but as we know things move all too quickly these days. In the 1960s Vernon and Hirsch produced the first dynamic theory to account for changes in the patterns of trade over time. They asked the question: Why are some products that used to be made at home, now imported from other countries, especially less developed ones? For example the UK used to be a major producer of textile products, but is no longer. Vernon (1966) suggested that as products mature, both the sales location and the optimal production location would change. As these change, so will the flow and direction of trade. Products move through different stages of their life cycle, and as they do, where they are produced and sold change too. For Vernon the product life cycle consisted of three stages: new, maturing, and standardized. Moreover, there were three types of nations: lead innovation nation (in the 1960s he saw this as the USA), other developed nations, and developing nations. Vernon observed, at the time, that most of the world's new products were developed by American firms and sold initially in the USA. He attributed this to the wealth and size of the US market. While demand was growing in the USA there would be only limited demand by high-income consumers in other advanced countries. Therefore, there would be little incentive for firms in foreign countries to produce the product, so other developed markets would be served by exports from the USA. But as demand for the new product grew in other advanced countries, foreign producers would begin to produce the product. US producers, in an effort to capitalize on foreign demand, would also begin to produce in the foreign markets. Exports from the USA slowed down as they were replaced by foreign production. As the US market and the foreign markets matured, the product became more standardized, and price became more important to consumers. Some foreign producers with lower wage costs exported to the USA market during this stage. Later, production shifted to developing countries where wages were even lower, and the USA became an importer of the product.

While the product life cycle theory was useful for explaining trade patterns for products like photocopiers that were developed in the 1960s and 1970s, today, given the effects of globalization and the integration of the world economy, the theory does not hold up well. Today, you can think of many products that were designed and introduced outside the USA, like video game consoles that were initially introduced in Japan, or Europe's wireless phones. In addition, many products are introduced simultaneously in the USA, Japan, and Europe. Production of these new products is often globally dispersed from the start.

In an effort to resolve some of the shortcomings of other theories, researchers in the 1970s began to look for other explanations of trade. This new vein of thought, called strategic trade theory, argued that because of the unit cost reductions that are associated with a large scale of output (economies of scale), some industries can support only a very few firms. Moreover, in some industries, to achieve economies of scale, firms need to have a major share of the world's market. The costs of developing new aircraft, for example, are so high, that firms have to hold a significant share of the world market in order to gain economies of scale. There are reasons why there are only two makers of large commercial aircraft in the world! *First mover advantage* is an important concept here. Firms that achieve first mover advantages will develop economies of scale, and create barriers to entry for other firms. Airbus, for example, should enjoy the first mover advantages associated with its A380 5550-seater super jumbo plane. Airbus had to sell at least 250 super jumbos just to break even on the project. The market over the next twenty years is expected to be just 400 to 600 planes, so Airbus has first mover advantages based on scale economies. Can Boeing compete? Should it?

This theory suggests that government should support certain strategic industries that can gain first mover, hard-to-replicate advantages. Typically these have high up-front entry costs, in terms of research and building capabilities, and are highly capital-intensive, thus creating high entry barriers. In our Airbus example above, the project received substantial subsidies from European governments. However, in other cases a government might lack the information or knowledge to identify a strategic industry, and where first mover advantage could be gained. Strategic trade theory supports comparative advantage theory because it actually identifies a source of comparative advantage. Governments might use this information to implement strategic trade policies that nurture and protect firms and industries where first mover advantages and economies of scale are important.

Bringing it to country level, have you ever wondered why some countries have certain industries that seem to be superior to those of other countries? Why is Japan so strong in the global auto industry? It wasn't always. Why does Switzerland dominate the pharmaceutical industry? In 1990, Michael Porter identified four factors that he argued promoted or impeded the creation of competitive advantage in an industry. Together, he called these factors the diamond of competitive advantage.

The first factor, called factor endowments, refers to a country's position in the factors of production that can lead to a competitive advantage – things like the skilled labour or infrastructure that were important to achieving a competitive advantage in a particular industry. For example, the forests and timber that are abundantly available can explain the paper industry in Scandinavia. High-tech industries gather around university cities, e.g. Cambridge, UK, Munich, Germany, because scientists and graduates are readily available there. Demand conditions, the second factor, refer to the nature of home demand for the industry's products/ services. For example, sophisticated and demanding Japanese customers for iPods, console games, and mobile phones have pressured Japanese consumer electronics firms to be highly competitive. The third factor, related and supporting industries, refers to the presence or absence of supplier and related industries that are internationally competitive and contribute to other industries. According to Porter, successful industries will be grouped in clusters in countries. If a country has world-class manufacturers of semi-conductor processing equipment, it will tend to have a competitive semi-conductor industry. The fourth factor - firm strategy, structure, and rivalry - refers to the conditions in the nation that govern how companies are created, organized, and managed, and the nature of domestic rivalry. When domestic rivalry is strong, there is greater pressure to innovate, improve quality, reduce costs, and invest in advanced product features.

Was Porter successful at increasing our understanding of trade patterns? Porter argued that a nation's success in an industry is a function of the combined impact of the four points on his diamond. He also suggested that government could play a role. For example, government imposed subsidies could affect factor endowments, or by imposing local product standards, a government could change demand conditions. Antitrust laws, and so on, could influence rivalry among firms. If his arguments are correct, his model ought to predict the patterns of trade we see in the real world but so far his theory is not well tested. He also puts too much emphasis on domestic conditions creating industry advantage. India's IT industry, for example, has arisen largely as a response to the export market, rather than India's domestic market.

1.8 National Institutions and International Trade: Free or Protected?

Free trade refers to a situation where a government does not restrict what its citizens can buy from another country or what they can sell to another country. Many nations today claim to support free trade, but, in reality, most countries are only nominally committed to free trade. They tend to intervene in international trade to protect the interests of politically important groups, and national interests. The global recession of 2008/9 led to an increase in protectionist policies in many countries. Countries and governments intervene in markets in several ways. Let us look at these.

- *Tariff barriers.* A tariff is a tax levied on imports that effectively raises the cost of imported products relative to domestic products. There are two kinds of tariffs. Specific tariffs are levied as a fixed charge for each unit of a good that is imported, and ad valorem tariffs are levied as a proportion of the value of the imported good. Tariffs are beneficial to governments because they increase revenues. They are also beneficial to domestic producers because tariffs provide protection against foreign competitors by increasing the cost of imported foreign goods, though of course, this means higher prices for consumers. There is general agreement that tariffs are unambiguously pro-producer and anti-consumer. It is also argued that tariffs reduce the overall efficiency of the world economy because they encourage domestic producers to manufacture goods that could be produced more efficiently elsewhere. Tariffs are often imposed because of special interest groups' ability to influence political decisions. An often cited example are farming interests and their influences in Europe, USA, and Japan, but you can point to many other sectors across the world protected by tariff policies.

- *Subsidies* are government payments to domestic producers. Governments can give subsidies in various ways including cash grants, low interest loans, and tax breaks. They can help domestic producers compete against low cost foreign imports, and they can help them gain export markets. One of the biggest recipients of subsidies in most countries is agriculture. Do subsidies help producers be more competitive, or do they tend to protect inefficient producers and promote excess production? One study showed that if developed countries eliminated their agricultural subsidies, we would see an increase in global trade in agricultural products, and a savings of $160 billion. Consumers typically absorb the costs of subsidies.

- *An import quota* is a direct restriction on the quantity of some good that may be imported into a country. In the USA for example, there is a quota on cheese imports. *A tariff rate quota*, which is common in agriculture, is a mix of a quota and a tariff where a lower tariff is applied to imports within the quota than to those over the quota. A quota rent is the extra profit that producers make when supply is artificially limited by an import quota.

- *Voluntary export restraints* are quotas on trade imposed by the exporting country, usually at the request of the importing country's government. In 1981, Japan established voluntary export restraints for the auto industry. Japan believed that by setting its own limits it could avoid potentially higher limits that could be set by the USA. As a result of the 1981 voluntary export restraints for example, Japanese producers earned an extra $1 billion from the higher prices charged to consumers because of the trade barriers. Import quotas and voluntary export restraints benefit domestic producers by limiting import competition, but they do raise prices of imported goods.

- *Local content requirements* are another form of trade barrier where the government demands that some specific fraction of a good be produced domestically. Like other types of trade restrictions, local content requirements benefit producers, but probably not consumers!

- *Administrative trade policies* are bureaucratic rules designed to make it difficult for imports to enter a country. The Japanese are known for this type of trade barrier that frustrates companies trying to break into the market. Since 2008 Indonesia and Malaysia have limited imports to certain ports. India has banned Chinese toys, citing safety concerns. As with other trade barriers, these policies can hurt consumers if they deny access to foreign products that may be superior to those available at home.

- *Antidumping policies.* Dumping is selling goods in a foreign market below their cost of production, or selling goods in a foreign market at below their fair market value. Dumping is viewed as a method by which firms unload excess production in foreign markets, and some dumping is considered to be predatory behaviour where producers use profits from their home markets to subsidize prices in foreign markets with a goal of driving indigenous competitors out of the market, and then later raising prices and earning substantial profits. To stop this type of behaviour, countries implement antidumping policies or countervailing duties designed to punish foreign firms that are dumping and protect domestic producers from this type of unfair competition.

1.9 Government Intervention and Free Trade: The Debate

Many argue that, economically over the long term, free trade is best. For example, it is argued that free trade can increase a country's stock of resources, e.g. since the 1990s Western companies have been investing in Eastern Europe increasing the amount of capital that's available to use there. Free trade can also increase the efficiency of resource utilization. Thus if firms can sell to a bigger market, they can gain from the economies associated with large-scale production. Studies show that countries that adopt a more open stance toward international trade tend to have higher growth rates than those that close their economies to trade. There may be times when restrictions on trade are counterproductive. For example, when they involve retaliation and trade wars, or efforts to further domestic policies. For example, strategic trade policies that are designed to establish domestic firms in dominant positions in the global market will probably result in retaliation. So when the European Union provided $15 billion in subsidies to Airbus, the USA took steps to protect Boeing. In the end, the subsidies probably cancelled each other out, and consumers and taxpayers footed the bill. Those who argue against such subsidy cite many such examples. A favourite one involves policies adopted by the European Union to protect consumers from imported agricultural products. It is often pointed out this may well do nothing more than protect inefficient farmers and politicians who relied on the farm vote, and actually cause consumers to pay more for food.

But still others argue that a country needs to protect its own domestic industries and also its new, emerging industries. One of the problems with the latter argument, though, is determining when an industry has grown up enough to stop government support. In fact, many people believe that protecting these industries is really no different from sponsoring the development of inefficient industries. Others argue that, regardless of the economic arguments, protectionism can advance a country's political, social and environmental agenda. The main political arguments for government intervention can be summarized:

- National security concerns are often evoked to protect defence-related industries in France, the USA and UK for example.

- Governments also claim that trade barriers are sometimes necessary to protect consumers. For example, the European Union has limited imports of hormone-treated beef for many years, and this has been a source of a huge conflict between the European Union and the USA.

- Sometimes governments intervene in markets to retaliate against moves made by other governments. China has been under fire in recent years for failing to take proper steps against product piracy, and many nations have threatened to implement trade barriers against Chinese products if the practice isn't stopped. China initially responded with threats of increasing its own barriers to trade, although it has since backed off.

- Governments also argue that intervention in the market is necessary to support their foreign policy objectives. A country might, for example, extend favourable trade terms to a country that it is trying to build a relationship with, or implement policies designed to punish countries. For example, the USA maintains trade embargoes against Cuba and North Korea.

- Protecting human rights is another argument used by governments that intervene in the market. The basic idea is that the best way to change human rights practices in a country is to encourage it to trade. This will raise income levels, which generally means that human rights practices improve.

- Environmental and social responsibility arguments are sometimes used to start trade intervention against certain countries, e.g. the USA banning shrimp imports from India, Malaysia, Thailand and Pakistan, arguing that their fishing techniques trapped also sea turtles, a protected species in USA waters.

1.10 Conclusion

This chapter has explored the major characteristics of globalization and provided a basic understanding of the global economy and its broad trends. We have sought to explain the major trends in globalization, and the major players in the globalization process. At the same time the chapter entered into the major globalization debates and assessed under what conditions and for whom globalization can be considered an advantage or disadvantage. It also articulated the implications of globalization for firms operating internationally. We also looked at the evolution of theories of trade, and entered into the debate about whether free trade or protectionism or a balanced mix of each worked best internationally and for which interested parties.

Hopefully this chapter raises questions for you, not least as a taxpayer, an employee, and as a global citizen and stakeholder. This means you have embarked on the fascinating journey of understanding the global context in which we all live, and in which organizations and businesses operate, though in contexts they can also influence. The next two chapters are about that context, but in much more detail. To start this, in the next chapter we look at the national, regional, and multilateral institutions that importantly shape the conduct of international business.

'Laws and institutions, like clocks, must occasionally be cleaned, wound up and set to true time'

H.W. Beecher, 1813-1887

'Countries differ greatly in the extent to which they are different from one another'

P. Ghemawat, 2007

CHAPTER 2
Political, Economic and Legal Environments: Diversity or Growing Uniformity?

2.1 Introduction

Of course you know that political, economic, and legal systems of countries differ. But you may not know what these differences are, the degree of difference (are countries actually becoming similar?) and how and why these differences are important to companies that do business in foreign markets. In practice, firms operating abroad should have a thorough understanding of the formal institutions of each country they are in, or are thinking of entering. In this chapter, we are going to explore these institutions and related systems, known collectively as the political economy of a country, and what they mean for businesses operating internationally. In doing so we are going to introduce something called 'an institution-based perspective'. The key functions of institutions are to reduce uncertainty, reduce transaction costs, and constrain opportunism. As we shall see, political, economic, and legal institutions establish the formal 'rules of the game' for operating in a particular country. We will look at the equally, and sometimes more important, informal rules in the next chapter.

In this chapter we also look at international institutions that are important contextual features of international business. Here we look at the roles of organized regional blocs using examples in Europe, Americas, and Asia Pacific, and the institutions of the international monetary and trading system.

2.2 An Institution-Based View of International Business

Peng, Wang and Jiang (2008) and Peng and Meyer (2011) argue that essentially a country's institutions establish the formal and informal rules of the game for operating in that country. Firms operating internationally need to know these because these 'rules' differ between countries, and because they shape greatly what can be achieved, and what is not possible. Institutions can be formal or informal. In this chapter we focus on the formal institutional framework - laws, regulations, and rules - of a country that controls individual and firm behaviour. As we shall see, different governments have regulatory power to coerce compliance to varying degrees. In the next chapter we will look at informal rules – norms, values, ethics shaped by culture, religion, and other social forces.

What do institutions do? Essentially their key role is to reduce uncertainty, and limiting the range of acceptable actions does this. Institutions have developed over time because the potential adverse consequences of uncertainty can be devastating. For example, if you were trying to do business in the Middle East in 2012, say in Egypt, Syria, Israel, Qatar, Libya, imagine the immense difficulties of just understanding the business context, let alone deciding what to do. Uncertainty increases transaction costs, a term made highly popular by Oliver Williamson, a Nobel Economic prize winner Williamson (1985). Transaction costs are the costs associated with carrying out an economic transaction or, in short, the costs of doing business – for example search, negotiation, getting to contract, monitoring supplier performance. Transaction costs will increase if others behave opportunistically, defined rather nicely by Williamson as 'self-interest seeking with guile'. Institutional frameworks can reduce the potential for such opportunistic behaviour. This is important for international business, because if transaction costs become prohibitively high in a country, people may choose not to undertake trade in that country at all.

Institutions are evolving all the time, and international business managers need to keep up with these changes. For example, in the last decade and more, China, Poland, Russia, and Vietnam have been moving from central planning to market competition, though each in different ways and at different speeds. These are often called transition economies. Institutional transition can be defined as fundamental and comprehensive changes to the formal and informal rules of the game that affect organizations as players.

In summary, Peng and Meyer (2011) argue convincingly, that, for international business, institutions matter. They suggest that at the heart of an institution-based view there are two core propositions. Firstly, managers and firms rationally pursue their interests and make choices within the formal and informal constraints of a given institutional framework. Secondly, although formal and informal institutions combine to govern firm behaviour, in situations where formal constraints fail or are unclear, informal constraints will play a larger role in reducing uncertainty and providing constancy to managers and firms. More on informal constraints in chapter 3, but try this out now if you want. Take an organization you are familiar with – a workplace, a university, a hospital maybe. There are formal ways of getting things done, for example assigning a task to someone with a deadline. What are they? What happens if they do not work? The chances are that it will be a mixture of formal and informal institutions that prevail to get the task assigned and the person to agree, and perform.

2.3 Political Systems

A political system represents the rules of the game on how a country is governed politically. It is helpful to think of political systems as having two dimensions: first, the degree to which they emphasize collectivism as opposed to individualism, and second, the degree to which they are totalitarian or democratic.

Collectivism versus individualism

Collectivism refers to a system that stresses the primacy of collective goals over individual goals. In other words, in a collectivistic society, the needs of a society as a whole are generally viewed as being more important than individual freedoms. In modern times collectivism has been equated with socialism, and state ownership of the basic means of production, distribution, and exchange. During the late 1970s, communism, with strong command economies, was a dominant force in the world. Think of the former Soviet Union for example, and its Eastern European neighbours like Poland, Czechoslovakia, and Hungary. Think also of China, Cambodia, and Vietnam, and of Angola and Mozambique, Cuba, and Nicaragua. By 2000, the world was a very different place. The Soviet Union for example, had been replaced by 15 republics that were structured as democracies. China, though it still limited political freedom, was moving away from its strict communist ideology. Today, only a few fringe states like Cuba and North Korea still practise a strong brand of communism. Social democracy, which believed in a mixed economy of central planning, state, and private enterprises has also been retreating, though at different speeds depending on the country. For example, countries like the UK, France, and Germany have placed less emphasis on state-ownership of the means of production and have seen moves towards privatization, i.e. selling state-owned enterprises to the private sector.

Individualism suggests that individuals should have freedom over their economic and political pursuits. People and economists such as Adam Smith, Milton Friedman and Friedrich von Hayek have championed this philosophy. Individualism is based on two key concepts: first, that individual freedom and self-expression are guaranteed, and second, that people are allowed to pursue their own self-interest in order to achieve the best overall good for society. For international companies there is a debate about how important individualism and the related idea of free market economics are for creating a favourable business environment, and about who gains from applying these concepts in international trading environments.

Totalitarianism

You can think of totalitarianism and democracy as being at opposite ends of a political dimension with, at one end, totalitarianism, where one person or political party exercises absolute control over all spheres of life, and opposing political parties are forbidden; and at the other end democracy as a political system in which government is by the people, and is exercised either directly or through elected individuals. While we generally think of democracy as going hand-in-hand with individualism, and totalitarianism being associated with collectivism, grey areas do exist. For example, China is still under totalitarian rule, but has adopted free market policies that tend to be associated with individualism. The world has seen four major forms of totalitarianism:

- *Communist totalitarianism* advocates achieving socialism through totalitarian dictatorship. While this form of totalitarianism is declining worldwide, countries like Vietnam, Cuba, and North Korea still follow the philosophy.

- *Theocratic totalitarian* system is where political power is monopolized by a party, group, or individual that governs according to religious principles. You can think of countries like Saudi Arabia or Iran when you think of this type of system. Both countries are greatly influenced by the principles of Islam, and both countries restrict political and religious freedom.

- *Tribal totalitarian system* is where a political party that represents the interests of a particular tribe monopolizes power. This type of system has occurred, for example, in some African nations like Zimbabwe and Tanzania.

- *Right wing totalitarian system* may allow individual economic freedom, but individual political freedom is restricted to avoid forms of socialism. A nation's military often backs this type of system. This type of system has been declining, but you might recall its presence in Germany and Italy during the 1930s and 1940s.

Democracy

A pure democracy is based in the belief that people should be directly involved in decision making. The most common form of democracy today, however, is representative democracy, where elected representatives vote on behalf of constituents. Some of the espoused characteristics of democracies include freedom of expression, free media, regular elections, a fair court system, and free access to state information. The political system is governed by institutions. The rules are usually laid down in a constitution, determining things like how elections are organized, how votes are translated into representation in a parliament, and how much power elected officials and representatives have. There are notable variations in representation methods, including:

- *Proportional representation versus first-by-the-post*. Countries such as Germany and Denmark have systems whereby all votes are added up and seats allocated to political parties in proportion to the number of votes they gained. Countries like India, USA, and UK have a first-past-the-post system where each constituency elects one representative based on who in the election wins the most votes.

- *Direct versus indirect elections of government*. Some countries have direct elections for certain posts, e.g. citizens of France and the USA directly elect their presidents with executive power to appoint ministers. In most countries citizens elect representatives who then, on the citizens' behalf, elect and monitor government and ministers.

- *Representative versus direct democracy.* In most countries citizens elect representatives to act on their behalf.

- *Centralization of power.* There are variations between countries in the degree of power held by central, regional and local governments. For example, in federated countries like Australia and the USA states wield quite a lot of power. In the UK central government has devolved quite a lot of functions to Scottish, Welsh, and Northern Irish assemblies.

Political systems matter for international business because they:

- Set the rules, and whose interests are served by the rules.

- Determine whether and how businesses can influence legislative processes through lobbying (mostly legal) or corruption (usually illegal).
- Influence how frequently, and in what ways the rules of the game for business change. This can be a major source of political risk, i.e. risk associated with political changes that may negatively affect domestic and foreign firms.

2.4 Economic Systems

Keep in mind that a nation's political system and its economic system are connected. As we mentioned before, in countries where individual goals are given primacy over collective goals, free market systems are likely to exist, but in countries where collective goals are dominant, markets are likely to be restricted and state-owned enterprises are common. All have implications for firms operating internationally! An economic system refers to the rules of the game on how a country is governed economically. Broadly there are three types of economic system:

- *Market economy.* Here goods and services are privately owned and production quantities are determined by supply and demand. In a market economy, governments encourage free and fair competition and discourage monopolies. Note that, amongst countries, there have been very few pure market economies! In 2001 Hong Kong had the highest degree of economic freedom, but there is still some noticeable government intervention in the economy. The 2008/9 financial crisis and its aftermath has seen increased government intervention in many countries across the world.

- *Command economy.* Here the government plans the goods and services that a country produces, the quantity in which they are produced, and the price at which they are sold. Businesses are state-owned and the government allocates resources for the good of society as a whole. An example was the former Soviet Union, and in 2012 was North Korea.

- *Mixed economy.* Here elements of a market economy and elements of a command economy are present. Governments often take control of industries that are considered vital to national interest. Examples include France, UK, and Sweden.

In the 21st century most countries are more or less market economies – they organize themselves by market forces but also have varying degrees of non-market coordination. The varieties-of-capitalism view embodies this reality.

The varieties-of-capitalism view (Hall and Soskice, 2001) suggests that, due to history, culture, resources, and other factors, countries can vary enormously on how they combine market and non-market mechanisms to coordinate economic activity. Moreover these economies will be constantly changing in the modern dynamic global environment. The view suggests two main types of economy:

- *Coordinated market.* This operates through a system of coordinating by market signals together with a variety of other means, for example Italy, Netherlands, and Japan. Such economies may well have more employment protection, and less ability to raise capital through the stock market. In Germany, for example, employees have representatives on corporate boards (unlike in UK) and government is much more directly involved in vocational training. In Asia, many countries have embraced liberal market principles but also have a strong state providing direction and investment supporting the economic development path, e.g. South Korea, Singapore.

- *Liberal market*. This operates through a system of coordination primarily through market signals. Hall and Soskice (2001) suggest UK, USA, Canada, and Australia as examples in 2000, though it is important not to understate the extent of government involvement in economic development even in these states. For example the 2008/9 crisis prompted the UK and US governments to nationalize some banks and tighten banking regulations.

2.5 Legal Systems

A legal system represents the formal rules that regulate behaviour, along with the processes by which the laws of a country are enforced and through which redress for grievances is obtained. Why is it important for international managers to be familiar with different legal systems? Because a country's laws regulate business practice, define the manner in which business transactions are to be executed, and set down the rights and obligations of those involved in business transactions. The legal system impacts the attractiveness of a country as a business investment or a potential target market (see also chapters 7 and 9). A country's legal system is influenced by its political system. So, countries that are collectivistic, totalitarian states restrict private enterprise, while individualistic market economies support private enterprise and consumer rights. There are three broad types of legal system, though many legal systems are influenced by multiple legal traditions:

- *Common law* is based on tradition, precedent, and custom. So, judges look at how previous cases have been treated to decide how to treat current cases. Then, as new precedents are made, laws can be amended if necessary. Thus an important part of common law is case law, which is a rule of law created by precedents of cases in court. Common law is English in origin but has stretched to many English-influenced countries (in Africa, Asia, South Africa, also Canada and the USA) and is based on statutes, customs and court decisions. Judges are arbiters, and juries are decision-makers. The implications for business are greater freedom to design contracts and codes of practice; detailed contracts are needed to fill in for gaps in the legal framework; more legal disputes involving much use of lawyers; greater legal burden may favour the more powerful companies.

- *Civil law* is based on a detailed set of laws organized into codes. This type of system, which is practised in more than 80 countries including Germany, Japan, and Russia, is less adversarial than common law because under civil law, judges only have the power to apply the existing law, not interpret the law. Here law is codified in books of law, and judges lead the proceedings including questioning and deciding. For businesses the implications tend to be relatively short contracts and codes of practice, and more consumer and employee protection available under the law. Businesses often complain about the bureaucracy of civil law, but civil law also often gives greater legal certainty. Examples include the French code civil, Germanic civil law and Nordic civil law.

- **Religious law** is based on religious teachings. Today, Islamic law is the most widely practised theocratic law system in the world. Examples include Iran, Libya, Saudi Arabia, and Morocco. In practice, Islamic jurors and scholars are struggling to apply the foundations of Islamic law to the modern world, and many Muslim countries today are actually practising Islamic law combined with common law or civil law.

Why is it important for international companies to be familiar with the legal system of the countries in which they operate? One key reason is because each system approaches the enforcement of contracts in a different way. So, suppose you come from a common law state, and you have signed an agreement with a company operating under a civil law system. Which law should apply? To deal with this type of scenario, about 70 countries have signed the United Nations Convention on Contracts for the International Sale of Goods, or CIGS, which established a uniform set of rules governing certain aspects of the making and performance of everyday contracts between sellers and buyers who have their places of business in different nations.

Issues For international businesses

Legal systems are also important for dealing with several other important issues for international businesses:

- **Property rights.** Property rights are the legal rights over the use to which a resource is put and over the use of any income that may be derived from that resource. As you have probably already guessed, the laws on property rights differ across countries. In some countries, even though there are laws protecting property, the laws are not consistently enforced. Property rights can be violated through private actions and through public actions. Individuals perform private violations like theft, piracy, or blackmail. Keep in mind that this type of violation can take place in any country, but countries with weak legal systems like Russia have a much bigger problem with it. When public officials like politicians and bureaucrats violate property rights, they might use legal mechanisms such as levying excessive taxes, as in Venezuela in the 2000s, or requiring special expensive licences, or even simply taking assets into state control.

- **Intellectual property issues.** Intellectual property rights are rights associated with the ownership of intellectual property – which can include anything from computer software or a chemical formula for a new drug to a screenplay or a music score. Intellectual property can be protected in three ways:

  1. A patent gives the inventor of a new product or process exclusive rights to manufacture, use, or sell the invention.

  2. A copyright is the exclusive right of authors, composers, playwrights, artists, and publishers to publish and dispose of their work as they see fit.

3. A trademark is a design or name that may be officially registered, that allows merchants or manufacturers to designate or differentiate their products.

Protection of intellectual property rights varies by country. China and Thailand are currently among the world's biggest violators of intellectual property rights. Pirated products like Rolex watches, Levi's jeans, and computer software are widely available in both countries. In Latin America, about 68 percent of all software is pirated, and in China some studies estimate that 86 percent of software is pirated. Nearly 200 countries have signed the Paris Convention for the Protection of Industrial Property to protect intellectual property rights and are part of the World Property Organization, but enforcement of property regulations is still lax in many countries. What can you do if your intellectual property is stolen? You can lobby your government to take action. You can also file your own lawsuit. For example, Starbucks was successful against a Chinese firm that opened stores that were virtually replicas of the traditional Starbucks store.

- *Product safety and product liability.* Product safety laws set certain standards to which a product must adhere and product liability involves holding a firm and its officers responsible when a product causes injury, death, or damage. These vary greatly across countries. This often leads to an ethical dilemma for companies. What should a company do if the standards in a foreign market are lower than the standards at home? Should they comply with home standards even if this puts them at a competitive disadvantage?

- *Corporate governance.* This involves the rules by which shareholders and other interested parties control corporate decision-makers. Variations across countries are closely related to differences in economic and legal systems. Generally, common law systems have evolved in ways that provide strong protection for financial investors, i.e. shareholders. In civil law countries, for example Germany and Denmark, the law tends to offer less protection for shareholders and more rights to other stakeholders in the firm – for example, non-managerial employees who tend to be represented on corporate supervisory boards.

2.6 Country Development: Political, Economic, and Legal Issues

The political, economic, and legal environments of a country can have a significant impact on its economic development, and on its attractiveness as a potential investment location or target market. Economic development levels can be measured using gross national income per person, or GNI. But GNI measures can be misleading because they do not take into account cost of living differences. So, we adjust these numbers by purchasing power. Using purchasing power parity or PPP, we can adjust the numbers to reflect how far your money actually goes in a particular country. What does this mean for companies? Well, looking at a PPI adjusted GNI for India in 2007, we would conclude that the average Indian could only consume about 6 percent of the goods and services consumed by the average American. Should US firms have discounted India as a potential market then? No, because if we look a little deeper we would find that the country has an emerging middle class of about 100 million people that represents a tremendous opportunity for foreign companies. Are there other ways to measure economic development? Nobel-prize winning economist Amartya Sen argues that rather than simply focusing on material output measures like GNI per capita, we should consider the capabilities and opportunities people enjoy when measuring economic development. Sen (1999) believes that economic progress includes things like removing impediments to freedom - such as tyranny, poverty, and the neglect of public facilities - and a democratization of political communities so that citizens have a voice in decisions. So, for example, Sen argues that providing basic health care and education is essential for economic growth. The UN has incorporated Sen's ideas in its Human Development Index, or HDI, which measures the quality of life in different countries. HDI is based on life expectancy at birth, educational attainment, and whether average incomes in a country are sufficient to meet the basic needs of life in that country.

Why do some countries succeed in economic development while others fail? Some argue that investment and technological progress explain capital accumulation, higher productivity and thus increasing economic success. Many policy makers and scholars contend that innovation and entrepreneurship are the engines of long-run economic growth, and that furthermore innovation and entrepreneurship require some form of market economy. In other words, new products and business processes can increase the productivity of labour and capital. Think of some of the innovations by Microsoft or Dell, both of which were formed by entrepreneurs, and how they have changed not only the way of doing business, but also how many people live today. Similarly, innovation and entrepreneurship probably require strong property rights. If the innovations by Microsoft were not given protection, there would have been little incentive for the company to continue to develop new software and other products.

Others argue that human capital is the key to prosperity, so developing countries must invest in higher education. Others relate success to market friendly macro-economic policies by government, including low inflation, stable exchange rates, low trade barriers and low government budget deficits. Peng and Meyer (2011) line up with the argument of North (2005) and see political, economic, and legal institutions as the basic determinants of a national economic performance because these influence incentives, and the costs of doing business:

- Institutions ensure that firms are able to make gains from trade.

- Lack of strong formal market-supporting institutions force firms to trade on a much more informal basis, incurring political, legal and economic risks in conditions of instability, and over-dependent on informal relationships.

- Emerging formal market-supporting institutions support foreign firms moving into complicated long-distance trade with a country because they can see reasons for specialization and growth in size, and making long-term commitments to international trade there.

- If property rights are protected, this will fuel innovation, entrepreneurship, more economic growth, and increased inward investment.

2.7 Beyond the Nation State: Regional Economic Integration

The idea behind regional economic integration is that without trade barriers, member countries will be better off. However, there is some concern that as more countries become involved in regional agreements, the trading blocs will begin to compete against each other. We can observe across the world five levels of economic integration:

- A *free trade area* removes all barriers to the trade of goods and services among member countries, but members determine their own policies toward nonmembers. The European Free Trade Area (EFTA) between Norway, Iceland, Liechtenstein, and Switzerland, is the most enduring free trade area. Another well-known free trade area is the North American Free Trade Area or NAFTA.

- A *customs union* eliminates trade barriers between members, and adopts a common policy toward nonmembers. The EU began as a customs union, but as we'll discuss later, it's moved beyond this level of integration. The Andean Pact between Bolivia, Columbia, Ecuador, and Peru is a current example of a customs union.

- A *common market* has no barriers to trading between members, a common policy toward nonmembers, and the free movement of the factors of production. This is a significant step up from a customs union, and requires members to cooperate on fiscal, monetary, and employment policies. The EU was a common market for many years before moving to the next level of integration. Eventually, MERCOSUR, an agreement between Brazil, Argentina, Paraguay, and Uruguay, hopes to become a common market.

The next level of economic integration is the *economic union* which involves the free flow of the factors of production between members, the adoption of a common external trade policy, a common currency, harmonization of tax rates, and a common monetary and fiscal policy. So, again, this is a significant increase in integration from the previous level. The EU is currently an imperfect example of an economic union. Not all members have adopted the common currency, and there are still differences in tax rates across the countries.

In a political union, independent states are combined into a single union where the economic, social, and foreign policy of members is coordinated. An example is the USA. The EU is also headed toward this level.

Countries integrate for both economic and political reasons. We know from our discussion of trade theory in chapter 1 that free trade can be beneficial to countries. We will see that, for various reasons, trade barriers still exist despite the efforts of the World Trade Organization (WTO). Regional economic integration offers countries a way to achieve the gains from free trade, at least on a limited basis, more quickly than would be possible under the process offered by the WTO. The political case for integration has two main points. First, by linking countries together, making them more dependent on each other, and forming a structure where they regularly have to interact, the chances of violent conflict and war decrease. Second, economic integration gives the bloc of countries greater power and makes them much stronger politically when dealing with other countries than if they were to act independently.

If integration is beneficial, why does it not occur more often? Two key issues limit integration. First, while a nation as a whole benefits from integration, some groups may actually lose. Critics of NAFTA, for example, were concerned about the potential for job loss in the USA if companies shifted production to take advantage of Mexico's low cost labour. Second, countries that integrate their economies lose some degree of national sovereignty. Integration requires that countries give up some control over monetary policy, fiscal policy, and trade policy. For example, most of the countries belonging to the EU have given up their currencies and adopted the euro instead. Some economists point out that integration only makes sense when the amount of trade it creates is greater than the amount that is diverting. Trade creation occurs when low cost producers within a free trade area replace high cost domestic producers, while trade diversion occurs when higher cost suppliers within a free trade area replace lower cost external suppliers.

2.8 Regional Integration in Europe

As we said, faced with the inevitable limitations of global institutions, many countries have chosen to organize themselves into regional blocs to pursue joint economic and sometimes political objectives. In this section we will look at some of the major economic blocs as examples only, remembering that there are many such blocs, though none as large as the ones described here.

Regional Integration in Europe

In Europe, there is the European Union (EU), which is the world's most integrated group of countries with 27 members. The EU Single Market is based on freedom of movement of goods, capital, people, and services. This is implemented though harmonization of regulation in some sectors, and mutual recognition of national regulation in others. The EU aims to facilitate free movement of people within the union, particularly to enable people to take up a job in another country. The euro has become a common currency in 16 countries that have transferred their monetary policy to the European Central Bank. EU competition policy aims to ensure that a competitive environment is maintained in cases of mergers and acquisitions, cartels, collusion and state aid. Formal political structures of the EU resemble a government, yet national governments wield power through the Council. The decision-making processes in the EU are based on democratic principles, yet they are often far removed from the individual citizens in member countries. Enlargement creates not only benefits but also costs for existing EU members, who thus may be less enthusiastic to admit further members. The UK has an ambiguous relationship with the EU grounded in its history and its political culture. For example, like several other European countries, it refuses to have the euro as its currency.

Today, the European Union consists of many countries. The original agreement between Belgium, France, West Germany, Italy, Luxembourg, and the Netherlands was expanded in 1973 to include Great Britain, Ireland, and Denmark. In 1981, Greece joined, then Spain and Portugal in 1986, and Austria, Finland, and Sweden in 1986. Ten more countries joined in 2004, and three more in 2007. The European Community was founded in 1957 by the Treaty of Rome. This became the European Union in 1993 after the Maastricht Treaty was ratified, and extended political cooperation, and committed members to adopt a single currency by 1999. This created the single largest currency zone in the world after the US dollar. Euro notes and coins started circulating in 2002. However, three members, Britain, Denmark, and Sweden opted out of the euro zone. Five institutions govern the EU.

- The European Council resolves major policy issues and sets policy directions.
- The European Commission is responsible for implementing EU law and monitoring member states to ensure they're in compliance.
- The Council of the European Union is the ultimate controlling authority.
- The European Parliament debates legislation proposed by the commission and forwarded to it by the council.
- The Court of Justice acts as the supreme appeals court for EU law.

For our purposes the most relevant aspect of the EU is the institutional framework it provides for business. Four aspects of EU policy shape greatly how international business can be done:

- *The 'single market'.* The EU has created an institutional framework that establishes many of the rules by which businesses compete. It has removed most internal trade barriers between member countries. Internal customs and passport controls have been abolished. A prime focus has been on establishing the four freedoms – free movement of people, goods, services, and capital amongst member countries. A common external tariff is applied to all imported goods across the customs union. The EU has attempted to harmonize, that is create common rules, standards and regulations on the free movement of goods, and has made considerable headway, but this has been a difficult and complex political process, national or local regulations sometimes being allowed to stand if deemed more effective than EU stipulation. The single market for services has been even more difficult to implement. Service sectors like banking and telecommunications have complex regulatory regimes. Services always have some local component and common standards may be difficult to apply across different cultures, and customers with differing expectations. Moreover, and a bigger point for goods and services, harmonization represents liberalization and threatens protectionism in local markets.

- *The free movement of people.* People from EU member states are free to work in other EU countries but there can be barriers. The EU has moved to guarantee mutual recognition of professional experience, qualifications, and training across EU countries. It has also encouraged the movement of EU students and the advancement of higher education across EU countries. The Schengen agreement laid the basis for passport-free travel across member states, but also tightened regulations and policing for non-EU state citizens arriving at EU borders - the so-called Schengen area.

- *European competition policy.* The European commission regulates for competition issues such as over-dominant players, or illegal collusion, but only in cases involving multiple countries. National authorities are the regulators where only a national market is affected. The EU commission also looks to regulate mergers and acquisitions, including foreign mergers, if they seem to represent a substantial impediment to effective competition within the EU. Note that the EU also regulates governments, for example, when 'state aid' or subsidies are being offered to subsidize companies or protect local jobs, or make attractive a particular location to a multinational looking to make a foreign direct investment. Competition policy has numerous exceptions however, not least during the 2008/9 financial crisis when governments bailed out their home country banks.

The euro as a common currency. Having one currency, rather than several, is easier for companies and individuals. The same currency is used across the bloc, so companies will save the cost and risks of converting currencies. Having a single currency will also make it easier to compare prices across Europe. Adopting a single currency will make it easier to do the same thing in Europe, and force companies to lower prices. The lower prices should then encourage producers to look for ways to reduce their production costs in order to maintain their profit margins. So, by adopting a common currency, we should see greater efficiency. Another benefit of the euro is that it should boost the development of a highly liquid pan-European capital market. Finally, the capital market will provide a greater range of investment options to individuals and institutions. While there are many benefits of adopting the euro, there are also some disadvantages. A major cost involved in adopting a common currency is that individual countries lose control over monetary policy. The three countries that opted out of the euro zone did so because they did not want to give up this autonomy. A second disadvantage of the euro is that the EU is not an optimal currency area, or an area where similarities in the underlying structure of economic activities make it feasible to adopt a single currency and use a single exchange rate as an instrument of macro-economic policy. In other words, because of differences in member economies - take Portugal and Finland for example - they might react differently to external shocks. So, a change in the euro exchange rate that helps Finland might actually hurt Portugal. Some critics have argued that instead of establishing the euro and then moving toward political union, the EU should have achieved political union status first.

2.9 Regional Integration in the Americas

We will look at just three trade blocs in the Americas, and assess their levels of success.

The North American Free Trade Agreement (NAFTA)

This became law in 1994. Under NAFTA, tariffs on 99 percent of the goods traded between Mexico, Canada, and the USA were abolished, and so were most of the restrictions on the cross-border flow of services. The agreement also protects intellectual property, removes most restrictions on Foreign Direct Investment between the three countries, and allows each country to maintain its own environmental standards. In addition, two commissions were established to intervene when environmental standards or legislation involving health and safety, minimum wages, or child labour are violated.

What are the benefits of NAFTA? NAFTA's supporters argue that it will provide economic gains to all members. Mexico should benefit from more jobs as companies from Canada and the USA shift production south to take advantage of lower cost labour. The jobs will help Mexico grow economically. Economically Mexico looked to getting preferential treatment for 80 percent of its exports. In the USA and Canada, consumers will benefit from the lower priced products that come from Mexico, and companies will benefit not only from low cost labour, but also from having access to a large and more prosperous market.

How did NAFTA's critics see the agreement? NAFTA's critics worried that the loss of jobs and wage levels that was to occur as a result of NAFTA would be detrimental to the USA and Canada. They also raised concerns that pollution would increase as companies shifted production to take advantage of Mexico's more lax environmental regulations. In addition, some critics raised concerns that Mexico would lose its sovereignty as the country became dominated by US firms that were not really committed to helping the economy grow, but rather just saw it as a cheap assembly location.

After the first decade of NAFTA, most people agree that both the critics and the supporters of the agreement were probably guilty of exaggeration. By most statistical measures NAFTA has been a success, with trade between the countries and FDI into Mexico growing very fast indeed. For example, studies showed that the concern over jobs turned out to be a non-issue. Jobs in Mexico boomed while job losses in USA were very small. Some US firms persevered because most components in Mexican assembly plants used US-made parts, unlike Asian- based assembly plants. One positive that has come from the agreement was increased political stability in Mexico. This, of course, may also be beneficial to the USA and Canada. Some Mexican critics point out that job gains have stagnated as USA and Canadian multinationals shift more work to China rather than Mexico. The future may well see some enlargement with several other Latin American countries including Chile indicating that they would like to join.

Andean Community and Mercosur

It is useful to look at regional blocs that are less successful. The Andean Pact between Bolivia, Chile, Ecuador, Columbia, and Peru was formed in 1969, and modelled on the EU. However, by the mid-1980s, it was clear that the Pact had more or less failed to achieve any of its goals. In the late 1980s though, many Latin American countries began to adopt free market policies, and in 1990 the Andean Pact was re-launched, and now operates as a customs union. In 2003, the Andean Community signed an agreement with MERCOSUR to work toward a free trade area.

Mercosur began in 1988 as a free trade agreement between Brazil and Argentina. It was expanded to include Paraguay and Uruguay in 1990, and has been making progress toward free trade between the countries. However, some critics have argued that rather than creating trade, Mercosur, by establishing high tariffs to outside countries, is actually diverting trade in some industries, and that companies in these industries would be unable to compete in global markets. In recent years, the future of this group has been unstable, not least because of politics. Venezuela pulled out of the Andean Community in protest against Colombia and Peru signing trade deals with the USA. Uruguay demanded the right to sign a separate trade deal with the USA despite being a Mercosur member. The central problem is that members of both trade blocs actually trade very little with each other but mainly with the USA. Other economic blocs have been proposed but seem hard to organize and sustain in the difficult political disunity of the continent.

2.10 Regional Integration in Asia Pacific

One of the most important efforts in Asia Pacific is the Association of South East Asian Nations, or ASEAN. ASEAN was formed in 1967 and includes Brunei, Cambodia, Indonesia, Laos, Malaysia, the Philippines, Singapore, Thailand, and Vietnam. ASEAN's goals are to promote free trade between members and achieve cooperation on industrial policy, but so far, it has made only slow progress. However, a new agreement came into effect in 2003 between the six original members to create a free trade area with the creation of the ASEAN Economic Community by 2015.

ASEAN suffers because members' main trading partners - the USA, Japan, China, and Europe - are outside the ASEAN bloc. On average intra-ASEAN trade represents only 27.6 percent of ASEAN country exports. Size of intra-ASEAN trade also varies from country to country so benefits of membership are unevenly distributed. Furthermore, ASEAN experiences internal political tensions, and much more economic, religious, and cultural diversity than say the EU. However ASEAN does act as a group in negotiating agreements with other countries, or groups like the EU for which it is an important trading partner. It has signed free trade agreements with Korea, Japan, Australia, and New Zealand, and the ASEAN China Free Trade Agreement (effective 2010), fundamentally converting a major rival into a potential partner in raising exports and GDP for all parties.

2.11 The Multilateral Monetary and Trade Systems

We have looked at formal institutions operating at country and regional level, but firms operating internationally also have to bear in mind the influence and impact on the business environment of two international institutions, namely the International Monetary Fund (IMF) and the World Trade Organization (WTO). Both have their supporters and detractors.

The International Monetary Fund

The IMF is a multilateral organization promoting international monetary cooperation and providing temporary financial assistance to countries with balance of payments problems. It has three primary activities on behalf of its 184 member countries:

- Monitoring the global economy.
- Providing technical assistance to developing countries.
- Lending to countries in financial difficulties.

The IMF's lending activity focuses on helping countries with severe balance of payment problems. The IMF acts as a lender of last resort, with loan repayments typically expected within one to five years. As one example, IMF bailouts in 2008/9 were to Hungary (US$157 billion), Iceland (2.1b.), Ukraine (16.4b.), Romania (17.1b.), Latvia (2.4b.), Georgia (0.75b.), Armenia (0.54b.), Belarus (2.46b), Pakistan (7.6b.) and Serbia (0.53b.). There have been quite a few since!

IMF loans come with strings attached. IMF **conditionality** typically imposes conditions that require 'belt-tightening' by pushing governments to embark on reforms that they probably would not have undertaken otherwise. To attack inflation and government deficits, the IMF typically looks for cuts in government expenditure amongst other things, in agreement with that government. In principle the conditions imposed are designed to also ensure the country can repay its IMF loans. In the 1990s and early 2000s the IMF often went into action in emerging economies including Mexico, Russia, Indonesia, South Korea, Turkey, and Brazil. The financial crisis of 2008 and subsequent events, for example the financial crisis in Greece, Spain, Ireland, and Portugal 2010-12, has led to renewed debates around the pros and cons of IMF conditionality. Criticisms include:

- The IMF's lack of accountability. It has very few officials, who are not elected and do not always have deep knowledge of the country being bailed out.

- The IMF's 'one-size-fits-all' economic strategy may be inappropriate. Some economists argue that balancing the budget may not be the best policy; that deficit spending has been a successful policy for pulling countries out of crisis; that cutting spending in more vulnerable developing countries undergoing a major economic crisis to balance the budget may make matters much worse, not better. On the other hand, some critics have argued that the IMF has sometimes not been tough enough, allowing countries to run up deficits not sustainable in the medium and long term.

- Bear in mind, of course, that it is difficult to say whether IMF policies are better or worse than the alternatives, because it is difficult to know what would have happened if a country had not adopted IMF recommendations.

- A major limitation identified in the 2008-13 crisis is that the IMF has no power over countries that do not need its loans despite having large budget or current deficits. Notable cases are the USA and the EU.

The World Trade Organization

In the late 1940s the world community developed several institutions to facilitate international trade and political integration. These included the United Nations, the International Monetary Fund and World Bank, together with the General Agreement on Tariffs and Trade (GATT), and its successor the World Trade Organization (WTO).

GATT was created in 1948 to reduce the levels of tariffs amongst participating countries. By the 1980s it had been successful but had left out trade in services and intellectual property protection. For trade regulation there were a lot of loopholes requiring reform. Moreover GATT's success in removing tariff barriers led to countries developing non-tariff barriers, and GATT did not have effective dispute resolution mechanisms for these. In 1995 participating countries extended GATT by creating the WTO.

The WTO is the main multilateral organization making rules for international trade, and resolving trade-related conflicts between nations. It has both political and economic functions. Peng and Meyer (2011) suggest that in recent years it has focused on:

- Handling disputes constructively. Its role here has increased in recent years.

- Making life easier for all participants. This involves setting out a common set of rules for international trading partners. For example, the WTO's *principle of non-discrimination* means that a country cannot discriminate against some trading partners and not others. If you lower tariffs for one WTO member country you must do so for all WTO members (regional trade groups are an exception here – see below).

- Raising incomes, generating jobs, and stimulating economic growth. The essential role here is cutting trade barriers, with the WTO estimating that if it helped cut trade barriers by a third, this would raise worldwide income by about US$600 billion. There is a debate however, about the environmental impacts of more trade, and how it is conducted and who benefits.

The WTO has six main areas:

- The umbrella agreement establishing the WTO.

- The old GATT agreement covering international trade of goods.

- A new agreement covering the trade in services – General Agreement on Trade in Services.

- An agreement covering intellectual property rights – Trade-Related Aspects of Intellectual Property Rights.

- Trade dispute settlement mechanisms.

- Trade policy review for looking at an individual country's trade policies.

Clearly, the WTO does a lot more than was previously done under GATT, though developing countries often complain that agricultural policies of developed countries were not included under the WTO remit. In recent years it undertook two major initiatives:

Trade dispute settlement. The WTO has a procedure to resolve conflicts between governments over trade-related matters. You can see these at work in the cases you will look at in the Activity below. The procedure is designed to avoid the weaknesses of the old GATT system, which saw long delays, blocking by accused countries, and lack of enforcement. The WTO first facilitates negotiations between the parties, but if consultation fails, it establishes a group of experts to hear the evidence, write a report and adjudicate. All within 12 months (or 15 months if there is an appeal). A limitation is that the WTO does not have its own enforcement capability. It makes a recommendation, not an order. It is up to the offending country to change its practices or not, though the WTO can authorize the winning countries to impose trade sanctions and tariff barriers to encourage compliance.

- *The Doha Development Agenda.* Also called the Doha Round, initiated in Qatar in 2001. This was the first time the WTO participating countries established the aim of promoting economic development for developing countries. The four ambitions were to (1) reduce agricultural subsidies in developed countries; (2) cut tariffs, especially in industries of interest to developing countries, e.g. textiles; (3) free up trade in services; and (4) strengthen intellectual property protection. You might guess which group of countries supported which aim! However, by 2003 numerous countries had failed to deliver on their promises of 2001.

Agriculture was a particular problem with developing countries demanding that Japan, the EU, and USA reduce farm subsidies, but this was rejected. Meanwhile, partly in retaliation, developing countries, led by India, refused to tighten protection on intellectual property and make concessions on service trade. By the 2006 round in Geneva there was still little movement on global agreements, though, outside the WTO altogether, regional and bilateral (between country) agreements were accelerating, and have been since then. One example is the Australia-New Zealand Closer Economic Relations Trade Agreement (ANZCERTA or CER). The USA has signed 17 bilateral free trade and investment agreements with countries as diverse as Australia, Singapore, Peru, Oman, and Jordan, while three more are in the process of ratification. Advocates of bilateral FTAs see them as a convenient substitute for global free trade. Critics argue they: permit countries with large markets to use their bargaining power more effectively, lead to a hub and spoke system of international trade that further strengthens the countries at the hubs, create fragmented rules for businesses operating in multiple countries, and increase trade diversion.

Other multilateral organizations

While the WTO and IMF are the most important multilateral organizations, there are others, not least the United Nations, whose mission is to secure world peace. Peng and Meyer (2011) usefully organize all these in terms of three agendas driving global collaboration and negotiation. The major initiatives are:

- *The development agenda*. As two examples, the World Bank supports major projects that otherwise would not get off the ground, particularly in developing economies. The European Bank for Reconstruction and Development serves transition economies, mainly in Central and Eastern Europe.

- *The climate change agenda*. A major global concern is the environmental impact of human activity. The chief focus has been on the detrimental global warming effects of greenhouse gas emissions. The 1997 Kyoto protocol got developed countries pledging to cut GHG emission levels by 6 percent from 1990 to 2012. Unfortunately the USA, the leading emitter, refused to sign the protocol. Nor did the protocol include India and China, which developed very fast, with China becoming by 2009 the leading source of GHG. The 2009 Copenhagen meeting of countries agreed that more action had to be taken, but sparked disagreements about exactly who had to do what by when. The result was a weak non-binding Copenhagen Accord. This remains a difficult issue on which to make global progress.

- *The financial sector regulation agenda*. Bank crashes can harm not just the home country but can have adverse consequences internationally. A country like UK for example, is responsible for regulating its own banks, including foreign subsidiaries, and can constrain foreign banks operating in the UK. The Basel Committee for Bank Supervision disseminates minimum regulatory standards, revised in 2004 and known as Basel II. This established minimum requirements for liquidity, and procedures for risk metrics. In the aftermath of the 2008 financial crisis these have been criticized as inadequate. Some argue that national regulation of international banks is not enough. However there is as yet (2013) no agreement as to how global bank supervision could be carried out.

2.12 Conclusion

In this chapter we introduced the institution-based perspective on international business and pointed out that there are both formal and informal institutions in countries, and that these may differ across countries. The key functions of institutions are to reduce uncertainty, reduce transaction costs, and constrain opportunism. In practice, firms operating abroad should have a thorough understanding of the formal institutions of each country they are in, or are thinking of entering.

We detailed the main types and characteristics of political, economic, and legal systems found in the world, the debates surrounding these different systems, and pointed out the implications of these in terms of establishing the rules of the game for and challenges in conducting business internationally. We then moved on to look at a five-type model of formal institutions at the regional level. The chapter then detailed the major examples of trading blocs, the first being the political institutions of the EU, and how and why the institutional framework created by the EU is pivotal for business. We then described the advantages and disadvantages of regional and bilateral economic integration in the Americas and Asia Pacific. Finally at cross-regional level, we assessed the multilateral institutions of the global monetary and trade systems, and their current challenges.

Clearly these national, regional, and global institutions are highly important shapers of how business can be conducted internationally. However, as we pointed out, they are not the only, and often not the most important, rules of the game that international business needs to contend with. In the next chapter we follow the institution-based perspective through into the area of informal institutions embracing culture, social norms, religion, language, ethics, and we then consider how business organizations respond to formal and informal institutional frameworks by exploring their approaches to corporate social responsibility.

'A nation's culture resides in the hearts and souls of its people'
M. Gandhi

'Present global culture is a kind of arrogant newcomer. It arrives on the planetary stage following four and a half billion years of other acts, and... declares itself in possession of eternal truths. But in a world that is changing as fast as ours, this is a prescription for disaster'
C. Sagan

CHAPTER 3
Cultural Social and Ethical Challenges: Towards CSR

3.1 Introduction

If you ever visit a foreign country, you will notice a lot of differences in how people dress, the food they eat, or their choice of transportation. Perhaps a particular religion influences how society works, or a different language is spoken. In time you will notice they also have different gestures and manners, and different rituals, codes of behaviour, and ways of working. All of these things are manifestations of culture. And just as you would adapt for differences at home, when doing business in foreign countries, firms need to adapt as well.

In this chapter we look at the informal institutions firms need to take into account when operating internationally. In particular we will focus on the differences between countries in culture, religion, language, ethics, and approaches to corporate social responsibility. Culture is a system of values and norms that are shared among a group of people and that, when taken together, constitute a design for living. Values are abstract ideas about what a group believes is good, right, and desirable, and norms are the social rules and guidelines that prescribe appropriate behaviour in particular situations. Long-standing cultural differences still influence how business is being done. Also, bear in mind that culture is dynamic, it is always changing. It is also important to consider how culture might affect the cost of doing business in a particular location.

We also discover in this chapter that managers and firms ignorant of foreign languages and religious traditions may end up making mistakes that harm their business. We also explore different approaches to ethics in international business, and how variations in ethics across countries can create ethical dilemmas, as can a range of differences about dealing with such issues as the environment, labour, human rights, and corruption. What relevance does the recent development of corporate social responsibility (CSR) have to such ethical dilemmas? We explore firms' different CSR strategies, and whether CSR is vital to, or a diversion from, what international firms need to be focusing on.

3.2 Cultures and International Business

Informal institutions come from socially transmitted information and are part of the heritage that we call culture. They tell individuals in a society what behaviours are considered right and proper, and what would be unacceptable. Typically, cultures have no clearly defined origin, but have evolved over time. Those within a society tend to perceive their own culture as 'natural, rational, and morally right'. This self-centred mentality is known as *ethnocentrism*. Culture can be seen as the collective programming of the mind that develops over time, which distinguishes the members of one group or category of people from another. Though we talk about French culture, and Chinese culture, culture is not necessarily divided by national boundaries. Some countries like Switzerland even have multiple distinct cultures. Similarly, some cultures transcend national boundaries. For example, you might think of how the values promoted by Islam influence many countries.

Culture has been described as 'the way things are done round here' and also as the shared norms, values and assumptions of a group, organization, or society that translate into distinctive behaviours. Values are a fundamental building block of culture. They provide the context within which a society's norms are established and justified. Values can include things like a society's attitudes toward individual freedom, loyalty, collective responsibility, and marriage. The social rules that govern people's actions toward one another are called norms, which you can think of as the routine conventions of everyday life like dress codes, social manners, and accepted codes of conduct. These may get translated into the actual laws of a country.

How is a culture shaped into being? The values and norms of a culture evolve over time and are a function of a number of factors at work in a society including religion, political and economic philosophies, education, language, and social structure. Social structure refers to the basic social organization of a society. There are two important elements to consider here: first, the degree to which the basic unit of social organization is the individual rather than the group – usually we think of the individual being dominant in Western societies, and the group being more important in other societies; second, the degree to which the society is stratified into classes or castes.

How can we understand differences in culture? It is usual to distinguish between three approaches:

The context approach. Context is the underlying background upon which interaction takes place. In low-context cultures (such as in North American and Western European countries), communication is usually taken at face value without much reliance on unspoken context. In other words, yes means yes. In contrast, in high context cultures (such as Arab and Asian countries) communication relies a lot on the underlying unspoken context, which is as important as the words used. For example, 'yes' does not necessarily mean 'yes, I agree', it might mean 'yes, I hear you'. Clearly, failure to understand context and differences in interaction style can lead to misunderstandings in international business. On this theory Chinese, Korean, Japanese and Arab cultures are high context, while German, Canadian and Swiss, for example are low context. This looks a bit simplistic! Critics point out that the context approach may exaggerate the lack of context in so-called 'low context' approaches, and that all cultures, national, business or otherwise, as products of history and tradition, have important unspoken aspects, which are as important as the words used. Also the context approach only looks at one dimension, unlike the dimensions approach detailed below.

The cluster approach. A cluster here is a group of countries that share similar cultures. There are three main theories of clusters. Ronen and Shenkar (1985) identified 14 clusters, while the Globe study (House et al., 2004) sees ten, of which five are similar to the Ronen and Shenkar study. The GLOBE study also used in its survey nine dimensions of culture, thus also falling into the 'dimensions' approach described below. Huntingdon (1996) proposed eight 'civilizations' – Slavic Orthodox, Islamic, Western, Hindu, African, Latin American Confucian, and Japanese. Which civilization do you belong to! All these studies have methodologies that have been coolly received by some scholars. However, the clusters are a useful way of looking at things, because we need to understand that in international business people will feel more comfortable doing business with countries and businesses from the same cluster. However, the approach tells us little about differences between countries within a cluster.

The dimensions approach. The most extensive studies exploring this have been done by an IBM psychologist called Geert Hofstede. He and colleagues identified five dimensions of culture:

- **Power distance** focused on how a society deals with the fact that people are unequal in physical and intellectual capabilities. A culture would rank high on this dimension if it allowed these inequalities to grow over time into inequalities in wealth and power, while cultures that ranked low on power distance played down the inequalities.

- **Individualism versus collectivism** focused on the relationship between the individual and her fellows. In individualistic societies, individual achievement and freedom are valued, and in collectivist societies the ties between individuals are stronger.

- **Masculinity versus femininity** looked at the relationship between gender and work roles. In cultures that were identified as masculine, there was a sharp distinction between sex roles, and traditional masculine values influenced cultural ideals, while in a more feminine culture, there was little differentiation between men and women in the same job.

- **Uncertainty avoidance** measured the extent to which different cultures socialized their members into accepting ambiguous situations and tolerating uncertainty. So, in a culture that ranked high on uncertainty avoidance, people placed a premium on job security, retirement benefits, and so on, while in a low uncertainty culture, people were more willing to take risks, and were less resistant to change.

- **Long-term orientation** – Hofstede later expanded his study to include a fifth dimension he called Confucian dynamism to capture attitudes toward time, persistence, ordering by status, protection of face, respect for tradition, and reciprocation of gifts and favours.

Note that Hofstede studies record only *relative* culture differences between countries. For example Austria, Israel, and Denmark scored low on power distance, so power is distributed more equally in those countries than in Malaysia and Guatemala who scored the highest on power distance. Likewise the USA is highest on individualism, while South American countries tend to be much lower. On long-term orientation Asia Pacific countries tend to be higher than West European countries and the USA.

It is important to note though, that while Hofstede's original study gave us many important insights into cultural differences, his study was flawed in that he made the assumption that there is a one-to-one relationship between culture and the nation-state, the research was culturally bound since it was conducted only by Europeans and Americans, and the study may have been biased since it took place within a single company, IBM. It is important for you to understand the strengths and limitations of Hofstede's work. It provides a good starting point for a cultural analysis that needs to be more fine-grained if it is to influence actual management practice. Each organization may well have its own distinctive culture of 'how things are done around here' and it is important to understand, for example, the culture of Toyota, compared with that of Ford when operating as an international car component supplier. It is an old study and undoubtedly cultures have changed in this period of time. There have been supportive studies subsequently though, and these ironed out some of the methodological weaknesses of the original study.

A further 'dimensions' approach to culture is offered by Trompenaars (1993) who built on the work of Hofstede to arrive at seven dimensions of culture in the workplace:

- *Universalism versus particularism*. In universalist cultures rules and regulations are applied in all situations, regardless of circumstance – Switzerland, Canada, and USA are given by him as examples. The most particularist countries were Korea, Russia and China.

- *Individualism versus collectivism.* As per Hofstede above.

- *Neutral versus emotional*. How often emotions are displayed and whether emotions and subjectivity are thought to be good bases for decision-making. Italy and France come out as the most emotional countries, while in his study the least emotional, in the workplace at least, are Japanese, Germans, Chinese, Swiss, and Indonesians.

- *Specific versus diffuse.* Do workplace hierarchical relationships stay specific to the workplace, or do they extend into the wider social context (diffuse)? Australia and Netherlands came out as the most specific, while China, Japan, India, and Singapore as the most diffuse.

- *Achievement versus ascription.* Are status, power, and authority achieved through merit or does the culture ascribe these by class, gender, age, and education? The former is found more in Norway, Sweden, UK, and USA for example. The latter more in Egypt, Turkey, and Argentina – again as examples only.

- *Sequential versus synchronic attitudes towards time.* Sequential refers to time seen as a sequence of events, and relates to punctuality, meeting deadlines. Synchronic refers to several events/tasks juggled at the same time and less concern about precision on time. Latin American, Arabic, and south Mediterranean cultures come out as more typically synchronic, while north European cultures tend to be sequential.

- *Attitude towards environment.* Does the culture emphasise subjugation and control of the natural environment, or working with nature in harmony with the environment?

Trompenaars' work provides a useful framework for investigating how culture plays out in particular countries and workplaces, and for discovering cultural differences and then how to deal with these. It also has the merit of using initial research involving 1,500 employees in 50 different countries, and in addition focused not just on culture at the country level, but also in actual business workplaces, thus being directly useful to practising managers. However, there may have been quite a lot of changes since the original study, though Trompenaars and colleagues have produced more up-to-date research that continues to monitor cultural diversity.

What are the implications of all of this for managers? It is vital for international firms to develop cross-cultural literacy. To be successful, you have to be able to conform and adapt to the value system and norms of the host country. One way you can gain knowledge of the local culture is to hire local citizens. Developing a cadre of cosmopolitan managers who have been exposed to different cultures can also be helpful. It is important to avoid being ethnocentric, or believe that your ethnic group or culture is superior to that of others.

A second reason for companies to be aware of cultural differences is the link between culture and competitive advantage. The value systems and norms of a country influence the cost of doing business, which of course then affects the competitive advantage of the firm. A society's class structure affects the relationship between management and labour for example – look at Japan's strong worker loyalty system, and lifetime employment guarantees affect the success of Japanese companies. Similarly, a more individualistic culture promotes entrepreneurial activities as compared to a culture that emphasizes collective behaviour. These differences provide companies with insight as to which countries are most likely to produce competitors, and which countries will be the best for investing or selling. For example, if you are comparing two countries with similar wage costs, you will recognize that the country with the better education system, less social stratification, and group identification is probably the better site for production facilities (see also chapter 9 on location attractiveness).

What should the corporate response be to the issue of cross-cultural management, as it has been called? Certainly firms need to develop an awareness of cultural diversity in their workforce, but also need to encourage adaptation in personal behaviour and organizational practices to suit the ever-changing mix of cultures within the firm, subsidiaries, and markets they serve. Clearly this has training and development implications for firms operating internationally. The better firms will also leverage the cultural diversity within the organization and combine the best aspects of different ways of doing things. Rugman and Collinson (2012) summarize a number of research studies and suggest that cultural diversity can be managed by:

- Recognising diversity – map the national culture and ethnic groups within the firm and use this to identify which elements of consistency and standardization can be promoted.

- Building diversity issues into such areas as recruitment, HRM planning, strategy. location decisions, and alliances. This helps avoid clashes and inefficiency.

- Identifying where and to what degree local divisions should be encouraged to take the lead in expressing and managing diversity.

- Encouraging cross-border discussion and interaction as well as focused training. Give international experience to fast-track managers (see also chapter 11).

- Getting a cultural balance in particular areas of strategic and tactical decision-making. For example changing brands for particular markets (see also chapter 7). Ensure a numerically balanced pool of managers to give diverse inputs into decision-making.

- Lead from the top with behaviours that signal the valuing of cultural diversity. Match the geographic diversity of the firm's business with a culturally mixed group of senior managers and board directors.

3.3 Languages

Let us look at how language defines culture. Language is how we communicate with each other both in the spoken form and in the unspoken form, and it is also how we perceive the world. Some countries have more than one language and distinct culture. Canada for example, has both an English speaking and a French speaking area – both with their own cultures. Belgium is divided into Flemish and French speakers, and four different languages are spoken in Switzerland. Chinese is the mother tongue of the largest number of native speakers (20 percent), though English is the most widely spoken language in the world.

Of the world's population 6 percent are English native speakers, 5 percent speak Hindi, 5 percent are native Spanish speakers, 4 percent speak Arabic, and 4 percent Russian. Other languages make up 56 percent of the world's native speaking population.

Many multinationals have adopted English as their official corporate language, to enable knowledge sharing and communication across borders, not least with customers, suppliers, and fellow employees. But note that, even though English is the 'lingua franca', i.e. the default global business language, sharing English as a language in a business meeting can still create problems. People from different cultures may understand the same words differently. For example, famously it is said that the USA and the UK are two nations divided by a common language.

What about unspoken language – why is it important? Well, think for a moment about how you stand when you are talking with another person. You probably stand about an arm's length away. But in Latin America people tend to stand much closer together. Now picture yourself at a business meeting with someone from Brazil. He might try to stand at his customary distance causing you take a step backward because he has invaded your personal space. You may be annoyed at him for standing so close to you, and he may interpret your response as aloofness. Your meeting is already off to a bad start. Similarly, consider the circle you might make with your thumb and forefinger. In the United States, you have signalled a positive response, but if you make the same gesture in Greece, you have just insulted someone (!). We could provide multiple examples of such international misunderstandings. Because facial expressions, hand gestures, and other types of unspoken language can mean different things in different cultures, it is important to do your homework before meeting with someone from another culture.

3.4 Religion and Ethics

Religion is another important determinant of culture, especially in countries where a single religion is dominant. Religion is the system of shared beliefs and rituals that are concerned with the realm of the sacred. Religions with the greatest following today are Christianity (1.7 billion), Islam (1 billion), Hinduism (750 million), and Buddhism (350 million). You might also include Confucianism with these. While not strictly a religion, Confucianism influences behaviour and shapes culture in many parts of Asia. Closely related to religion are ethical systems, or sets of moral principles or values that guide and shape behaviour. So, you might think of Christian ethics or Islamic ethics.

Most followers of Christianity live in Europe, the Americas, or other countries settled by the Europeans. Christians are divided into Roman Catholics, those who belong to the Orthodox Church, and Protestants. Muslims are found in more than 35 countries, particularly in the Middle East. Islam is an all-embracing way of life – prayers take place five times a day, women dress in a certain manner, and pork and alcohol are forbidden. How does Islam affect business? The Koran, which is the sacred book for Islam like the Bible is for Christianity, supports free enterprises and legitimate profits, and the right to protect private property, but advocates using profits in a righteous socially-beneficial manner. The central tenets of Hinduism, which is mainly based in India, are spiritual growth and development. Many Hindus believe that the way to achieve nirvana is through material and physical self-denial.

Hinduism, at least in its pure form, creates interesting challenges for companies. For example, because the religion emphasizes spiritual rather than individual achievement, the drive for entrepreneurial behaviour that is so common among Protestants, for example, is not present. So, it may well be that a devout Hindu may not see promotion or additional responsibilities as being desirable. Buddhism's followers are located mainly in Central and Southeast Asia, China, Korea, and Japan. Buddhism stresses spiritual achievement and the afterlife over involvement in this world. As with Hinduism, there is a lack of emphasis on entrepreneurial behaviour.

Confucianism is practised mainly in China and teaches the importance of attaining personal salvation through right action. Moral and ethical conduct is important, as is loyalty. What do the principles of Confucianism mean for business? The key principles of the ideology - loyalty, reciprocal obligations, and honesty - could translate into making the costs of doing business lower.

Knowledge of religions is crucial even for non-religious managers. Religious beliefs and activities affect business through religious festivals, daily and weekly routines that vary across religions (e.g. prayer times, sacred days, fasts) and activities and objects with symbolic values - positive or negative - that lead to rules as to what the believer can and cannot do. For example, in India cows are holy in Hindu religion and may not be disturbed or eaten. Some objects or practices are taboo or banned – for example Muslims are not supposed to eat pork. Recall the international furore over the Danish newspaper publishing cartoons involving the Muslim prophet Mohammed. Religious differences, more than any other differences, tend to raise emotions and thus are challenging to handle for businesses. Showing respect for other religions and associated values will help you by avoiding conflict and creating a basis for doing business. An individual's religion may also help shape his/her attitude toward work and entrepreneurship.

Ethics

Ethics refers to the principles of right and wrong, standards and norms of conduct governing individual and firm behaviour. Ethics are not only an important part of informal institutions but are also deeply reflected in formal laws and regulations. Business ethics are the accepted principles of right or wrong governing the conduct of business people. An ethical strategy is a course of action that does not violate these principles.

Managing ethics overseas is challenging because what is ethical in one country may be unethical elsewhere. How to deal with ethical dilemmas that arise when operating internationally? *The Friedman Doctrine* argues that the only responsibility of business is to increase profits. Milton Friedman (1970) claimed that as long as the firm stayed within the letter of the law, ethics did not enter the equation. So, in other words he would argue that it is not the responsibility of a company to take on social expenditures beyond what the law mandates, and what is required to run a business efficiently. What Hill (2011) calls the *naïve immoralist* approach argues that if a manager of a multinational company sees that firms from other countries are not following ethical norms in a host country, that manager should ignore the norms as well. Peng and Meyer (2011) suggest three approaches. *Ethical relativism* follows the cliché, 'When in Rome, do as the Romans do'. *Ethical imperialism* refers to the absolute belief that 'There is only one set of ethics and we have it'. Firms often run into problems adopting either of these two approaches. Therefore Donaldson (1996) suggests a *"Middle of the road"* approach in international business by observing three principles when overseas – respect for human dignity and human rights, respect for local traditions, and respect for institutional context. In practice these principles may clash in specific circumstances, leaving the business manager to behave as diplomatically as he/she can in the prevailing situation. For example, where do you draw the line on gifts, or appointing family members to jobs, or hiring children under the working age in your own country, but not in the country where they are working for you? Then there is corruption, defined as the abuse of public power for private benefit, usually in the form of bribery (in cash or in kind). What is acceptable in which cultures and what is not acceptable and therefore corruption?

Ethics provides a useful bridge between culture, language, religion, and the subject of a major way forward - corporate social responsibility-which we will now look at.

3.5 Corporate Social Responsibility Challenges

People involved in business run into ethical situations daily. In international business, they are often magnified because of differences in things like legal, political and economic systems, and culture. How can firms deal with the ethical dilemmas that arise when operating internationally? A major approach is corporate social responsibility (CSR), defined as the consideration of, and response to issues beyond the narrow economic, technical, and legal requirements of the firm in order to accomplish social benefits along with the traditional economic gains the firm seeks.

As we shall see, globalization has created many concerns in its wake (see also chapter 1). Moreover, a stakeholder view of the firm sees a business as responsible not just to its shareholders for its performance, but also to a much wider constituency. There are primary stakeholder groups on whom the firm directly relies for its continuous survival and prosperity – managers, employees, customers, shareholders, and governments. There are also secondary stakeholder groups who do not engage in transactions with the firm, but influence or are affected by the firm, though not essential for its survival. If you take an *instrumental view* you will take notice of all stakeholders because this may indirectly improve the firm's financial performance. If you take a *normative view*, your firm will be self-motivated to fulfil social obligations because it is the right thing to do. As a result of rising global concerns and the stakeholder view, firms increasingly develop CSR *triple bottom line strategies* that take into account their economic, social, and environmental performance. International businesses are faced with at least four major CSR concerns:

- **Environment** is currently a high profile topic, especially the irreversible damage that man-made pollution is causing. A key concern is *sustainability*, defined as the ability to meet the needs of the present without compromising the ability of future generations to meet their needs. Because many countries are establishing strong environmental regulations to try to limit further damage, companies have to adopt new, often costly, measures to abide by the laws. For example, new regulations may be forcing your company to take expensive steps to stay within the law. You know that these regulations have not been imposed in some other countries, known as 'pollution havens', particularly those that are less developed and/or trying to attract inward investment – a so-called 'race to the bottom'. Should you shift your production to another country where the laws do not exist, or are only loosely enforced? Your first response might be that the ethical approach is to stay home and adopt the costly compliance measures. But, you might worry that competitors that do not take this approach will have an advantage. This brings up a phenomenon called the tragedy of the commons. It occurs when a resource held in common by everyone, like the ocean or the atmosphere, is overused by individuals, and degraded. What are the social consequences of this? If everyone else is pumping pollutants into the ocean, should you do otherwise? Thus an MNE could choose to lower standards when operating abroad, seeing it as an opportunity to lower costs by producing where regulations impose least costs, and using the threat of relocation to prevent the foreign government from raising legal requirements. On the other hand there may be some advantages in raising standards when operating abroad. This may be to satisfy closer monitoring by stakeholders; to achieve scale advantages from common practices and standards throughout the organization; to lower the risk of catastrophic disruptions; and perhaps achieve first mover advantage in new technologies and practices that are environmentally friendly. One should not underestimate also the public relations advantages of raising standards.

- **Employment practices** frequently present ethical dilemmas. Suppose work conditions in a host country are inferior to those in the home country. Which standards should you apply – the home country standards or the host country standards? Nike found itself in the midst of a huge controversy in the mid-1990s when it was reported that the working conditions at some of its sub-contractors were poor. While neither the subcontractor, nor Nike was actually breaking the law, there was strong reason to suspect that workers were being exploited. For example, in one factory in Vietnam, women were paid just 20 cents an hour, well below the living wage of $3 per day, to work with toxic materials six days a week. Nike was forced by public pressure to establish a code of conduct for all of its subcontractors, and implement a monitoring system to ensure that the code was followed. The pressure to lower conditions in foreign operations is particularly strong with 'footloose plants' that are labour intensive and can easily relocate when local regulations get tighter. Another problem area is where an MNE buys products or components from foreign firms. Is Adidas, Nike, or Starbucks responsible for labour and work conditions of another, foreign firm? MNEs like Adidas sometimes introduce standards of engagement on their suppliers. These are written policies and standards for corporate conduct and ethics. But what happens if suppliers fail to meet standards or provide misleading evidence? MNEs can be more pro-active, e.g. by joint problem solving and diffusing best practices.

- *Human rights.* You may not think much about your human rights – things like freedom of association, freedom of speech, freedom of assembly, and so on are often taken for granted in many countries. But these freedoms are not respected in all countries. Think about the apartheid system that denied basic political rights to black people in South Africa, for example, or the situation in the Darfur region of western Sudan where the Sudanese government has been accused of genocide by several other countries. Should companies do business in countries with repressive regimes? Some people argue that the presence of multinational companies actually helps bring change to these countries; for instance, it is some people's belief that change is occurring in China because investments by multinationals are helping to raise living standards. Others, however, argue that some countries like Myanmar, which has one of the worst human rights records in the world, are so brutally repressive that no investment can be justified.

- *Corruption.* Is it necessary to be ethical when dealing with corrupt government or individuals? This is something firms have to consider. At what point does 'gift giving' become bribery for example? From a government perspective, bribery is invariably not allowed. The Organization for Cooperation and Development (OECD) passed an anti-bribery measure in 1997 that obligates member states to make bribery of foreign public officials a criminal offence. Despite laws like these, bribery continues to be a common practice for some firms. In fact, some economists believe that in certain cases speed payments, or payments made to speed up approval for business investments, can be justified if they enhance public welfare by creating jobs, and so on. Others argue however, that corruption can become ingrained as a way of doing business, and hard to stop if part of a country's way of getting things done.

3.6 Institutions and CSR Strategies

What are the moral obligations of firms operating internationally? The formal and informal institutions operating in a country greatly influence types of CSR strategies firms can adopt, and the levels of success experienced. In liberal market economies like the USA and the UK firms have a high discretion over their activities. So far as they undertake CSR this will be *explicit* corporate activity undertaken voluntarily as policies, programmes, and strategies, with the extent of these actions dependent on the expectations of different stakeholders of the firm. In more coordinated market economies, for example in Germany and Scandinavia, much more *implicit* CSR takes place with CSR being part of the fabric of the legal, political, and social and cultural institutions, and indeed may not only be morally demanded but legally demanded, e.g. in Germany paying health care benefits for all those employed for more than 20 days a month. Note however that, amongst developed countries in particular, there has been some convergence towards more CSR regulation.

Do companies have a responsibility to take into account the social consequences of their actions when they make business decisions? Should companies always choose the path that has both good economic and good social consequences? You might answer yes, firms have a social responsibility simply because it is the right way to operate. Many people believe that companies need to give something back to the societies that have made their success possible. Others, however, do not share this view. Peng and Meyer (2011) suggest firms adopt different responses to ethical challenges:

- *Reactive strategy* – deny responsibility and do less than required. An example of a *reactive strategy* is when Ford marketed the Pinto in the early 1970s knowing that its gas tank was designed badly and could explode under certain conditions. Ford did not recall the Pinto or make improvements, seeing high costs. After frequent accidents it only recalled the vehicle in 1978 under intense government and media pressure.

- A *defensive strategy* involves regulatory compliance while rejecting informal pressure from the media and interest groups to do more. An example is Nike in the early 1990s, accused of running 'sweatshops' while the incidents took place in contractors' factories in Vietnam and Indonesia. As legislators considered changes to the law, Nike acknowledged an ethical responsibility beyond the legal boundaries of the firm, though at the time seeming to see CSR as a cost and nuisance.

- An *accommodative strategy* accepts responsibility to apply norms and standards commonly held but not enshrined in law. Typically here top managers see CSR as a worthwhile policy and social obligation. Nike, Adidas and the sportswear industry have in recent years been much more accommodative on CSR and by 2000 Ford had also become more willing. When Ford Explorer vehicles equipped with Firestone tyres had a large number of fatal rollover accidents, it recalled all vehicles, launched a high profile media campaign and terminated its relationship with Firestone.

- A *proactive strategy* involves anticipating social responsibility and doing more than is required. For example, anticipating future concern, BMW enabled their cars to be recycled by designing easier-to-disassemble cars and signed up high quality dismantler firms as part of an exclusive recycling infrastructure. It also campaigned to establish its approach as the German national standard for automobile disassembly. In such a strategy a firm like BMW can lobby regional, national, and international policy discussions, build alliances with CSR interest groups on the environment etc, and engage in voluntary activities that go beyond what is required by law.

Sometimes, it can very difficult for companies to decide how to behave in some situations. Managers will be influenced by their personal ethics, and cultural perspective, which may or may not be appropriate in a given situation. However, there are several things that managers can do to be sure that ethical issues are considered when decisions are made.

- Firms can hire and promote people with well-grounded personal ethics. While it may seem obvious that you should hire people with a strong sense of business ethics, it can be hard to know whether a person fits this category. So businesses often require references, or give prospective employees tests as a way of finding out more.

- It is also important for individuals to find out about the ethics of a prospective employer. You might ask, for example, whether a firm has a formal code of ethics, or how senior managers are viewed, and so on.

- Firms can build an organizational culture that places a high value on ethical behaviour. To develop this, they need to articulate values that place a strong emphasis on ethical behaviour. Some firms do this by establishing a formal code of ethics. Once a code has been developed, leaders need to emphasize it and act on it. Companies can encourage employees to adopt the code by offering incentives and rewards to employees who behave in an ethical manner.

- Firms can make sure that leaders articulate the rhetoric of ethical behaviour and act in a manner that is consistent with that rhetoric.

- Managers can develop moral courage. Companies can strengthen the moral courage of employees by committing themselves to not retaliate against employees who exercise moral courage, say no to superiors, or otherwise complain about unethical actions.

- Firms can put decision-making processes in place that require people to consider the ethical dimension of business decisions.

3.7 Conclusion

In this chapter we have looked at cultural differences across countries and workplaces, and how firms need to take into account cultural issues within their own organizations as well as in the countries and markets in which they operate. It becomes clear that cultures systematically differ from each other, are deeply rooted and need to be worked with carefully, in an adaptive mode, in international settings. We have reached an understanding of what culture is and detailed several useful frameworks that attempt to delineate the dimensions of culture. We have also articulated two of culture's creators and manifestations, namely language and religion, and pointed to the importance of taking these into account when undertaking international business.

The chapter has also introduced the subject, and importance, of business ethics, and the challenges likely to be experienced on the international stage. A related set of challenges, but also ways forward, were identified with the topic of corporate social responsibility. Firms can be reactive, defensive, accommodative, or pro-active on corporate social responsibility, but failing to take the CSR issues on board is to ignore both the wider stakeholder community that the MNEs are increasingly answerable to in a globalising world, and the power of the formal and informal institutions described in this chapter and in chapter 2 to shape the path MNEs can take, when they embark on the task of strategy that we turn to in the next chapter.

'All can see these tactics whereby I conquer, but what none can see is the strategy out of which victory is evolved'

Sun Tzu

'However beautiful the strategy, you should occasionally look at the results'

Sir Winston Churchill

CHAPTER 4
Strategy in Global Context:
One Size Fits All?

4.1 Introduction

This chapter provides an introduction to international business management strategy. In order to go international all firms must first develop a strategy and identify how to create more value by operating in foreign, as well as domestic, markets. An important part of strategy is to design the firm's value chain of primary and support activities to ensure that it has the processes and activities necessary to create and optimize value. The managers of a firm must also understand the economics of international enterprise, and in particular how they can achieve economies of location, scale, and (from experience) effects.

With this in place, the firm needs to carry out an environmental analysis to identify the key factors that can support or constrict strategic action in different markets. This is a way of linking our learning from Part One of this book to generating strategic options. We provide three frameworks - PESTEL, CAGE, and SWOT - to facilitate such an analysis.

Finally, the firm needs to choose a strategy. We introduce four types of strategy commonly pursued in international business, how such strategies evolve, and detail Ghemawat's aggregation, arbitrage, and adaptation (AAA) strategy triangle as a basis for designing strategy for international contexts.

4.2 Strategy and Value Creation

A firm's strategy has been defined variously as a long-term plan, a set of actions and/or as an integrated set of commitments. For example:

- "A set of concrete plans to help the organization accomplish its goal" (Oster, 1994).

- "The creation of a unique and valuable position, involving a different set of activities ... making trade-offs in competing ... creating fit among a company's activities" (Porter, 1996).

- "The determination of the basic long-term goals and objectives of an enterprise, and the adoption of courses of action and the allocation of resources necessary for carrying out these goals" (Chandler, 1962).

- "An integrated and coordinated set of commitments and actions designed to exploit core competencies and gain a competitive advantage" (Hitt, Ireland, and Hoskisson, 2003).

Here we will work with the Hitt et al. (2003) definition, recognising that strategy looks at long term (3 years or more) direction, while planning actions for short (1 year) and medium term (3 year) goals. Strategy asks, and seeks to answer, three fundamental questions:

- Where are we now?

- Where do we want to be/must we be?

- How do we get there?

These questions form the essence of strategy as shown in Figure 4.1. You can apply this framework to identify, analyze and make strategy recommendations for any organization. Note that in Figure 7.1 not all espoused strategies work, and some aspects may be modified or dropped (unrealized strategy). On the other hand, not all strategies that eventually get enacted appear in the original plan. They may emerge in the course of events, as managers respond to circumstances, take opportunities, or have to react to unexpected events (emergent strategy). You can test the usefulness of Figure 4.1 now. Take a large company you know well, e.g. SingTel in Singapore, Tata in India, Barclays Bank in the UK. Apply the framework to the period 2007-

Figure 4.1
The Essence of Strategy

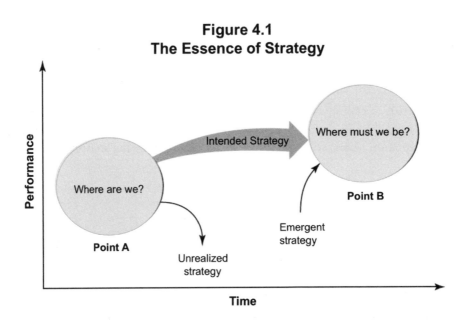

2013. Strategically, where was the company in 2007? Where did it want to get to? What strategy did it follow to get there? You can use the company's annual reports, available on the internet, to help you with this task.

Value creation and the value chain

A business firm needs to pursue strategies that increase profitability and profit growth. Profitability is the rate of return the firm makes on its invested capital. Profit growth is the percentage increase in net profits over time. In general, higher profitability and profit growth increases the value of a firm to its owners. A firm can increase profitability by adopting strategies that (a) reduce costs, and/or (b) add value to the firm's products/services, thus allowing it to raise prices. A firm can increase the rate of profit growth by selling more products/services in existing markets, or pursuing strategies to enter new markets. Generally speaking, firms expand internationally because they experience restrictions and competition in their domestic markets, and see international business as a way of increasing profitability and their profit growth rates.

In practice a firm is always trying to find the optimal, that is the most profitable, balance between (a) keeping its own costs low, and (b) differentiating its products/services in ways that allow it to increase prices to levels at which enough customers will still buy those offerings. The trick is to identify the market segment, that is the group of customers, to whom your product/service and price is more attractive than those offered by the competition. This is not easy! Take US hotel chains that operate internationally. The Four Seasons positions itself as a luxury chain and stresses the high value of its product offering. It can thus charge a premium price for its differentiated product, but at the same time will incur increased costs of operation, e.g. more service staff per customer, better quality of food and restaurant. The Marriott and Sheraton and Westin chains aim to offer sufficient value to attract international business travellers but do not compete in the luxury market, though they do compete against each other. Cutting costs can enhance profitability, but will this affect the quality of the product/service and so the customer experience? Will this then drive customers to rival hotels? Improving the product/service and customer experience could attract customers, allowing price increases, but at what point do higher prices drive customers elsewhere? And what are the adverse cost impacts of improving quality? We will revisit these issues in the next chapter when discussing Michael Porter and Cost versus Differentiation strategies.

The Firm as a Value Chain

The international hotel chains mentioned above, like all businesses, will only create superior value if they organize their operations efficiently. Operations here are defined as the different value creation activities a firm undertakes. These include, in a manufacturing firm, production, marketing and sales, R&D, human resources, information systems, logistics and infrastructure. Figure 4.2 is an example only and does not exhaust the possibilities. For example, a service organization like Singapore Airlines or British Airways will have its primary activities organized around producing its services – selling the right plane seat, providing responsive service to or at the airport, during and after the flight.

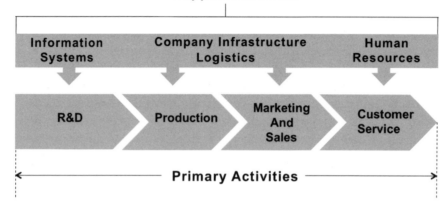

Figure 4.2
A Firm's Value Chain

Primary activities have to do with the design, production and delivery of the product/service, its marketing, and its support and after-sales service (see chapter 7 for more discussion of Marketing and Research and Development – R&D). All create value in various ways:

*   ***R&D*** – value is added through the design of products, services, and production processes, e.g. banks compete by designing new financial products like mortgages, insurance policies, and processes like on-line banking, smart money cards.

*   ***Production*** adds value to a product by converting raw materials into an item, e.g. a car, a computer. In a service like health care 'production' consists of delivering the service, e.g. a heart operation, a prescription.

*   ***Marketing and Sales*** can increase the perceived value of a product/service through global branding ('your promise to the customer') and advertising, e.g. Gillette differentiating its razors from non-branded razors or more local products.

*   ***Customer service*** can give support through the whole customer's buying experience from awareness of the product/service through to the actual buying event, to after-sales support. As one example, US-based Caterpillar manufactures heavy earthmoving machines and vehicles, and can get spare parts to a customer anywhere in the world within 24 hours after a malfunction.

The support activities of the value chain provide inputs that allow the primary activities to occur. Typical support activities that we will deal with in detail in later chapters are:

*   Logistics (sourcing and supply chain management – see chapter 9).
*   Information Systems management (chapter 10).
*   Human Resource management (chapter 11).

Do not be misled. These can be as important, and sometimes even more important, than 'primary' activities. For example, Amazon began making worldwide sales through being an internet 'pure play' in the 1990s and, with no retail outlets, dominates the book market and has been able to move into other business lines – CDs, electrical goods. Its IT infrastructure capability has allowed it to develop a 'cloud' (internet) based business renting digital storage space to other businesses worldwide. Major consultancy companies like McKinsey, PA Consulting Group, and Bain and Company are crucially dependent on their HR capability in the so-called 'war for talent', i.e. getting the best, skilled and motivated employees in sufficient numbers to service clients' needs. Logistics deals with sourcing decisions and, in a semi-conductor manufacturer based in Taiwan, for example, the transference of physical material through the value chain from procurement, through production into distribution. Efficient logistics creates value by lowering costs. When computerized the cost reductions can be dramatic. But better still, excellent logistics can provide raw materials, components and finished goods to where they are needed faster, reducing bottlenecks in internal operations, and improving end service, and even creating a point of competitive differentiation by 'delighting' the customer. The firm's infrastructure provides the support for all these other activities, and includes finance and accounting, organization structure and control systems (see chapter 8), and IT infrastructure services (see chapter 10).

To show the relevance of value chain analysis in the age of the internet, Figure 4.3 portrays the value chain of an internet start-up company looking to compete against Amazon. Note that it is a service rather than a manufacturing firm, and that, like most organizations with international, or even global, ambitions it is highly dependent on information and communications technologies throughout the value chain.

4.3 Going International - Economies From Scale, Location, and Experience

Firms operate on the international stage in order to expand their markets. The success of firms that expand internationally depends first on the goods or services they sell, i.e. the competitiveness of their value proposition or offering to international customers. In chapter 5 we shall see that carrying out *competitive positioning analysis* can enhance this. Second, international success depends on core competencies – skills within the firm that competitors cannot easily match or imitate. Core competencies enable the firm to reduce the costs of value creation and/or to create perceived value so that premium pricing is possible. In the next chapter we shall see the importance of taking a ***resource-based approach*** to competitiveness. In addition, in domestic and international business, three ways of achieving cost advantage regularly come up in management thinking. We note them here because the terms will occur frequently in subsequent chapters.

Figure 4.3
Value Chain for Internet Start-Up

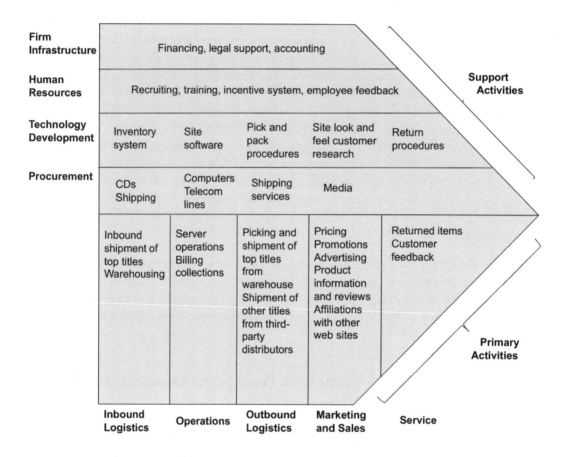

Economies of scale refer to the reductions in unit cost achieved by producing a large volume of a product. Sources of economies of scale include: spreading fixed development and production costs over a larger volume of output; utilizing production facilities more intensively; increasing bargaining power with suppliers. Going international can help economies of scale in several ways. For example the cost to a pharmaceutical company like Pfizer of developing a new major drug and bringing it to market can exceed US$900 million and take 12 years. Companies like Pfizer therefore look to sell their products worldwide to reduce average unit costs by spreading fixed costs over an increasing sales volume. The highly competitive global automobile industry faces intensive cost pressures in every product type, from luxury cars to the cheapest. An efficient factory needs to scale at, say, 200,000 units per year. The only way to sell cars in that number is to serve international as well as domestic markets, so using its factory assets more intensively.

Growth in output and size, fuelled by international sales, may also have another scale benefit. As demand for resource inputs increases so does bargaining power with suppliers. Thus retailers like Wal-Mart generate huge sales volumes and can negotiate down prices it pays to suppliers of goods sold in Wal-Mart stores.

Location economies. Here value creation activities are dispersed to locations where they can be performed most efficiently and effectively. Location economies arise from performing a value creation activity in the optimal location for that activity, wherever in the world that might be. A location might be more attractive cost-wise because of favourable political, legal, and economic factors, for example. Also due to differences in factor costs certain countries have comparative advantage when producing certain products, for example, historically, pharmaceuticals in Switzerland, semiconductors in South Korea, computer software in the USA. This was one reason why initially so many firms moves their IT work to Indian centres like Bangalore and Mumbai, though relative labour costs there have been rising in recent years. By achieving location economies, firms can lower the costs of value creation and achieve a low cost position, and can also differentiate their product offering. Firms that take advantage of location economies in different parts of the world create a global web of value creation activities. Different stages of the value chain are dispersed to locations where perceived value is maximized or where the costs of value creation are minimized. An example is Lenovo, the Chinese computer company that bought IBM's personal computer operations in 2005. The products are designed in the USA, case keyboard and hard drives are made in Thailand, the memory and display screen in Thailand, the wireless card in Malaysia and the microprocessor in the USA. Meanwhile the ThinkPad is assembled in Mexico, and then shipped to the USA for final sale. Note that location economies can vary over time and this Lenovo setup may well change in the future.

Experience curve effects. This refers to systematic reductions in production costs over product lifetime. Studies have tended to show, for example in the airframe industry, that whenever output doubles, the cost per unit declines to 80 percent of the previous cost. This comes mainly from learning effects, as people learn to work more productively and management achieves efficiencies in how work is organized. Where learning falls off after a few years, then economies of scale - whereby increasing the scale of production spreads costs more thinly over each unit produced - will also contribute to this cumulative effect.

The utilization of any of these three sources of economies can have significant strategic impacts for a firm. In certain industries, once a firm establishes a profitable low cost position that can form a real barrier to new competitors. For example in the 1970s Matsushita, the Japanese electronics company, at first lagged behind Philips and Sony in the race to get a commercial videocassette recorder on the market. Matsushita's strategy was to build sales volume world wide and fast by producing from one Japanese factory, which reaped huge learning effects and economies of scale. The objective was to get its VHS standard for videocassette recorders accepted worldwide (Sony and Philips had Betamax standard). Lower costs of production enabled Matsushita to drop its prices by 50 percent within five years of launching its first VHS videocassette recorder. By 1983 it controlled 45 percent of the global market and had a major scale and cost advantage over its rivals.

4.4 Analysing the International Environment

So far you have gained an understanding of strategy, and the economics and activities that underpin any strategy. We now focus more specifically on how firms can move into internationalizing their businesses. There are three very helpful frameworks for diagnosing the environment, and the national and international factors likely to have a high impact on the success or failure of a firm's strategy.

The PESTEL Framework

Recall chapters 2 and 3. The PESTEL framework categorises environmental influences into six main types:

- political
- economic
- social
- technological
- environmental
- legal

PESTEL provides a comprehensive list of influences on the possible success or failure of particular strategies. PESTEL summarises for international management purposes, i.e. from the firm's perspective, the critical factors discussed in chapters 2 and 3:

- *Political Factors.* For example, Government policies, taxation changes, foreign trade regulations, political risk in foreign markets, changes in trade blocks (EU).

- *Economic Factors.* For example, business cycles, interest rates, personal disposable income, exchange rates, unemployment rates, GDP trends.

- *Socio-cultural Factors.* For example, population changes, income distribution, lifestyle changes, consumerism, changes in culture and fashion.

- *Technological Factors.* For example, new discoveries and technology developments, ICT innovations, rates of obsolescence, increased spending on R&D.

- *Environmental ('Green') Factors.* For example, environmental protection regulations, energy consumption, global warming, waste disposal, re-cycling.

- *Legal Factors.* For example, competition laws, health and safety laws, employment laws, licensing laws, IPR laws.

Here are some rules for using PESTEL:

- Apply *selectively* – identify specific factors that impact on the industry, market and organisation in question.

- Identify factors that are *important currently* but also consider which will become *more important in the next few years.*

- Use *data* to support your points, and analyse trends using up-to-date information.
- Identify *opportunities and threats.*

Now is also a good time to carry out a preliminary SWOT analysis:

> S – Strengths of the firm.
>
> W – Weaknesses of the firm.
>
> O – Opportunities for the firm.
>
> T – Threats to the firm.

Here SW refers to the internal firm's capabilities, while OT refers to the PESTEL environment, plus (as discussed in chapter 5) competitive rivalry at industry level. There is a neat way of performing a SWOT analysis and deriving some provisional views of strategy. It is called a 'MiniMax' analysis (see Figure 4.4). Here ask yourself four questions:

- How can the firm maximize its strengths to take advantage of its opportunities?
- How can a firm leverage its strengths to minimize threats?
- How can a firm maximize opportunities to minimize its weaknesses?
- What actions do the firm need to take to minimize its weaknesses and threats?

**Figure 4.4
Minimax Analysis for Creating Strategies**

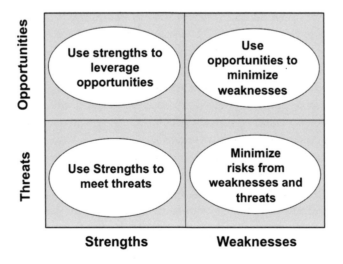

Here you can see the firm is at its strongest using its strengths to take advantage of opportunities. For example Amazon is very good at running an online book service. Many bookstores have not been so good. One solution has been to use Amazon to run their online book service. A business can also use its strengths to meet and minimize threats. In a very competitive industry like newspaper publishing, in some countries your strength just might be control of the distribution chain and speed of delivery. Potentially you could make life quite difficult for a new start-up newspaper! If your business has weaknesses, for example a call centre facility that is costly and underutilized in the Netherlands, maybe the opportunity is to outsource it to South Africa. The firm is at its weakest where weaknesses and threats come together. Typically this arises because another firm is attacking you at your weakest point. For example you offer a poor, or at least very variable and high-priced service to your customers in a hotel chain across the world. Local hotels are eroding your market share. A response is needed! One might be to sell the non-competitive parts of the hotel chain. Another might be to institute radical improvements to establish standards and pricing that customers will appreciate and that are competitive in different countries.

The CAGE Distance Framework

We mentioned Ghemawat's work on *Distance Still Matters* in chapter 1. He developed a CAGE framework to provide a richer understanding of what he means by distance – it is not just geographical distance he is referring to. You will recall that Ghemawat argues, and produces evidence for the fact that, for global strategy, distance still matters. Despite Thomas Friedman's 'The World Is Flat,' (see chapter 1) there are important differences between countries. The world is not globalised but semi-globalised. In practice firms recognise this by trading less in parts of the world that are more distant from them in cultural, administrative/political/institutional, geographic, or economic terms. Firms need to pay attention to the distinctively large differences that arise at national borders, and devise international business strategies that take these differences into account. Ghemawat argues that pure global standardization and localization strategies will not work. International business strategy always needs to take into account the CAGE factors shown in Figure 4.5. CAGE, as you can see, stands for Cultural, Administrative, Geographical, and Economic differences. Note that the Figure shows typical bilateral differences between the USA and several Asian mainland countries. Clearly, distance and differences between the USA and these Asian mainland countries are not just geographic. There are also cultural differences for example language, race/ethnicity, social norms and values; administrative, political and institutional differences; and economic differences, e.g. personal incomes, infrastructure, human talent. Each country will also have what Ghemawat calls 'unilateral' CAGE attributes – distinct attributes that a PESTEL analysis would highlight, and which will influence the design of international business strategy. For example Singapore has English as its language, is multi-ethnic, has strong legal institutions, is a small island (that has been made bigger!) but strategically located, and has historically had strong government intervention in the economy, and a protected bank system.

Ghemawat also points out that a CAGE distance analysis at country level may not suffice. In Ghemawat (2010) he argues also for a CAGE industry-level analysis and discusses the case of Mexican-based multinational CEMEX and its internationalization strategy. One of the notable parts of CEMEX's rise to globalism over 25 years has been the care with which it entered markets that shared affinities with Mexico on several of the CAGE dimensions. Its international excursions began in 1992 with the acquisition of two Spanish companies (Mexico is Spanish speaking). Then it acquired small cement companies in Latin America and the Caribbean, then in Colombia and Venezuela. Note that its acquisition policy over the years recognises that CAGE factors are so important that local companies are needed in order to gain local market share. By the mid-2000s CEMEX had become Mexico's top multinational with operations in 30 countries across five continents, and was the first firm from a developing country to enter the list of the world's top 100 transnational firms.

Figure 4.5
The CAGE Distance Framework: Country-Level Analysis

	Cultural Distance	Administrative Distance	Geographic Distance	Economic Distance

Bilateral (or Multilateral) Attributes	• Different languages
	• Different ethnicities/lack of connective ethnic or social networks
	• Different religions
	• Differences in national work systems
	• Different values, norms and dispositions
		• Lack of colonial ties
		• Lack of shared regional trading bloc
		• Lack of common currency
		• Different legal system
		• Political hostility
			• Physical distance
			• Lack of land border
			• Differences in climates (and disease environments)
			• Differences in time-zones
				• Differences in consumer incomes
				• Differences in availability of:
				  ✧ Human resources
				  ✧ Financial resources
				  ✧ Natural resources
				  ✧ Intermediate inputs
				  ✧ Infrastructure
				  ✧ Supplier/ distribution struct
				  ✧ Complements
				  ✧ Organizational capability

Unilateral Attributes	• Traditionalism • Insularity • Spiritualism • Inscrutability	• Nonmarket/closed economy (home bias versus foreign bias) • Lack of membership in international orgs. • Weak legal institutions/ corruption • Lack of govt. checks and balances • Societal conflict • Political/ expropriation risk	• Landlockedness • Geographic size • Geographic remoteness	• Economic size • Low per capita income • Low level of monetization • Limited resources, inputs, infrastructure, complements capability

4.5 Ghemawat's AAA Model for Strategy Development

How to deal with the international environments-regions, countries, and industries-and the characteristics and differences uncovered by analyses like PESTEL and CAGE? Ghemawat provides an answer in his AAA framework. When looking to globalize, the firm will experience a tension between the need to be responsive to local conditions and markets (Adaptation), and the need to achieve economies of scale and other advantages through global integration (Aggregation). At the same time it will want to take advantage of any absolute economies it can get from operating in a different country (Arbitrage). Let's look at these concepts in more detail (see Figure 4.6). In a foreign marketplace:

Adaptation provides the most obvious strategy for dealing with differences. The strategy is to *adjust* to those differences. Faced with different customer preferences, offer different or modified products or services and tailor policies, positioning, advertising, and pricing. But such variation can be expensive, and sub-strategies will be needed to reduce the costs of such variation.

- *Aggregation.* The strategy here is to *overcome* differences. Use grouping devices and intragroup coordination mechanisms to create greater economies of scale/scope than country-by-country adaptation can provide. Standardization of products/services is just one Aggregation strategy amongst many other possibilities. Particularly important are regional strategies that aggregate based on geography. This involves establishing for example regional hubs, shared service centres, and marketing and sales platforms regionally. Recall that more than one half of international trade and foreign direct investment (FDI) takes place within regions. One reason is that countries in a region often have commonalities in the cultural, administrative and economic, as well as geographic, dimensions of the CAGE distance framework. But firms also aggregate along other dimensions. For example, Tata Consultancy Services (TCS), based in India, and one of the largest Indian IT services companies, aggregates partly by language. Uruguayan operations service Spanish-speaking markets; Hungarian operations service German-speaking countries; while TCS has also set up in Morocco to service French-speaking markets. Recall CEMEX, and how initially it focused on emerging markets – representing an aggregation strategy along an economic dimension. Later it shifted to an aggregation strategy based on geography.

- *Arbitrage*. As a strategy, this *exploits* differences between national or regional markets by locating different parts of the supply chain in different places. As such, arbitrage represents a production strategy, where the firm focuses on absolute economies rather than scale economies gained through standardization. Find the location where there are lower labour costs, lower resource (minerals, raw materials) or assembly costs or cheaper capital, and perhaps tax advantages. In practice, firms in every industrial and service sector have multiple arbitrage opportunities across the world, and we shall deal with this issue of sourcing and supply chain management in much more detail in chapter 9.

The key to successful global competitiveness is to look at the trade-offs between the three As when entering a specific country and industry, and form an integrated AAA strategy. Figure 4.6 summarizes Ghemawat's views on what each strategy offers and how they often pull in different directions. You can see first of all that there are real tensions between the three strategies in terms of first the objectives of going international, where best to locate overseas, how international operations should be organized, what to watch out for strategically, and which public issues need to be addressed. International business management is about clarifying and dealing with these tensions inherent in the strategic choices made.

Figure 4.6
Integrating Adaptation, Aggregation, and Arbitrage Strategies

AAA Strategy	Adaptation	Aggregation	Arbitrage
Competitive Advantage: Why globalize at all?	To achieve local relevance through national focus (while exploiting some scale)	To achieve scale and scope economies through international standardization	To achieve absolute (nonscalar) economies through international specialization
Configuration: Where to locate overseas?	To limit the effects of cultural – administrative-geographic-economic differences by concentrating on foreign countries that are similar to home		To exploit (selected) differences by operating in more diverse countries
Coordination: How should international operation be organized?	By country: emphasis on adjustments to achieve a local face within borders	By business: emphasis on horizontal relationships to achieve economies of scale across borders	By function: emphasis on vertical relationships, including across organizational boundaries
Checks: What to watch out for strategically?	Excessive variety or complexity	Excessive standardization	Narrowing spreads
Corporate Diplomacy: Which public issues need to be addressed?	Potentially discreet and robust given emphasis on cultivation of a local face	Appearances of and backlash against homogenization or hegemonism (especially on part of US companies)	The exploitation or displacement of suppliers, channels, or intermediaries: potentially most prone to political disruption

Ghemawat helpfully discusses the example of De Beers the Africa-based diamond mining and retail multinational. He argues that, even before its more recent strategy shift, De Beers used all three AAA strategies to engage with cross-country differences. Thus De Beers *adapted* to adjust to country differences by focusing on owning mines in 'weak governance countries', presented different marketing campaigns for different countries while obscuring the country of origin, strove for market and product development in different markets and tended to have a global mindset in its management cadre. De Beers also *aggregated* to overcome country differences. Infrastructure and other activities were subject to large-scale economies. Global demand was managed by stockpiling to keep the price up and by global advertising. And it built up bargaining power over its distribution channels through leveraging size and control. At the same time De Beers undertook *arbitrage* to exploit differences. For example, it sourced where material costs were low, for example Africa, Russia, and Australia. On labour costs it used India for absorbing the smallest stones. It gained attractive terms from certain countries needing contracts. It arbitraged to reduce its tax burden. And it retained superior information on optimal locations for its range of activities.

4.6 Choosing a Strategy for International Business

We have one more framework to look at! There are four basic strategies to compete in international markets (see Figure 4.7). The appropriateness of each strategy depends on the pressures for cost reduction and local responsiveness in the industry.

Figure 4.7
Four Basic International Business Strategies

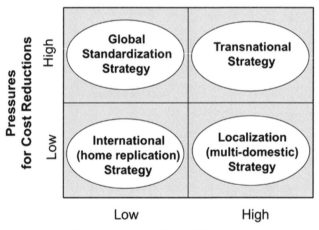

Let us look at the vertical axis first. Pressures for cost reductions are greatest:

- In industries producing commodity type products that fill universal needs (needs that exist when the tastes and preferences of consumers in different nations are similar if not identical) where price is the main competitive weapon.

- When major competitors are based in low cost locations.

- Where there is persistent excess capacity.

- Where consumers are powerful and face low switching costs.

Pressures for local responsiveness arise from:

- Differences in consumer tastes and preferences. Strong pressure emerges when consumer tastes and preferences differ significantly between countries.

- Differences in traditional practices and infrastructure. Strong pressure emerges when there are significant differences in infrastructure and/or traditional practices between countries.

- Differences in distribution channels – there is a need to be responsive to differences in distribution channels between countries.

- Host government demands – economic and political demands imposed by host country governments may require local responsiveness.

  1. *International (home replication) strategy,* which stresses the advantages of replication internationally of home country-based competencies, e.g. brand, distribution network, products, and services. Taking products first produced for the domestic market and selling them internationally with only minimal local customization makes sense when there are low cost/global integration pressures and low pressures for local responsiveness.

  2. *Localization (multi-domestic) strategy,* which considers each country or region as a stand-alone local market worthy in itself of significant adaptation and attention. This responds to Ghemawat's Adaptation requirements in strategy. The strategy involves increasing profitability by customizing goods or services so that they match tastes and preferences in different national markets. This makes sense when there are substantial differences across nations with regard to consumer tastes and preferences and when cost pressures are not too intense.

  3. *Global standardization strategy,* which seeks to develop and distribute standardized products/services worldwide to reap the benefits of economies of scale and shared product development. This is Ghemawat's Aggregation goal, namely to increase profitability and profit growth using economies of scale, learning effects, and location economies. This makes sense when there are strong pressures for cost reductions and demands for local responsiveness are minimal.

  4. *Transnational strategy,* which aims to capture the 'best of both worlds' by endeavouring to be both cost efficient (Aggregation focus) and locally responsive (Adaptation focus). This tries to simultaneously achieve low costs through location economies, economies of scale, and learning effects, differentiate the product offering across geographic markets to account for local differences, and foster a multidirectional flow of skills between different subsidiaries in the firm's global network of operations. This makes sense when cost pressures are intense and pressures for local responsiveness are strong.

An International/home replication strategy may not be viable in the long term. To survive, firms may need to shift to a global standardization strategy or a transnational strategy in advance of competitors. A Localization strategy may give a firm a competitive edge, but if the firm is simultaneously facing aggressive competitors, the company will also have to reduce its cost structures. This would require a shift toward a more Transnational strategy. As we shall see in chapter 6 international strategies become outdated and inevitably evolve to fit with changes in strategic choices and environment. Another issue is 'fit' or alignment with the organization structure and operations – we will deal with these in chapters 6 and 8.

4.7 Conclusion

In this chapter we have arrived at an understanding of what strategy is, how it is a design for value creation, and how the value chain of a firm is vital to deliver on the value promise inherent in the strategy. These concepts have been applied to firms operating internationally with worked examples illustrating the concepts and principles. You were also introduced to economies from location, experience effects and scale, and should be able to apply these ideas to strategy development in international business. This chapter stressed the importance of your learning from chapters 1, 2, and 3 and described the major components of an environmental analysis capturing this learning through PESTEL and CAGE frameworks.

We also showed you how to apply these frameworks to actual cases, and generate strategies from the analyses, not least by using the simple but powerful MiniMax box. This chapter introduced a major means for developing international business strategy for an organization in detailing Ghemawat's AAA model. We also discussed the four basic international strategies types, namely International (home replication), Localization, Global Standardization, and Transnational strategies and the inevitably of evolution from these simple models to deal with changes in strategic choices, levels of success and environmental dynamism. This sets us up for the next chapter, which looks at how firms can compete internationally. We will look at competitive positioning, resource-based and institution-based perspectives on this issue.

'You may not be interested in strategy, but strategy is interested in you'

Leon Trotsky

'The essence of strategy is choosing what not to do'

Michael Porter

'If you know the enemy and know yourself, you need not fear the result of a hundred battles. If you know yourself but not the enemy, for every victory gained you will also suffer a defeat. If you know neither the enemy nor yourself, you will succumb in every battle'

Sun Tzu

CHAPTER 5
International Competitive Strategy: Debating Approaches

5.1 Introduction

At this point, we make a distinction between three types of strategy. Business-level or competitive strategy-the subject of this chapter-focuses on how individual businesses should compete in their particular markets. There is also corporate level strategy that concerns the overall scope of a firm, and how value is added, and synergies achieved across the firm's several business units if taken as whole. We deal with this issue in chapter 6. Then there are the operational strategies, where the focus falls on how the components of an organization deliver effectively the corporate and business level strategies in terms of resources, processes, and people. Operational strategies are primarily covered in the book's later chapters on organization, sourcing, information systems, and human resources.

An *industry* is a group of firms producing goods (products/services) that are similar to each other. There may be thousands of firms offering similar goods/services in perfect competition. Here entry barriers are low, there are many equal rivals each with similar products, and information about competitors is freely available. An example is taxicab services in large cities throughout the world. More typically there are relatively few organizations in direct competition. At the other extreme, a monopoly is where only one firm provides the goods/services for an industry. A duopoly is where two firms dominate the industry. An oligopoly is where a few firms control an industry. A *market* is a group of customers for specific products or services that are similar to each other. Thus Honda operates in the world's automobile market and will sell its range of cars in markets like USA, Europe, Japan, with intensive competition from other automakers like Toyota, BMW, General Motors, Citroen, across its entire car range. To compete successfully, Honda needs to understand the competitive dynamics of its industry, globally, the strategies available to it, the resources it needs to create and leverage to compete, and where it needs to cooperate with other firms in its competitive effort and in its supply chain.

In this chapter we focus on the three major approaches to competitive strategy – the competitive positioning, resource-based and institution-based perspectives, and debate and offer insights into the usefulness of each.

5.2 Porter's Five Forces Framework

Michael Porter has been a pioneer in developing the competitive positioning perspective. His five forces model identifies an industry's structure, and whether or not it is an attractive industry for a business unit to compete in. It provides a useful starting point for identifying whether competing will be profitable, and if not, what actions a firm can take, what levers to pull, as it were, to become more profitable. Porter's framework helps a business to position itself advantageously relative to its competitors. The five forces are shown in Figure 5.1.

Figure 5.1
Five Forces Framework for Competitive Analysis

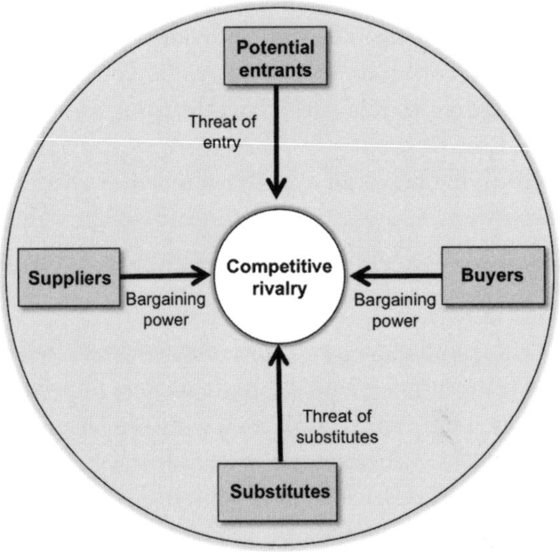

Rivalry between competitors

Competitive rivals are organizations with similar products and services aimed at the same customer group, and are direct competitors in the same industry/market (they are distinct from substitutes.) For example Air France and British Airways compete for airline passengers in Europe. Trains are a substitute service. The degree of rivalry is increased when:

• Competitors are of roughly equal size. This leads to more intense struggles for dominance between the firms.

- Competitors are aggressive in seeking leadership.

- The market is mature or declining. Think about this. If the market is expanding, the strong growth rate in sales allows firms to grow with the market. But if the products/services are mature, or the market is declining, then firms are competing for a shrinking share. As a result there may be high price competition and low profitability, involving intensive rivalry.

- There are high fixed costs. Industries requiring high capital equipment costs, e.g. the steel industry, or high research and development costs, e.g. pharmaceuticals, will seek to spread their fixed costs across increased sales, thus competing intensely with rivals.

- The exit barriers are high, for example due to high costs of redundancy or the decommissioning of capital equipment that is not easily resaleable. In a declining industry this puts pressure on rivals to fight to maintain market share.

- There is a low level of differentiation. Differentiation can be made for example by providing goods/services with different attributes, e.g. colour and shape of tennis racquet, battery length in a portable computer, or by pricing the goods/services differently, or by branding – customers are willing to pay more for Adidas or Nike sports shoes than for non-branded shoes.

Figure 5.2 gives an example of competitive rivalry in the global automobile industry. Note that there are different markets for different types of car, and that products and related services are differentiated from one another by factors like price and prestige. Looking at Figure 5.2 from a customer perspective, there are three markets – mass, luxury, and ultra luxury. We call each a *market segment*, i.e. a group of customers with similar needs, different from customer needs, in other parts of the market.

Figure 5.2
Three Strategic Groups in the Global Automobile Industry

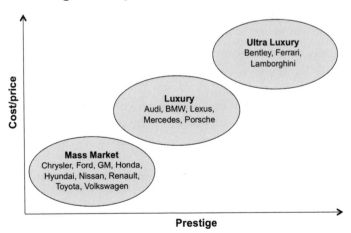

The Threat of Entry by New Rivals, and Barriers to Their Entry

Barriers to entry are the factors that need to be overcome by new entrants if they are to compete in an industry. The threat of rival entry is low when high entry barriers keep them out, such as:

- Economies of scale/high fixed costs. The steel, semi-conductor, and pharmaceutical industries are just three examples.

- Non-scale-based advantages, for example patents, difficult to imitate know-how, superior information about customers; such factors are resource-based. See below for more discussion.

- High experience and learning needed to succeed in the industry

- Difficult access to supply and distribution channels. In many industries firms have built control over their suppliers, by contracts, or by direct ownership for example large supermarket chains in Europe and the USA. This can be overcome of course. For example in the 1990s Dell Computers built a highly successful global business selling computer equipment on-line, with no retail outlets, and focused on controlling manufacturing and the supply chain.

- High differentiation and market penetration costs – typical for the products shown in Figure 5.2.

- Difficult government restrictions (e.g. licensing, tax regimes). For example the Indian government historically, has banned large-scale entry by foreign retailers like Wal-Mart and Tesco.

- Possible retaliation by incumbent (existing) firms in the market, for example slashing prices against a new rival setting up in the UK newspaper industry.

Threat of Substitutes

- Substitutes are products or services that offer a similar benefit to an industry's products or services, but by a different process. For example, in India Tata's 'one lakh' car may become a substitute for motorcycles and rickshaws, initially in Indian cities, but then as an export abroad. Customers will switch to alternatives (and thus the threat increases) if:

- The price/performance ratio of the substitute is superior, e.g. aluminium may be more expensive than steel but it is more cost efficient for some car parts.

The substitute benefits from an innovation that improves customer satisfaction, e.g. high-speed trains can be quicker than airlines from city centre to city centre – as one example in Europe, London to Paris. But note in this example that the price Eurostar can charge for train travel, despite Eurostar being a monopoly, is still limited by the cost of air travel to the same destination. Note also that the substitute may come from outside what you have defined as the industry – in this case, air travel.

The Bargaining Power of Buyers

Buyers are the organization's immediate customers, not necessarily the ultimate consumers. For example, for companies like Unilever and Proctor and Gamble (that make detergents, shampoos, and hundreds of related products) their customers are stores like Carrefour, Marks and Spencer. If buyers are powerful, then they can demand cheap prices or product/service improvements to reduce profits. Buyer power is likely to be high when:

- Buyers are concentrated, that is where a few buyers account for the majority of sales. Thus hundreds of automobile component suppliers try to sell to a small number of carmakers like Honda, BMW, Ford, and Citroen. This can give the automakers a lot of bargaining power. Look at Toyota in Guangzhou China, where the Toyota factory is surrounded by more than 30 supplier factories. Suppliers had to locate this closely because Toyota wanted low transaction costs, and strong control over its suppliers.

- Buyers have low switching costs, meaning they can switch easily between suppliers, for example a global retail chain like Starbucks could switch between coffee suppliers easily. Switching costs are low when the item bought is a weakly differentiated commodity, and is easily available, e.g. sugar.

- Buyers can supply their own inputs (backward vertical integration). For example some Chinese steel companies have gained power over their iron ore suppliers by acquiring iron ore sources for themselves, which puts them in a strong bargaining position relative to their existing suppliers.

The Bargaining Power of Suppliers

Suppliers are those who supply what organizations need in order to produce the product or service. Powerful suppliers can eat into an organization's profits. Supplier power is likely to be high when:

- The suppliers are concentrated, that is there are very few of them. Suppliers provide a specialist or rare input. For example, for Coca-Cola bottlers there is only one supplier - Coca-Cola - of Coke syrup. If Coca-Cola changes the price, there is little the bottlers can do but pay.

- Buyers represent only a small part of sales by the supplier. Thus Boeing will not offer lower prices for new aircraft to small airlines, but may well offer large discounts to Singapore Airlines, Malaysian Airlines, or British Airways.

- Switching costs are high, that is where it is disruptive or expensive to change suppliers. Thus Microsoft is a powerful supplier in the PC industry because of the high switching costs of moving from one operating system to another. Likewise Intel for microprocessors.

- Suppliers can integrate forwards. For example, low cost airlines have cut out the use of travel agents. Nike supplies shoes to traditional footwear stores, but has also established a number of retail outlets, such as Nike City, in major cities.

Use and Criticisms of The Porter Five Forces Framework

With the Five Forces framework you are trying to assess the attractiveness of an industry, and how to make it more attractive, from a business perspective. It is important, therefore, to ask:

- Should we enter or leave this industry?

- What leverage can we exert to improve our chances of success?

- How are competitors reacting to the five forces, and how will they react to moves we make?

The Five Forces framework is a useful tool but must be applied carefully:

1. Apply the framework at the most *appropriate level* – not necessarily the whole industry. For example, the European low cost airline industry must be separated out from the airlines industry globally.

2. A Five Forces analysis may assume too much stability. In most modern competitive environments, there is a higher dynamism than Porter assumed when he designed the framework back in 1985. For example, there is the phenomenon of *hypercompetition* where the frequency, boldness, and aggression of competitor interactions create constant disequilibrium and change. Think of the global mobile phone industry from 2008-12 (Samsung, Nokia, Apple iPhone, Google's Nexus One) and its destabilizing innovation, aggressive price cuts, and expensive marketing efforts.

3. Industry boundaries are constantly changing. Many industries, especially in hi-tech areas, are converging. Think of digital industries and convergence between mobile phones, cameras, and MP3 players, for example. This leads to blurred industry boundaries, rendering the Five Forces analysis more difficult, and needing constant updating.

4. Five Forces analysis tends to neglect the growing importance of *complementors*. Some commentators argue that in fact complementors represent a sixth force. An organization is your complementor when (a) customers value your product more if they use it along with the other firm's product/service than when they use your product alone, and (b) it is more attractive for suppliers to provide resources to both you and the other organization, rather than to you alone. Thus Microsoft Windows and McAfee computer security systems are type (a) complements. Boeing in its relationships to airlines is a type (b) example. Here, Boeing invests huge sums in innovation because it has so many airlines as potential customers. Boeing and its customers find it advantageous to cooperate on aircraft development in order to compete on other activities. The complementors to the PC industry are firms that produce software applications. When a complementor produces a new winning computer game, for example, then demand for both PCs and the game increases.

5. Are all Five Forces potential threats? This neglects the rise of strategic alliances between firms to achieve wider goals together, for example a foreign and local firm trying to dominate the Chinese market in a specific industry (see chapter 11). Also because of the costs of competition, even competitors are found these days cooperating. Thus GM and Toyota manufacture cars together. South Korean based Samsung provides computer chips to Japan-

based Sony. Such firms cooperate in order to compete – not the prime message of the original Five Forces framework!

6. The view of competition inherent in the Five Forces framework assumes that in conditions of high market uncertainty the firm is best advised to integrate backward to compete with suppliers, or forward to compete with buyers, in order to lessen the threats from these two sources. But is such integration advisable? It can be costly, and acquisitions to achieve integration can fail all too easily. Moreover critics argue that in conditions of high uncertainty, less integration is advisable, because it is easier to get rid of suppliers than one's own internal capability. This gives the firm more flexibility in the face of uncertainty. Furthermore, it is argued, outsourcing can give you closer control over suppliers and over cost and quality (see chapter 9). The interesting example, historically, has been to compare Toyota with a company like US-based GM. The Japanese company has always had a lot fewer full-time employees than GM but has uses its keiretsu network of strategic suppliers with whom it has very strong relationships to, for example, co-develop technologies, deliver materials just-in-time, and support the financial position of Toyota in times of market difficulty.

7. The industry-positioning perspective that the Five Forces framework represents has been challenged by the resource-based perspective on competition – see below and Peng (2001). It has also been challenged by the idea that the industry-based view ignores industry history and the importance of institution-specific determinants of firm performance – you will recall chapters 2, 3 and 4!

5.3 Generic Strategies

Having analyzed the macro-environment and the competitive forces in industry and marketplace, the firm needs to make strategic choices. Porter's work again is a useful starting point. He suggests three generic strategies to choose from (see Figure 5.3). Let us look at these in more detail.

Figure 5.3
Three Generic Competitive Strategies

	PRODUCT DIFFERENTIATION	MARKET SEGMENTATION	KEY FUNCTIONAL AREAS
Cost Leadership	Low (mainly by price)	Low (mass market)	Manufacturing and materials management
Differentiation	High (mainly by uniqueness)	High (many market segments)	Research and development, marketing and sales
Focus	Low (mainly by price) or high (mainly uniqueness	Low (one of a few segments)	Any kind of functional area

Cost Leadership

This competitive strategy centres on competing through low costs and prices. It is achieved through approaches such as the relentless pursuit of cost reductions and overhead control, avoidance of marginal customers, and cost minimizations in non-key areas like R&D, marketing, service, and perhaps advertising. The idea is to offer better value to customers through the same value at a lower price. Following this strategy, a firm will target average customers in a mass market and offer little product/service differentiation. The firm takes a high volume, low margin approach. The important issue here is to become the cost leader if at all possible. One example is Primark, the low-price clothing retailer in several markets worldwide. A second example is Wal-Mart. Both drive their cost bases down low so they can sell at lower prices and still make higher profits than their rivals. Buying in massive bulk also gives such firms leverage over their suppliers, whose dependence is increased, while their bargaining power is reduced.

The strategy has some weaknesses. A relentless drive to cut costs might compromise value that customers desire. Competing on price alone leaves little room for competitive manoeuvre if a competitor finds ways of reducing its own costs, e.g. innovating in its supply chain, or finding a substitute product. Consider the impact on world markets if Tata exported its 'one lakh' car mentioned above. The Tata Nano car sold initially for US$3,000 in India, while abroad, competitors' cheapest cars were selling for US$8-10,000.

Differentiation

A differentiation strategy delivers products/services that customers perceive to be valuable and different, even unique. Here a firm targets customers in smaller, well-defined segments who are willing to pay premium prices. It takes a low volume, high margin approach. The strategy is dependent on products/services with unique attributes (actual or perceived), for example in terms of quality, sophistication, prestige, or luxury. Of course, it can be quite a challenge to identify unique attributes that are valued by customers in each market segment, especially if the firm is selling into a mature market where most differentiation has already been tried or delivered. Thus key functional areas are research and development (as a source of innovation), marketing/sales, and after-sale services. Differentiation also erodes and becomes commoditized as competitors find ways of replicating the original product. In the fashion industry, new designs of dresses can sometimes be replicated by competitors and on the High Street at much lower prices within a few days of the original design being launched.

Focus (or Niche) Strategy

Here a firm concentrates on serving the needs of a particular segment or niche of an industry such as a geographical market, type of customer, or product line. A specialized differentiator has a smaller, narrower, and sharper focus than a large differentiator. For example, Japanese shipbuilders tend to build high quality vessels at premium prices for the global market. Scandinavian shipbuilders tend to narrow their focus to building icebreakers, cruise ships, and other specialized vessels.

A specialized cost leader deals with a narrower segment compared with the traditional cost leader. Focusing will be particularly successful when a firm possesses intimate knowledge of a particular market segment. India's large IT outsourcing firms such as TCS, Wipro, and Infosys throughout the early and mid 2000s competed successfully against much larger firms such as Accenture, Hewlett Packard, and IBM because they focused on providing good quality at lower costs for IT support, maintenance, and development work. Lower costs came from lower labour costs in India, and the adoption of process methodologies.

Looking across these strategies, one of the principles that Porter always argued is 'don't get stuck in the middle!' In other words do not get compromised by adopting more than one of these strategies. This has probably played well in a lot of strategic situations over the years, but in more modern environments increased competitive pressure has meant that firms have tended to have to BOTH reduce costs and differentiate, even in the same market segment. This has become true across a number of industries, not least the car industry where even cheap cars are expected, in many global markets, to be reliable and good quality. Firms in the supermarket industry regularly stress 'value for money'. For a time UK-based Sainsbury's had as its motto 'Good food costs less at Sainsbury's.' If this is a product of increased competitive pressure, not least from foreign firms, then 'middle' strategies are also massively enabled by more advanced technologies now available. For example, in the car industry, scale economies used to be everything in terms of establishing low price. These days flexible manufacturing systems and advanced automation have made mass customization possible, whereby quality cars can be produced in smaller batches at highly competitive prices.

5.4 A Resource-Based Perspective on Competitiveness

The industry-based view detailed so far focuses on competitive positioning in relation to external Opportunities and Threats. The resource-based view we now discuss focuses on the resources and capabilities needed to compete, and deals with the internal Strengths and Weaknesses of the firm. The most fundamental questions asked by the resource-based view are – do the resources add value? Do they enable a firm to exploit an external opportunity and/or neutralize an external threat?

Resources are the tangible and intangible assets a firm uses to choose and implement its strategies. Capabilities are a firm's capacity to technically deploy those resources to deliver strategy.

Look at Figure 5.4. Tangible assets are those that are observable and more easily quantified. Financial assets include internal funds such as shareholders' capital and retained profits, as well as external capital, like loans provided by banks. Physical assets include plants, offices, infrastructure, and equipment, as well as inventories of raw materials, components, and finished goods. Technological resources include patents, trademarks, and copyrights that entitle the firm to intellectual property rights and enable it to generate valuable products.

Intangible assets are also found on companies' balance sheets, but they are harder to value, difficult to codify, and tough to observe. Reputational resources are the firm's goodwill, brand names, and business relationships. Goodwill is the value of abilities to develop and leverage the firm's reputation as a solid provider of goods and services, an attractive employer and/or a socially responsible corporate citizen. Reputation can be regarded as an outcome of a competitive process in which firms gain and signal prestige in specific areas important for competing effectively, e.g. reputation for quality (cars), for corporate responsibility (banking), as a good employer (management consultancy). Innovation capabilities are increasingly highly valued across industries, though prevalent in hi-tech firms like Samsung, IBM, and Microsoft.

Figure: 5.4 Examples of Resources and Capabilities

TANGIBLE RESOURCES AND CAPABILITIES	EXAMPLES
Financial	• Ability to generate internal funds • Ability to raise external capital
Physical	• Location of plants, offices, and equipment • Access to raw materials and distribution channels
Technological	• Possession of patents, trademarks, and copyrights
Organizational	• Formal planning, command, and control systems • Integrated management information systems

INTANGIBLE RESOURCES AND CAPABILITIES	EXAMPLES
Human	• Knowledge • Trust • Managerial talents • Organizational culture
Innovation	• A supportive atmosphere for new ideas • Research and development capabilities • Capacities for organizational innovation and change
Reputational	• Perceptions of product quality, durability, and reliability among customers • Reputation as a good employer • Reputation as a socially responsible corporate citizen

Sources: Adapted from (1) J. Barney, 1991, Firm resources and sustained competitive advantage (p. 101), Journal of Management, 17: 101; (2) R. Grant, 1991, Contemporary Strategy Analysis (pp. 100–104), Cambridge, UK: Blackwell; (3) R. Hall, 1992, The strategic analysis of intangible resources (pp. 136–139), Strategic Management Journal, 13: 135–144.

Human resources (or human capital) are embedded in the individuals working in an organization. They include:

• Individual employees' skills, talent and knowledge.

• Individual employees' capacity for collaboration and communication, and their abilities for interpersonal interaction that are not captured by the firms' formal systems and structures.

• Employees' shared values, traditions, and social norms within an organization.

Financial analysts may take human resources for granted, but many firms regard them as a foundation of all their capabilities. Knowledge and associated routines and practices are known as capabilities. Knowledge capabilities are these days highly valued as firm-specific intangible abilities to use resources to achieve organizational goals.

No firm can generate competitive advantage by relying only on primary resources. As we saw in chapter 4, most goods and services are produced through a chain of vertical activities (from upstream to downstream) that add value – in short, a value chain. Many of the most important capabilities in today's business world relate to abilities to connect different stages of the value chain. Here are some examples:

- Capabilities in innovation. A firm's assets and skills to (1) research and develop new products and services, and (2) innovate and change ways of organizing.

- Capabilities in operations. A firm's ability to effectively implement its regular activities, notably the manufacturing process.

- Capabilities in marketing enable firms to develop and sustain brand's awareness and values and to induce consumers to buy these brands.

- Capabilities in sales and distribution enable firms to manage interactions with (potential) customers and in bringing products to the right customer at the right time.

- Capabilities in corporate functions include a firm's planning, command, and control systems, and structures.

While all such capabilities can contribute to competitive advantage, some may become primary for a firm in specific circumstances. For example, Wal-Mart today is the biggest retail company in the world. It does not make a single thing. All it "makes" is a hyper- efficient supply chain. Its logistics capabilities were born from being initially located in low cost Arkansas, USA. Its logistics capabilities give Wal-Mart speed, scale, and cost advantages over rivals, and also enable Wal-Mart to provide logistics advice and services to other companies.

One of the critical questions on capabilities a firm must answer is whether a capability is critical enough to be kept in-house, or whether it is not a core critical capability and can be outsourced, or be the subject of a strong partnering relationship with another firm, or service supplier. As one example, many booksellers found they could not develop the capability to run an on-line book service. So they hired Amazon to run their websites and service. It is an interesting question whether this was a good move in terms of long-term competitiveness. What do you think? We address this question in depth in chapter 9.

5.5 Resource-Based Competition: The VRIO Framework

Peng and Meyer (2011) propose a resource-based framework that focuses on the value (V), rarity (R), imitability (I), and organizational (O) aspects of resources and capabilities. This is called a VRIO framework. You may also come across the VRIN framework. The difference here is the N! In the VRIN framework N stands for Non-substitutability. This refers to products/services, but also importantly to non-substitutable competencies. Peng (2001) argues for the need to replace this attribute with the more general one of Organization, seeing the distinctive characteristics and abilities of the organization built over years as a guard against easy competence substitution. Here we work with Peng's VRIO framework. VRIO poses four fundamental questions:

Value. Do resources and capabilities exist that are valued by customers and provide potential competitive advantage? Adding value is necessary for achieving competitive advantage. For example, throughout the 1980s and 1990s IBM sold PCs but this became highly competitive and its focus on hardware became a disadvantage. IBM moved into the more lucrative software and services areas, and indeed sold its PC division to China's Lenovo in 2004.

Rarity. How rare are the valuable resources and capabilities? Do capabilities exist that no, or few, competitors possess? Valuable but common resources do not give an advantage, e.g. water as a cooling agent in wet weather countries. However, in hot, dry countries water might be both valuable and rare and access prized. Valuable and rare can give a temporary advantage. Advantage is temporary because competitors catch up, and the differentiation becomes commoditized. An interesting example is the quality advantage Japanese cars had in US and European markets for many years. The quality across carmakers is now comparable but quality is no longer rare, and has become a minimum requirement to compete in the industry.

Imitability. How easy is it to replicate the resources/capability? Generally, it is easier to imitate tangible resources/capabilities, for example a manufacturing plant, than intangible ones, for example tacit knowledge, managerial talent, superior motivation. There are two ways to imitate – direct duplication and substitution. Direct duplication is the more difficult:

- It is hard to acquire in a short time what competitors have developed over a long time.

- Difficult for a competitor to identify the causal determinants of your firm's performance. An interesting case is Toyota (Qumar 2010). Until recently Toyota was the number one automaker in the world and was much admired and studied over many years for something called 'The Toyota Way', i.e. the way it combined all factors and resources in a distinctive way that other organizations tried and rarely succeeded in replicating.

- Substitution – less challenging, but not always easy.

Organization. How is a firm organized to develop and leverage the full potential of its resources and capabilities? For example, in the movie business film stars are valuable, rare, and hard to imitate, but they need a studio and an organization to make the film into a success. This involves using complementary assets - film crews, directors, make-up artists, business managers - this can be a long list! It also involves socially complex ways of organizing, for example overcoming cultural differences, establishing strong human relationships by which activity can be facilitated. Thus distinctive organization that gives competitive advantage is dependent on using complementary assets effectively; managing social complexity successfuly; and leveraging invisible relationships that can add value – because this makes imitation much more difficult.

Figure 5.5 shows the growing competitive advantage from developing firm specific resources and capabilities that are valuable, rare, non-imitable and are supported by distinctive organizational capabilities. Valuable, rare, but imitable resources/capabilities can give temporary advantage. Only valuable, rare and hard-to-imitate resources/capabilities backed by distinctive organization can provide a sustained competitive advantage.

Are there limitations to the resource-based perspective? Critics point to several issues. The first is the conceptual blurring of the notions of resources and capabilities. At what point do resources convert into capabilities and how is the combination arrived at? It is all too easy for managers to look at a group of resources and say they add up to a capability; but what makes them a capability rather than just a group of resources? Secondly, and relatedly, a capability is potential. It can only be proven in performance. Firms can mislead themselves in believing they have distinctive competitive capabilities because they have not really had to utilise them, or do not know the capabilities of competitors very well. The US car industry felt it had world-class capability in building cars in the late 1980s until comparisons were made with Japanese factories both in Japan and the USA in the early 1990s. The inferior US performance led to much analysis of Japanese capabilities and the distinctiveness of their work practices, labour policies, and supplier network systems. Thirdly, resource-based competition involves building from the bottom-up, and capabilities, as Peng and Meyer (2011) point out, may take a long time horizon to develop and achieve differentiation in. Do modern firms have the time to do this? Basically a firm has to make a strategic bet on a capability. But by the time it is built, perhaps the dynamic competitive marketplace will have moved on and the capability is no longer needed, and/or does not differentiate in any meaningful way.

Figure 5.5
VRIO Framework

Criterion	Question	Resource 1	Resource 2	Resource 3	Resource 4
Value Creating	Does the resource add value?	No	Yes	Yes	Yes
Rare	How rare is the resource	-	No	Yes	Yes
Imitability	How difficult is it for others to imitate the resource	-	No	No	Yes
Organization	Are other policies and procedures organized to support the exploitation of this resource	No	Yes	Yes	Yes
		↓	↓	↓	↓
Competitive implications		Disadvantage	Parity	Temporary advantage	Sustained advantage

Sources: Adapted from (1) J.B.Barney, 2002, *Gaining and Sustaining Competitive Advantage*, 2nd ed. (p. 173), Upper Saddle River, NJ: Prentise Hall (2) R.E. Hoskisson, M.A. Hitt, & R.D. Ireland 2004, *Competing for Advantage* (p.118), Cincinnati, OH: Thomson South-Western.

5.6 Debates and an Institution-Based View of Competition

Finally, there are a number of controversies that are worth pointing to when it comes to the resource-based approach:

1. One interesting question is whether the competitive industry positioning approach that Michael Porter and others advance helps a firm compete better than the firm-specific resource-based approach. While many arguments and much evidence are marshalled to answer this question, the truth is that they are probably best seen as complementary lenses. Both provide different, useful insights on how a firm can compete successfully in international business.

2. In the last 10 years there has been much greater emphasis on the need for dynamic capabilities that are most frequently knowledge-based. There are dangers in investing in static capabilities whose differentiating, valuable, rare and organizationally- supported attributes commoditize and become less valuable over time. Dynamic capabilities are needed in fast moving and highly competitive environments typical of most industries in emerging and developed economies today.

3. Should the firm's resources and capabilities be retained in-house or can they be outsourced? Can they be offshored? What are the limits to offshoring and outsourcing? How can we avoid 'hollowing out' the organization? We will look at these issues in detail in chapter 9.

4. What about international capabilities? Do firms that are successful domestically have what it takes to win internationally? In the mid-2000s the US fashion retailer Limited Brands had 4,000 stores throughout the USA, brands like Victoria's Secrets, Bath & Body Works, but still refused to go abroad, even to Canada. This scepticism is backed by some evidence that it takes additional capabilities to move into overseas markets. Thus in the mid-2000s Wal-Mart withdrew from Germany and South Korea. Its main French-based competitor Carrefour also exited Japan, Mexico, Slovakia, and South Korea. At the same time, the Scandinavian furniture company IKEA has found its style of flat-pack packaging and sales is popular in many global markets. Unlike Limited Brands, companies like Zara, United Colors of Benetton, and Gucci are successful in major cities around the world. Reasons for success can be found in chapter 6 when we discuss modes of entry and the factors and choices that render international business performance effective.

5. We dealt with an institution-based view of competition in chapters 2 and 3. Peng and Meyer (2011), and Peng, Wang and Jiang (2008) are particularly strong on this perspective. They point out that, especially when it comes to international competitiveness, formal and informal institutions greatly affect and shape the strategies that are possible in specific countries and markets – something that the industry positioning and resource-based approaches tend to downplay, and even neglect.

5.7 Conclusion

In this chapter we have focused on competitive business strategy, as applied to international contexts. We saw the usefulness, but also the limitations of competitive positioning frameworks and approaches. In particular we looked at Porter's work on the Five Forces and generic strategies. While Porter's frameworks have been much criticised, they have also been much used over the years, not least by practising strategists. Much of the criticisms come from the original frameworks (developed in the 1980s) not always addressing the realities of the global marketplace of the 21st century. Thus we see how some have argued for a sixth force - complementors - being added to the framework for industry analysis. Such improvements can always, must always, be made in the fast-moving, globalizing management field. This should not detract from the importance of carrying out competitive positioning analysis when embarking on international business.

The chapter also gave an understanding of the resource-based approach to competition, in particular the VRIO framework, and how tangible and intangible resources and capabilities can be utilised to achieve competitiveness. To some extent the resource-based view of the firm is also a critique of competitive positioning approaches as represented by Porter, but it is best to see the perspectives as working in tandem, as it were, along with an understanding of the PESTEL and CAGE environments that comes from an institution-based perspective. To put it another way, a practising manager would gain much from applying only one of these perspectives, but the real advantage will come from applying all three when designing and crafting strategy for international business.

'Before you journey, observe the wind carefully, detect its direction, and then follow it. You will get to your destination twice as fast with half the effort'

Chin-Ning Chu

'The relationship between commitment and doubt is by no means an antagonistic one. Commitment is healthiest when it is not without doubt, but in spite of doubt'

Rollo May, The Courage to Create

'And the day came when the risk to remain tight in a bud was more painful than the risk it took to blossom'

Anais Nin

CHAPTER 6
Market Entry and Evolution: Commitment Versus Risk

6.1 Introduction

Throughout earlier chapters you read about foreign direct investment. FDI occurs when a firm invests directly in facilities to produce and/or market their products or services in a foreign country. Once a firm undertakes FDI it becomes, by definition, a multinational enterprise or MNE. However, entering a foreign market is not that simple! There are major choices: why enter a foreign market, which market(s) to enter, when to enter the market(s), and on what scale? There are also major options available as to how to enter a foreign market.

In this chapter, we discuss foreign direct investment in detail and the conditions under which it becomes a viable strategy. However, we also discuss options and their advantages and disadvantages. You will learn about exporting, turnkey projects, licensing, franchising, joint ventures, as well as fully owned subsidiaries. You will also learn about when to establish strategic alliances, and how to make these work. Finally, and connecting back to chapter 4 you will learn how firms evolve their international strategy in order to seek optimal location, organizational arrangements and returns.

6.2 The Decision to Enter Foreign Markets

The decision to enter a foreign market breaks down into four decisions that we will discuss here. If you are a small or medium enterprise (SME) your reasons and decisions may well be very different from those of a multinational (MNE). We will consider both kinds of enterprises here, though the main focus will be on MNEs.

Why enter a foreign market?

The obvious reason to seek foreign markets is to expand sales revenues. The home market may be too small to grow the business, but foreign markets for the product or service, when added together, could represent an enormous business opportunity, and also a source of funding.

Increased sales may well provide increased production economies of scale feeding into lower costs and more competitive pricing. Increased profits, and profitability can lead to further investment in the development of the business and its products/services. Consider the Russian company Kaspersky Lab. The product here is anti-virus software for home and company use, which is easily adaptable for international markets. The company started very small in 1997 but by 2008 was the fourth largest supplier in the world. They did this by gaining funding initially through foreign licensing agreements, expanding using foreign sales partners, then launching local offices, initially in the UK, Poland, Holland, and China, but then other countries were gradually added. Its dramatically successful growth is one that many SMEs would seek to replicate, though each would have its own distinctive set of challenges on the road to internationalization.

Some MNEs, on the other hand, may well have sufficient financial resources and be mature enough to act on a larger-scale and longer term basis and be able to invest directly in establishing subsidiaries abroad. Peng and Meyer (2011) suggest that such investments have one or more of four common objectives:

- *Natural resource seeking.* For example oil exploration in the Middle East, Russia, minerals in Africa, where the issues are quality, quantity, and cost of resources.

- *Market seeking.* For example luxury consumer goods in emerging countries, where the objective is to find strong market demand and customers willing to pay.

- *Efficiency seeking.* For example manufacturing in Guandong, China, logistics in Rotterdam, where the objective is to achieve economies of scale, use low-cost skilled labour, with sufficient transport, supplier, and communications, plus energy infrastructure.

- *Innovation seeking.* For example IT in Silicon Valley USA, and Bangalore India, biotech firms in Cambridge UK, where the objective is to seek out clusters of innovatory firms or individuals, or educational institutions.

More often, a firm's first entry into foreign markets is the start of a long-term evolution towards internationalization, and becoming a multinational. In this respect, consider the history of Pearl River Piano. Founded in 1956, it became China's leading brand, but by the 1980s faced strong competition in its domestic market. It started exporting to US importers, and only in 1999 established a US subsidiary, in California. In 2000 it also bought a prestigious German brand piano company to position itself in the higher priced end of the European Market. Global competition pushed a strategy of exports, Greenfield investments, and acquisitions over time.

Which markets to enter?

The answer to this question depends on the firm's objectives. A *market seeking* firm looks at size of market, and the present and future purchasing power of consumers there. Large markets such as India, China, and Indonesia will still differ in terms of living standards and economic growth. Thus weak economic growth in Indonesia makes it a less attractive target for foreign investment than India or China. Our earlier chapters established a range of factors that shape the overall attractiveness, or otherwise, of a particular regional, national, or intra-national marketplace (see also chapter 9 for a comprehensive framework). Also important is the level of domestic and foreign competition experienced in that foreign market. Thus Tesco, the British grocery chain, has expanded its foreign operations over the last five years in emerging countries where markets lack strong local or multinational competitors, and where there may be large potential demand.

Natural resource seeking firms, for example, looking for oil or gas deposits, seek quantity, quality, and low cost resources, as do efficiency seeking firms wanting - typically - low cost, productive and reliable local workforces, e.g. software developers and engineers in India, call centre operatives in South Africa. But for *efficiency seeking* firms total cost, not just labour costs, is a vital calculation.

When to enter?

Entering a market in advance of competitors can give first mover advantages. These include:

- The ability to pre-empt rivals by establishing a strong brand name.
- The ability to build up sales volume and ride down the experience curve ahead of rivals, and gain a cost advantage over later entrants.
- The ability to create switching costs that tie customers to products or services, making it difficult for later entrants to win business.

However being a first mover can also have risks and disadvantages, including:

- The risks and costs of business failure if inexperience in the foreign market leads to major mistakes, e.g. underestimating costs or cultural differences in customer preferences.
- Pioneering costs where the foreign business environment is so different that major time, effort, and expense has to be incurred in learning from experience.
- Costs of promoting and establishing a product offering and brand, including cost of educating customers.

As one example of the advantages of being a late entrant, look at McDonald's' experience in China. As an early US fast food chain KFC incurred considerable costs in setting up the business, but its US rival McDonald's learned from KFC's experience, and as a later entrant has capitalized on the market in China. Late movers, then, can gain certain advantages that first movers may not enjoy. Examples include taking advantage of a first mover's investments in educating customers, and learning about the market, and what works managerially; letting the market and technological uncertainties be sorted out by the first mover before entering the market; being able to leapfrog the early mover by being in a position to differentiate its products/services more precisely.

Scale and Ownership

Clearly, entering a foreign market incurs risk. Therefore it is important to decide whether you are making a strategic commitment, i.e. committing large resources and investments rapidly or wish to proceed incrementally, taking less risk. If the decision is to seize a large market opportunity and make a strategic commitment, then MNEs will look at the importance of ownership and control. To maintain control they might choose to start a new business in the foreign country as a *wholly owned Greenfield site.* Alternatively they might acquire, that is buy, an existing business with market presence in the country they wish to enter – this would be a *full acquisition,* giving better control, protection of know-how, and ability to coordinate globally.

Less control and ownership can be had from choosing a *newly created joint venture* with another business, to share costs, risks and profits, and gain access to the partner's knowledge, assets, and market presence. *Partial acquisition* of another business will give less ownership and control, and the potential of conflicts with the co-owners, but is a means of getting size, presence, and existing know-how in the foreign market.

6.3 Foreign Direct Investment

Having spelt out the decision points on market entry, let us look in more detail at foreign direct investment as an option. Foreign direct investment, or FDI, occurs when a firm invests directly in facilities to produce and/or market their products or services in a foreign country. Once a firm undertakes FDI it becomes, by definition, a multinational enterprise or MNE. There are two main forms of FDI. As we said above, Greenfield investment involves establishing a wholly owned new operation in a foreign country. The second type of FDI is an acquisition or merger with an existing firm in the foreign country. Most firms make their investments either through mergers with existing firms, or acquisitions. Firms prefer this route because mergers and acquisitions tend to be quicker to execute than Greenfield investments, it is usually easier to acquire assets than build them from the ground up, and because firms believe they can increase the efficiency of acquired assets by transferring capital, technology, or management skills.

Let us look at the bigger picture before we look at firm level decisions. The flow of FDI refers to the amount of FDI undertaken over a given period of time. Outflows of FDI are the flows of FDI out of a country, while inflows of FDI are the flows of FDI into a country. The stock of FDI refers to the total accumulated value of foreign-owned assets at a given time. There has been a marked increase in both the flow and stock of FDI in the world economy. In 1975, the outflow of FDI was about US$25 billion; by 2008 it was US$1.4 trillion! Together, six countries accounted for almost 60 percent of all FDI outflows from 1998 to 2006 – USA, UK, Netherlands, France, Germany, and Japan. Why has there been such a significant increase in FDI outflows?

- Firms are worried about protectionist measures, and see FDI as a way of getting around trade barriers.

- Changes in the economic and political policies of many countries have opened new markets to investment. Think, for example, of the changes in Eastern Europe that have made it possible for foreign firms to expand there.

- Many firms see the world as their market now, and so are expanding wherever they feel it makes sense. For example, Spain's Telefónica is pursuing opportunities in Latin America and in Europe.

- Many manufacturers are expanding into foreign countries to take advantage of lower cost labour, or to be closer to customers, and so on. For example, China has become a hot spot for firms that are attracted to the country's low wage rates, and large market.

Why do Firms Become MNEs by Engaging in FDI?

The answer to this question will help you understand how firms choose between the different foreign modes of entry - exporting, licensing, turnkey projects, franchising, joint ventures, fully-owned subsidiaries - discussed below. Dunning and Lundan (2009) developed a useful OLI framework that says firms will undertake FDI if there are:

Ownership advantages – resources of the firm transferable across borders that enable the firm to obtain competitive advantage abroad. Ownership advantages arise when a firm finds resources it owns that are not location-bound, but are internationally transferable, e.g. managerial capability to manage large hotels like Marriott, or a brand and product that travels well, e.g. IKEA and its style of furniture.

Locational advantages – location-specific advantages available to the firm in the foreign locality, conditions that it would not enjoy at home, e.g. raw materials, human resources. These advantages are not constant but grow, evolve, and even decline. These are dealt with in more detail in chapter 9, but here we will mention four types of locational advantages:

Markets – there are often advantages in being close to existing or potential markets – one reason why so many firms have sought to set up in the rapidly developing, hugely populated country of China. These advantages include:

- Avoidance of local protectionism.
- Reduction in transportation costs; where direct interaction with the local customer is essential, e.g. after sales service, component manufacturer needing to be close to the foreign car plant it supplies.
- Dealing with services where production and sale cannot be separated, e.g. hotels, consultancy, Spanish banks using local branches in South America to serve their clients there.
- Local marketing assets, e.g. acquiring local distribution networks and brand names.

Resource endowments – the locality may have specific resource advantages that the MNE can tap into, e.g. in land, labour, weather, infrastructure. For example, a recent development has seen Chinese MNEs seek natural resources around the world in oil, gas, minerals, and also agriculture and land. Other companies from India and China buy technology and brand names in Europe and the USA to combine these with their own resources and compete on the global stage.

Agglomeration – refers to the location advantages arising from the clustering of economic activity in certain locations. Think of Silicon Valley in the USA and the cluster of suppliers, manufacturers, research firms, and market leaders. Think of the City of London as a global financial centre. Advantages arise from:

- Knowledge spillovers whereby knowledge flows amongst closely located firms.

- Locally transferable skilled labour force.

- The creation of co-located specialized suppliers and buyers.

Institutions – A country may well offer tax advantages, business opportunities, legal recourse, subsidies, access and the like in order to attract foreign direct investment from multinationals. For assessing location attractiveness see also chapter 9.

Internalization advantages arise if the MNE can organize activities better and cheaper internally, within the MNE, than if using a third party that incurs prohibitive transaction costs; see also chapter 9 (sourcing) where this issue is discussed in depth.

The OLI framework and the advantages accruing are shown in Figures 6.1. and 6.2.

Figure 6.1
Dunning's Theory – O and L Advantages

Types of O-Advantages	Examples
• Resources created in one country that can be exploited in other countries	• Proprietary technology and managerial know-how (e.g. VW)
• Sharing of resources across business units	• Sharing of business model and brand name across stores (e.g. IKEA)CVCV
• Capabilities arising from combining business units in multiple countries	• Logistics based on superior co-ordinations between business units in different locations (e.g. Wal-Mart)
• Capabilities arising from organizational structures and culture	• Operation manuals, codes of conduct, organizational norms and practices (e.g. IKEA, Carrefour)
Types of L-Advantages	**Examples**
• Markets	• Size and growth consumer demand (e.g. China), presence of key clients (e.g. Antolin), high income consumers (e.g. Haier in the USA)
• Location-bound resources	• Human capital, such as a skilled labour force, natural resources, such as oil and gas deposits (e.g. Shell, BP) and agriculture (e.g. land in Africa)
• Agglomeration	• Geographic cluster of potential customers and suppliers (e.g. cars in Slovakia)
• Institutions	• Incentive schemes to attract FDI (e.g. Hungary)

6.4 Governments and Foreign Direct Investment

Let us return to an institution-based perspective on this subject for a moment. How does a government's attitude affect FDI? You can think of ideology toward FDI as being on a continuum where at one end is the radical view that is hostile to all FDI, and at the other end is the non-interventionist principle of free market economies. In between these two extremes is a more pragmatic nationalism. In recent years more countries have adopted friendlier FDI policies, but retain institutions that restrict and regulate FDI:

- Outright banning, e.g. nationalization of the oil industry in Venezuela in the new century.

- Case-by-case approval of FDI with registration and authorization requiring a range of conditions and negotiations to be gone through.

- Ownership requirements which disallow full foreign ownership but allow joint ventures perhaps, or minority foreign ownership, e.g. for security reasons the USA does not allow majority foreign ownership of domestic air transportation.

- Local business regulations will have to be complied with and may be restrictive if applied inflexibly.

Figure 6.2
Dunning's Theory – Internalisation Advantages

I-Advantages: Types of Market Failure	Examples
• Asset specificity	• FDI versus exports (e.g.aluminium industry)
	• FDI versus outsourcing (e.g. Flextronics, Wipro)
• Information asymmetry	• FDI versus exports where assessing the quality of the goods is difficult (e.g. database access in consultancy
	• FDI versus outsourcing where monitoring of the actual process is important(e.g. Nike, adidas)
• Dissemination risk	• FDI versus licensing of technology (e.g. automotive components)
	• In-house versus outsourcing of complex manufacturing processes (e.g. consumer electronics manufacturing)
• Tacit knowledge transfers	• FDI versus licensing/franchising of complex knowledge (e.g. Marks & Spencer)
• Strategic control	• FDI versus licensing as market entry strategy (e.g. Starbucks)

Source: Based on Multinational Enterprises and the Global Economy, 2nd ed. By J.H.Dunning & S. Lundan, 2008, Reproduced with permission from Edward Elgar Publishing Ltd and Professor S. Lundan

Local content conditions requiring that a certain part of the value of the goods made or sold in the country should originate from that country, e.g. European countries introduced legislation demanding that Japanese automakers use components that had partly originated in the host country rather than being made wholly in Japan and assembled in the host country.

Clearly Governments may be very suspicious of FDI and will need to weigh up the costs and benefits of FDI to the host country as shown in Figure 6.3. Quite a useful exercise for you is to also think through what the advantages and disadvantages for the home country of the MNE might be of DFI elsewhere. What do you think?

If the host country sees FDI as beneficial it might encourage FDI. It might reduce MNE risk by offering a government-backed programme covering the major forms of risk like the risk of expropriation, war losses, or the inability to repatriate profits. Some countries have also developed special loan programmes for companies investing in developing countries, created tax incentives, and encouraged host nations to relax their restrictions on inward FDI.

Figure 6.3 Benefits and Costs of FDI

	Possible benefits of FDI	Possible negative effects of FDI
Consumers	• Access to international quality products and brands • Lower prices due to scale economies and competition	• Reduces variety of traditional local brands (if local firms are crowded out)
Suppliers	• Technology transfer enhancing productivity • Opportunity to become an international supplier	• Crowding out by international sourcing
Competitors	• Technology spillovers enable learning • Competition may trigger upgrading and innovation	• Crowding out by overwhelming competition
Workers	• Employment opportunities • Typically higher labour standards than local firms • Training and knowledge transfer	• Often less labour intensive production (thus less work places) than local firms
Government	• Tax revenues • Economic growth	• Costs of subsidies and other incentives
Natural environment	• MNE's often have higher environmental standards than local firms	• MNE's may locate highly polluting activities in places with less stringent regulation

Note: These are possible effects that vary across FDI projects

Sources: (1) 'Perspectives on Multinational Enterprises in Emerging Economies', K.E. Meyer, 2004, *Journal of International Business Studies*, 34, pp. 259-277, Palgrave Macmillan; (2) 'When and where does foreign direct investment generate positive spillovers?' K.E. Meyer and E. Sinani, 2009, *Journal of International Business Studies*, 40, pp. 1075-1094, Palgrave Macmillan; (3) 'Multinational corporations and spillovers' Blomstom M. and Kokko, A., *Journey of Economic Surveys*, 12, pp 247-277, 1998, Blackwell; (4) Editors' Introduction in *Multinational Enterprises and Host Economies*, K.E. Meyer, ed., 2008, Edward Elgar Publishing. Reproduced and permission of Palgrave Macmillan, Wiley-Blackwell and Edward Elgar publishing Ltd.

To discourage outward FDI, countries regulate the amount of capital that can be taken out of a country, use tax incentives to keep investments at home, and actually forbid investments in certain countries – for example, as the USA has done for companies trying to invest in Cuba and Iran. In Sweden for example, foreign companies are not allowed to invest in the tobacco industry. In Japan, until the early 1980s, most FDI was prohibited unless the foreign firm had valuable technology. Then, the foreign firm was allowed to form a joint venture with a Japanese company because the government believed this would speed up the diffusion of the technology throughout the Japanese economy.

6.5 Major Modes of Entering Foreign Markets

OK, so government may be favourable or not favourable to FDI. But FDI does not exhaust the options. There are six major ways we see firms entering foreign markets. These are (with variants): exporting, turnkey projects, licensing, franchising, establishing joint ventures with a host country firm, or setting up a new wholly owned subsidiary in the host country. Each mode of entry has its advantages and disadvantages. As a firm's positioning in a foreign market evolves, you will also see shifts in ownership and modes of operating in order to achieve further revenue growth and competitive advantage.

Exporting

Exporting is the sale of products made by firms in their home country to customers in other countries. Exporting is a common first step for many manufacturing firms. Later, feeling limited in terms of revenue growth and lack of control, such firms may switch to another mode. Exporting is attractive because:

- It avoids the costs of establishing local manufacturing and service operations.

- It helps firms achieve experience curve and location economies.

- Lack of trust on payment can be overcome by a ***letter of credit***. For example if a US exporter does not trust a Chinese importer, it can draw up a financial contract that states that the importer's highly reputable bank will pay a specific sum of money to the exporter's bank on receipt of the goods/service.

- Export intermediaries are usually available in the exporting country with the expertise to help facilitate exports to a range of other countries. These are especially used by SMEs. The exporter can also employ its own sales agents, on commission fees, in the foreign country, or sell the products to a distributor, who is a local intermediary in the foreign country trading on their own account.

However, exporting may also be unattractive because:

- There may be lower cost locations for manufacturing the products abroad that are not being taken advantage of. Exporting from a home market base may not be the most effective policy.

- High transport costs and tariffs can make it uneconomical.

- Agents in a foreign country cannot be closely controlled, and may not act in an exporter's best interests.

- There will be restrictions on the amount of revenue growth that can be achieved using this channel.

Turnkey Projects

In a turnkey project the foreign contractor agrees to handle every detail of the project for a local client, including training personnel. After designing and constructing the new facility, the contractor completes the contract by handing the client the 'key' to the plant that is ready for full operation – thus the term ***turnkey***. A variant is the build-operate-transfer model, which includes the contractor managing the facility for fees after the construction has been completed. Turnkey projects are most common in the metal refining, pharmaceutical, petrol refining, and chemical industries. All these use complex and expensive production technologies. Turnkey projects are a means of exporting such know-how to foreign countries that lack these competencies. The approach is also popular in the construction and engineering industries for large infrastructure projects – for example airports (a Spanish firm Ferrovial operates London Heathrow and other British airports; Athens airport was built largely by German companies), power stations, and motorways.

Turnkey projects are attractive because:

- They are a way of earning economic returns from the know-how required to assemble and run a technologically complex process.

- They can be less risky than more conventional forms of foreign direct investment.

However the problems with turnkey projects include:

- The contractor firm has no long-term interest in the foreign country so market growth may be small.

- The contractor firm may create a local competitor that can grow to compete globally.

- If the contractor firm is supplying process technology or know-how that is its own source of competitive advantage, then selling this through a turnkey project is also selling competitive advantage to potential competitors.

Licensing

A licensing agreement is where a licensor grants the rights to intangible property to another entity (the licensee) for a specified period, in return for a royalty fee paid by the licensee. Intangible property includes patents, inventions, formulas, processes, designs, copyrights, and trademarks. As one example, Xerox signed an agreement with Fuji Photo in order to enter the Japanese market, creating Fuji Xerox. Xerox then licensed its xerographic know-how to Fuji Photo in exchange for a royalty fee of 5 percent of net sales revenue, earned from photocopier sales. The agreement was for 10 years and has been extended several times, with direct sales restricted to the Asia Pacific region.

Licensing has several advantages:

- The firm avoids development costs and risks associated with opening a foreign market.

- The firm avoids barriers to investment, e.g. in the Xerox case above, the Japanese government prohibited Xerox from setting up a fully owned subsidiary in Japan.

- The firm can capitalize on market opportunities without developing additional marketing, administrative, and operational capabilities itself.

At the same time licensing may be unattractive because:

- The firm does not have the tight control over manufacturing, marketing, and strategy needed to gain economies from an experience curve and location advantages.

- For a technology-based firm, lack of control over the technology and IP may become a problem.

- The firm's ability to coordinate strategic moves across countries is constrained.

- Proprietary or intangible assets could be lost. This risk can be lessened by using cross-licensing agreements. These are increasingly common in hi-tech industries. Here a firm licenses use of its proprietary know-how in exchange for a license to use the other firm's know-how. For example, US biotechnology firm Amgen licenses Japanese sales of its product Nuprogene to Japanese firm, Kirin. In exchange Kirin licenses Amgen to sell some of Kirin's products in the USA. Risks can also be reduced by forming a joint venture as was the case with Fuji Photo (above).

Franchising

Franchising is a specialised longer-term form of licensing where the franchiser not only sells intangible property to a franchisee (e.g. a trademark), but also insists on tight rules on how it does business. The franchiser will also often assist the franchisee to run the business on an ongoing basis. Like licensing, typically the franchiser receives a royalty payment, usually a percentage of the franchisee's net revenues. Whereas licensing is used primarily by manufacturing firms, franchising is used primarily by service firms. The obvious example globally is McDonald's, whose strict rules include control over the menu, cooking methods, staffing policies, design, and location. McDonald's also organises the supply chain for its franchisees, and provides management training and financial assistance.

The advantages of franchising include:

- It avoids the costs and risks of opening up a foreign market.

- A firm can quickly build a global presence.

However a firm needs to take into account certain risks, including:

- It may inhibit the firm's ability to take profits out of one country to support competitive attacks in another.

- Geographical and administrative distance from the franchisee may make it difficult to detect poor quality; likewise if there are many thousands of franchisees across the world. One way in which firms like KFC and McDonald's have reduced these risks is by establishing a joint venture with a local firm in each country or region. This firm then acts as a master franchisee, controlling the local firms' performances.

- Poor quality at one branch can hurt the brand globally. For example, travellers expect the same quality of experience in a Four Seasons Hotel in Hong Kong as in New York. If they experience variable quality they may be dissuaded from staying in this brand hotel in the future.

Joint Ventures

A joint venture (JV) involves establishing a firm that is jointly owned by two or more otherwise independent firms, e.g. Fuji Photo described above. US multinational General Electric has in recent years used joint ventures to enter foreign markets like Spain and South Korea where its units lacked a strong presence. GE switched its policy in the 2000s because of the rising costs of foreign acquisition, and because it recognised it could lower risks and gain local knowledge through JVs, while navigating difficult legal, political, economic, and cultural markets like China.

JVs are typically 50-50 owned by the partners, but minority ownership is also frequent, although sometimes creating issues around power, direction and control.

Joint ventures can be attractive because:

- Firms benefit from a local partner's knowledge of local conditions, culture, language, political systems, legal know-how, and business systems.
- The costs and risk of opening a foreign market are shared.
- JVs often satisfy local political considerations for market entry.

But joint ventures run a number of risks, which we will discuss in more detail below when we look at strategic alliances:

- The firm risks giving control of its technology to its partner.
- The firm may not have the tight control needed to realize economies from the experience curve, or from location economies, or to coordinate attacks against rivals on a global basis. Thus Texas Instruments instead established a fully owned subsidiary in Japan to check Japanese market share of the world semi-conductor market. TI required the subsidiary to take instructions from TI's US-based corporate centre and run at a loss if necessary – something few JV partners would be willing to accept.
- Shared ownership can frequently lead to conflicts and battles for control if goals and objectives differ or change over time, or power imbalances develop between the parties.

Fully Owned Subsidiaries

Here the firm owns 100 percent of shares in the subsidiary. A fully owned subsidiary can be defined as a subsidiary located in a foreign country that is entirely owned by the parent multinational.

Wholly owned subsidiaries are attractive because:

- They reduce the risk of losing control over core competencies.
- The firm gains 100 percent of the profits earned in the foreign market.
- They can help in protection of key technologies and intellectual property – particularly important in hi-tech, pharmaceutical, and electronics industries worldwide.
- They give a firm tight control over operations in different countries necessary for engaging in global strategic coordination.
- They may be required in order to gain location and experience curve economies. This is important where a firm wishes to establish a fully optimized global production system, or where there are intense cost pressures in the specific industry, for example:

- Firms pursuing global standardization or transnational strategies (see chapter 8) tend to prefer establishing wholly owned subsidiaries, which allow them more opportunity for creating an integrated global strategy.

Wholly owned subsidiaries may also be unattractive because:

- The firm bears the full risk and cost of setting up overseas.

One additional decision a firm needs to make if going down the wholly owned subsidiary route is whether to adopt a *Greenfield* or *Acquisition* strategy. In a Greenfield strategy the firm builds the subsidiary from the ground up, as opposed to acquiring an existing company.

The main advantage of a Greenfield venture is that it gives the firm a greater ability to build the kind of subsidiary company it needs. Firms also often discover that it is very difficult to transfer organizational culture and ways of operating to acquired firms. But Greenfield ventures are slower to establish, and are also risky. They also might lead to market entry being pre-empted by a rival who uses an acquisition strategy to gain a quicker foothold in the same market.

Alternatively, as we mentioned above, a firm can acquire an established company in the host nation and use that firm to promote, or even manufacture its products/services. As one example, insurance major ING entered the US insurance market by acquiring existing US firms rather than trying to build an operation from scratch. Acquisitions can be attractive as a mode of entry because:

- They can be quicker to execute.
- They enable firms to pre-empt their competitors in the foreign market.
- They may incur less risk than Greenfield or other options. You buy a set of assets that are producing a known revenue and profit stream. You also gain tangible assets – factories, logistics systems etc., and also intangible assets, e.g. brand name, managers' local knowledge of markets, existing customer relationships.

However, acquisitions have been known to fail due to:

- The acquiring firm overpaying for the acquired firm.
- Clash of cultures between the two firms.
- Attempts to realize synergies running into roadblocks (for example incompatible technologies and human resource policies) and take much longer and are more expensive to realize than forecast.
- There is inadequate pre-acquisition screening.

For these reasons firms that are frequently on the acquisition trail – for example Cisco Systems, develop a core expertise in carefully screening the firm to be acquired, ensuring they do not pay too much for the acquisition, and moving rapidly to implement a pre-developed integration plan.

Part of this will be an HR plan to allay the fears of the management and talented staff of the acquired firm, and to deal with other HR issues (for example resistance to change, the need for redundancies) that are likely to arise (see chapter 11).

6.6 Assessing the Relevance of Strategic Alliances

Strategic alliances (SAs) are collaborations between independent firms using equity modes, non-equity contractual agreements, or both. SAs can form between potential or actual competitors. Formal joint ventures are one form of strategic alliance. But an SA may also take the form of business unit joint ventures or short-term contractual agreements to cooperate on a particular strategic task, for example joint marketing, production, or distribution arrangements. The number of strategic alliances has exploded in recent decades as firms have sought to expand, and recognised that they do not necessarily have all the resources available to do so at the desired speed.

Why choose a strategic alliance? Because it:

- Facilitates entry into a foreign market.

- Can be a stepping-stone to a full acquisition, allowing the parties to learn how to work together, so smoothing the path to full acquisition.

- Allows a firm to share the fixed costs and risks of developing new products or processes.

- Helps a firm to establish technological standards for the industry that will benefit the firms.

- Brings together complementary skills and assets that neither partner could easily develop on their own.

But SAs have been criticised as an entry mode because:

- An SA may give the competitor you ally with a low cost route to technologies and market. For example, many US companies in the semiconductor and machine tool industries were criticised for their SAs with Japanese firms which, it was argued, allowed the Japanese companies to keep high paying high value-added jobs in Japan while gaining valuable US project engineering and production process skills, thus reducing US firms' competitive advantage. At the same time some US-Japanese SAs clearly work, for example the Microsoft-Toshiba alliance and the Boeing-Mitsubishi alliance to build the 787 aeroplane.

- The failure rate for SAs is very high. Historically, two thirds run into serious financial and managerial trouble within two years of their formation, and one third of these are subsequently rated as failures.

This suggests that SAs need to be carefully entered into and managed. One approach is to look for a limited SA first. Thus some firms enter into a business unit JV, where existing business units from two firms are merged. This works if the two firms can achieve something, e.g. market leadership, technological innovation, which neither could achieve on their own. It may also be a sensible option if a full takeover is not practicable. Also where the merged unit depends on inputs (such as technologies) from both parties that would be disrupted by legal separation. Another form of SA is operational collaboration, consisting of collaboration in operations, marketing, or distribution. For example, in the airline industry, national airlines form alliances to connect to all major travel destinations, and also share frequent flyer programmes, and share facilities and resources such as passenger lounges.

The success of an alliance is a function of:

- *Partner selection.* An effective partner helps the firm achieve its strategic goals and has capabilities the firm lacks and values; has a shared vision on the alliance's purpose; and does not exploit the alliance just for its own ends.

- *Alliance structure.* This should make it difficult to transfer technology not meant to be transferred; have contractual guarantees to guard against partner opportunism; and allow for swopping of skills and technologies with equal gains.

- *Management capability.* This requires the building of strong interpersonal relationships - called relational or social capital - amongst the two managements. It also seems to require learning from the alliance partner. Successful SAs see the partners perceiving the SA not just as a cost-sharing or risk-sharing device, but also as an opportunity to learn from a potential competitor how to do business better. This learning then needs to be diffused throughout the organization.

6.7 Going International: Growth Through Evolution

It is important to understand that foreign market entry is only the start of what is often a very long journey for a firm. If you refer back to chapter 4, you will recall how a firm will seek to evolve and grow its international business. An ***international strategy*** will seek to sell domestic products in foreign markets with minimal customization. Or a firm may choose a ***localization strategy*** to give itself a competitive edge in the foreign market. However, pressures to reduce costs together with the requirement to grow market size may well lead to the development of a ***global standardization strategy***. Alternatively where there are pressures to reduce costs, retain local responsiveness, and grow the market globally, the firm may well move to a ***transnational strategy***. In chapter 5 we saw that competitive markets are highly dynamic, and firms are continually seeking to match, outpace, or respond to competitors, these days increasingly on a global stage. In chapter 8 we will see how firms continually have to adjust their organization structures to fit with their emerging strategies to expand operations, revenues and profits, and adjust to changes in location and market attractiveness.

All this means that the initial mode of entry may well be only the temporary starting point for a firm's globalizing strategy. Much depends on the assessment of costs, risks, and benefits and how the changing trade-offs between these three factors suggest to a firm changes in commitment of resources, scale of operations, and ownership in the foreign market. A firm can make a relatively low commitment to a market through exporting, licensing and franchising, or by small-scale or partial acquisitions, or by limited joint ventures/alliances.

They may also see a low risk approach such as using the internet to extend their business beyond national boundaries. However to grow further they may need to make bigger commitments through wholly owned subsidiaries, large-scale joint ventures, and/or large mergers/acquisitions. In doing so they will need to integrate their internet business strategy relative to their other modes of operating in foreign markets.

6.8 Conclusion

In this chapter we have looked at the major decisions a firm needs to address when considering entry into foreign markets. A firm needs to answer four questions – why enter, which market(s) to enter, when to enter, and at what scale and level of ownership. The objectives of the firm, whether it is natural resource seeking, market seeking, efficiency seeking, or innovation seeking, will shape greatly the resulting decisions.

That decision might be to make foreign direct investments into a country to secure ownership, locational, and internalization advantages. But government institutions may well have a part to play in the degree to which these advantages can be gained in the targeted country. But FDI does not exhaust the options. In fact there are six major approaches we looked at, though each with advantages and potential disadvantages. These are exporting, turnkey projects, licensing, franchising, joint ventures, wholly owned subsidiaries. We saw in chapter 4 how CEMEX rose to a global position through a series of acquisitions. But strategic alliances are another way to gain a strong foothold in a foreign market, though the risk of failure, according to the evidence, is high.

The important concluding point is that entry is usually part of a long journey and therefore the firm needs to plan an evolution from the optimal starting point. Of course it will make mistakes along the way, or even in its initial decision. But going abroad is invariably a risky affair, which gives added justification for being very aware of the advantages and disadvantage of different modes of entry discussed in this chapter.

A key part of entering a foreign market is making strategic decisions on market segmentation, on areas such as product/service, price, promotion, and distribution channels. Such decisions have to tie in with the higher-level international business strategy and give it what is called 'granularity', i.e. detail. This is the subject of the next chapter.

'Marketing takes a day to learn. Unfortunately it takes a lifetime to master'

Phil Kotler

'If the circus is coming to town and you paint a sign saying "Circus Coming to the Fairground Saturday", that's advertising. If you put the sign on the back of an elephant and walk it into town, that's promotion. If the elephant walks through the mayor's flowerbed, that's publicity. And if you get the mayor to laugh about it, that's public relations. If the town's citizens go the circus, you show them the many entertainment booths, explain how much fun they'll have spending money at the booths, answer their questions and ultimately, they spend a lot at the circus, that's sales. And, if you planned the whole thing, that's marketing'

Unknown

'(You) that will not apply new remedies must expect new evils; for time is the greatest innovator'

Sir Francis Bacon (1561-1626)

CHAPTER 7
International Marketing and R&D Strategy: 'Seeing the Business Through the Customers' Eyes'

7.1 Introduction

This chapter covers international marketing strategy, market segmentation, and the four P's mix of Product, Price, Promotion, and Place. Marketing strategy leads to a focus on new product and market development, R&D, and R&D offshoring, as well as distribution channels (place).

Marketing is *"the activity, set of institutions, and processes for creating, communicating, delivering, and exchanging offerings that have value for customers, clients, partners, and society at large."* (AMA, 2007). Peter Drucker gave marketing a more customer focus when he described it as 'seeing the business through the customers' eyes'. Business to consumer marketing is the process by which companies create value for customers and build strong customer relationships, in order to capture value from customers in return. Business to business marketing creates value, solutions, and relationships (either short term or long term) with another company or brand.

International marketing refers to marketing carried out by companies overseas or across national borderlines. Firm-level marketing practices across borders include market identification and targeting, strategic decisions to compete in international markets, entry mode selection, and marketing mix choices.

7.2 Marketing Strategy and the Marketing Mix

When you go to another country, you will see some familiar products on the shelves at local shops. Many companies today sell their products all over the world. In fact, you probably buy imported products on a regular basis. Have you ever thought about how international companies sell their products? Does the product meet the same need in every country, or do companies have to develop different messages about their products depending on where they're being sold? International marketing is like domestic marketing in that it still involves the basic 'marketing mix' elements of product attributes, distribution strategy, communication strategy, and pricing strategy, but because international marketing involves selling products/services in different countries, with different literacy rates, currencies, levels of economic development etc., international marketing can be far more complex.

Are markets and brands becoming global? Can a firm sell the same product the same way everywhere? Probably not, especially with consumer products. For example, just looking at major US brands, while McDonald's is available around the globe, the company does make menu changes, e.g. a McArabia in the Middle East, and a Croque McDo in France. McDonald's also changes its distribution strategy. Levi's, too, standardizes certain elements in its marketing mix, but localizes others. Similarly, Microsoft, another global brand, has adapted its marketing mix to meet the needs of consumers in India. As we saw in earlier chapters, although the world is moving towards global markets, because cultural and economic differences continue to exist among nations (see chapters 2 and 3), any trend toward global consumer tastes and preferences is limited. In other words, while people around the world might drink Coke, how the brand is perceived, how it is marketed, and so on, still differs from country to country. Keep in mind too, that such factors as trade barriers and differences in product and technical standards also limit a firm's ability to standardize its product and marketing

International marketing strategy must be consistent with the firm's corporate and business strategies. Marketing strategy focuses on choices over products/services and markets. The Ansoff matrix (Ansoff, 1988) helps us here, and suggests four strategic choices (see Figure 7.1):

Figure 7.1
Ansoff Matrix

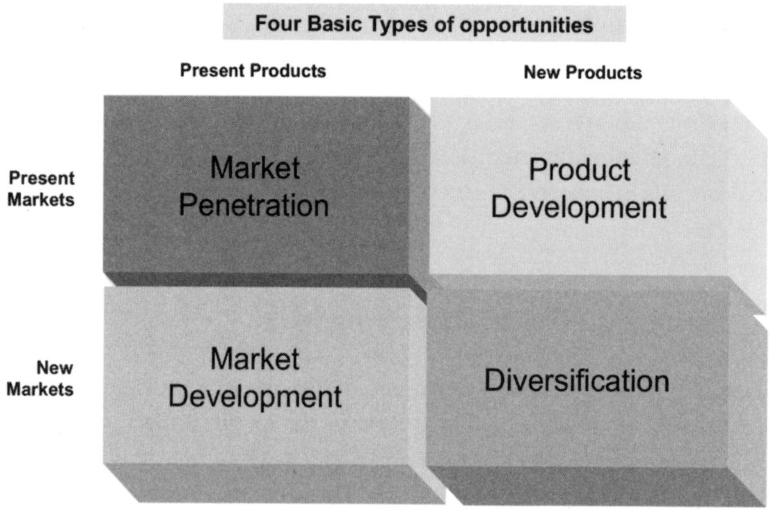

Four Basic Types of opportunities		
	Present Products	**New Products**
Present Markets	Market Penetration	Product Development
New Markets	Market Development	Diversification

- *Market penetration strategy* involves increasing the share of current markets with the current product/service range. We know that firms go international because this strategy often does not meet its growth needs domestically, in limited or overcrowded markets, or where products are mature.

- *Market development strategy.* Selling existing products in new markets. This strategy can see firms marketing abroad to new markets to extend the life of their products, and fnd opportunities to grow revenues and profits. This may also entail some ptoduct development (e.g. new styling or packaging). It can take the form of attracting new users (e.g. exending the use of aluminium to the automobile industry). It can take the form of new geographies (e.g. extending the market to cover new areas – international markets being the most important). However, it must discover and meet the critical success factors for that new market if it is to succeed, and may require new strategic capabilities, especially in marketing.

- *Product development strategy.* New products in existing markets, which involves varying degrees of related diversification (in terms of products). The strategy can be expensive in terms of R&D and marketing and high risk, may require new strategic capabilities, and typically involves project management risks. It can be relevant internationally when a firm is already in a foreign market and is developing new products/services for that market.

- *Diversification strategy.* New products in new markets. This strategy is the riskiest approach to internationalization, which explains why firms often try to mitigate risks, for example by joint venturing with local firms, or spreading R&D costs through collaboration. According to Johnson et al., (2011) the main drivers for diversification are exploiting economies of scope – efficiency gains through applying the organisation's existing resources or competences to new markets or services; stretching corporate management competences, exploiting superior internal processes, and increasing market power.

The *marketing mix* (the choices the firm offers to its targeted market) is comprised of 'the 4 Ps':

1. P – Product attributes.

2. P – Pricing strategy.

3. P – Promotion, i.e. communication strategy.

4. P – Place, i.e. distribution strategy.

Firms have to decide which elements of the marketing mix can be standardized, and which need to be adapted to the local market. Standardization versus customization is not an all-or-nothing concept. Most firms standardize some things and customize others. Firms should consider the costs and benefits of standardizing and customizing each element of the marketing mix. How do you figure out which elements in the marketing mix need to be customized to the local market and which can be standardized across markets? You can start by segmenting markets.

Market segmentation involves identifying distinct groups of consumers whose purchasing behaviour differs from others in important ways. You can segment markets in many ways, for example sex, age, income level, education level. Typical criteria for segmentation into customer groups are by:

- Geography.
- Demography.
- Socio-cultural factors.
- Psychological factors.

In Figure 7.2 we see how, on a bigger view of international differences (remember CAGE in chapter 4!), environmental variables help in the process of identifying the customer market segments your firm wishes to target.

Figure 7.2
Market Segmentation

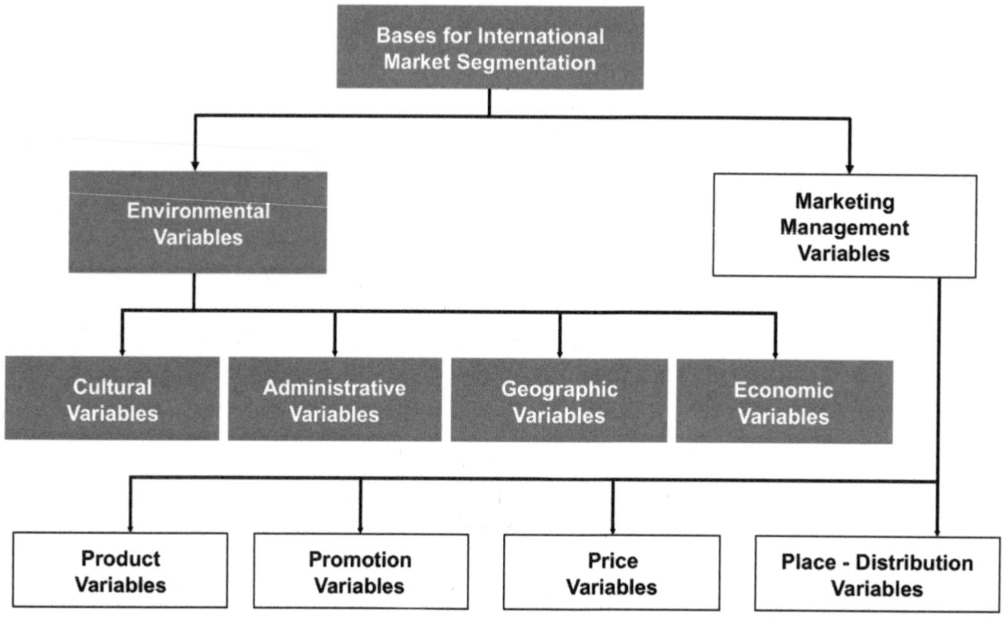

Once you have identified different segments, you can adjust the marketing mix accordingly. Toyota for example, sells its Lexus line to high-income consumers, but attracts lower income buyers with its Corolla (see chapter 8 case study). Firms not only need to adjust their marketing mix from segment to segment, they also need to identify segments that transcend national borders, and understand differences across countries in how the segments are structured. Sometimes segments that transcend national borders include consumers who are very similar, and have similar purchasing behaviour. When these types of similarities don't exist though, firms need to customize the marketing mix if they want to maximize their performance in the market.

Two key international market segmentation issues are: the differences between countries in the structure of market segments, and the existence of segments that transcend national borders. When segments transcend national borders, a global strategy is possible. Remember also that global market segments are more likely to exist in industrial products than in consumer products.

An overview of the marketing strategy planning process we have talked through, and how it fits with environmental analysis and business strategy appears in Figure 7.3.

Figure 7.3 Overview of the marketing strategy planning process

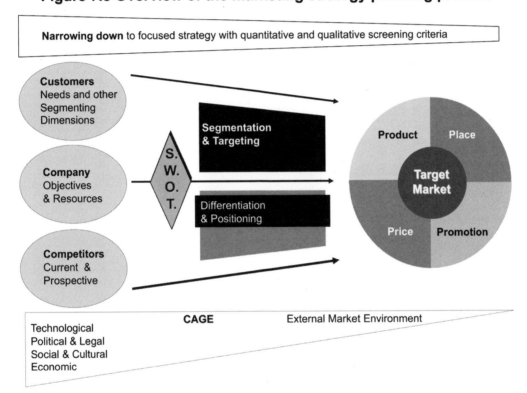

7.3 Product Strategy

Let us look at each element in the marketing mix beginning with product. A product is a bundle of attributes. Stop there and think. What attributes does a product actually have that you find attractive? Take for example a car. You might be buying its content, that is its superior performance and technical, aesthetic physical features. You might be buying the aura – what the car 'says' about you as a symbol of status and taste. You might be buying support aspects – for example the expertise that surrounds a luxury BMW, or a high degree of service personalization that used to surround a Rolls Royce. Figure 7.4 suggests that a product is actually more complex than you first think. For example if you buy an electronic dishwasher, what sort of warranty -

insurance of performance for a defined time period - would you prefer? Clearly there are very many ways to differentiate a product, even a humble product like a potato, for example!

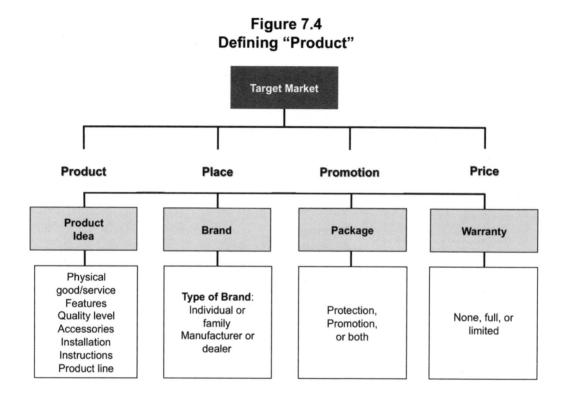

Figure 7.4
Defining "Product"

Products sell well when their attributes match consumer needs, and you can probably guess that if consumer needs were the same everywhere, a firm could sell the same product everywhere. But, what do you do when consumer needs vary from country to country because of cultural differences, or differences in levels of economic development, or different product/technical standards? Clearly there is plenty of room for product differentiation but let us explore three international dimensions a little more.

Cultural differences. What are the cultural differences between countries? Countries differ along a range of cultural dimensions including tradition, social structure, language, religion, and education (see chapter 3). To identify where standardization is possible and where the marketing mix must be customized, firms need to look for evidence in the selected marketplace. Nestlé, for example, sells frozen food in multiple countries, but offers different menus depending on local preferences. Nestlé sells fish fingers in Great Britain, but coq au vin in France, yet it is able to sell Lean Cuisine dinners in the same way in both Europe and the USA. Coca-Cola builds on its brand name in Japan by offering a tonic drink that appeals to local consumers in addition to its traditional cola.

Level of economic development. Consumers in highly developed countries tend to demand a lot of extra performance attributes. Consumers in less developed nations tend to prefer more basic products. What does a country's level of economic development mean to the marketing mix? Firms that are based in highly developed countries tend to build lots of performance features into their products. Think about your car for example. You have probably got power steering and power windows, maybe a CD player or DVD player. In contrast, we know that consumers in less developed countries tend to prefer more basic products, but want high product reliability. But even this will not be true of every market segment. Think of India and China. How easy is it to generalize across whole countries and billions of people? Marketing is more complicated than you think.

Product and technological standards. Sometimes firms have to customize their marketing mix to meet national differences in product and technological standards. For example, differences in technical standards between Great Britain and the USA mean that producers of DVD equipment have had to adapt their product to each market. In the 1970s RCA failed to account for technical differences in television signal frequency. Some Asian countries adopted the American standard, but Malaysia, Singapore, and Hong Kong adopted the British standard, and as a result could receive a picture but no sound. Not a good marketing result!

A little exercise might help you here. Take a local beer, e.g. Tiger beer in Singapore, Cobra beer thought of as an Indian product, Singha beer from Thailand. Find out how the beer you have selected is marketed. What are the attributes of the product, what is the market segment, what is the message of the brand? Now repeat the exercise for marketing the beer in another country with which you are familiar. Note and give reasons for the marketing differences and the similarities.

7.4 Pricing Strategy

How should a firm price its product in foreign markets? Should prices be different in different markets? Are there any regulations that might influence how a product should be priced? A firm can maximize its profits by using ***price discrimination*** where consumers in different countries are charged different prices for the same product. In other words, the firm charges whatever the market will bear. You might be wondering why someone would be willing to pay more for a product in one country if they know they can get it cheaper elsewhere. How can a firm get away with this strategy? Why, for example wouldn't a Malaysian person who is buying a new car simply go to Singapore to buy it if it's priced lower there? For price discrimination to work, the firm has to be able to keep its national markets separate. In other words, the car manufacturer might not be able to price the cars differently say in France and Germany, but could charge a higher price in France and Germany than the price charged in Britain because right hand drive cars are sold in Britain, while left hand drive cars are sold in both France and Germany.

Firms can also use price discrimination when different price elasticities of demand exist in different countries. Demand is elastic when a small change in price produces a large change in demand. Demand is inelastic when a large change in price produces only a small change in demand. Tommy Hilfiger for example, in 2007, successfully priced its jeans in Europe at roughly three times the price of its North American jeans. The price elasticity of demand is a measure of the responsiveness of demand for a product to changes in price. We say that demand is elastic when a small change in price produces a large change in demand, but inelastic when a large change in price produces only a small change in demand.

In general, firms can charge higher prices when demand is inelastic. What determines elasticity of demand? Income level is one factor that determines demand elasticity. When income levels are low, people tend to be more price conscious, and demand is more elastic. In parts of India for example, products like TVs (that are considered necessities in the USA) are still thought of as luxury items. The other main factor that affects price elasticity is the number of competitors in a market. The more competitors, the greater the bargaining power of consumers, and the greater the elasticity of demand.

What about strategic pricing? Firms can set prices to achieve certain strategic goals. There are three aspects of strategic pricing:

Predatory pricing involves using profits earned in one country to support aggressive pricing in another market as part of a strategy to drive out competitors in that market. Once the competition leaves, the firm then raises its prices. Matsushita in the 1980s allegedly used this type of strategy to gain market share in the USA.

Multipoint pricing refers to the fact that a firm's pricing strategy in one market may have an impact on how a rival prices products in another market. For example, if a firm uses aggressive pricing in one market, its rival may resort to aggressive pricing in another market. Kodak and Fuji Photo have been playing this game for years. When Fuji started a competitive battle in the USA in the late 1990s, rather than responding by dropping prices in its home market, Kodak dropped prices in Japan instead. To avoid being in this type of situation, managers need to continually monitor prices around in the world.

Experience curve pricing. Here a firm will set low prices worldwide as a way of quickly building sales volume. Firms using this type of strategy are willing to take a loss initially because they believe that in the future, once they've moved down the experience curve, they'll have a cost advantage over less aggressive competitors. Recall from chapter 4 that firms further along the experience curve have a cost advantage relative to firms further up the curve.

As we mentioned earlier, sometimes firms have limits on how they can price their products because of regulations in the target market. So, a firm that wants to use a price discrimination strategy or multipoint pricing for example, may find that it cannot. Ways in which a firm's ability to set its own prices can be limited through antidumping regulations and through competition policy. 'Dumping' occurs whenever a firm sells a product for less than the cost of producing it. So, both predatory pricing and experience curve pricing can be problematic when antidumping regulations are in place. Antidumping regulations set floors under export prices and limit a firm's ability to pursue this dimension of strategic pricing.

Many countries also have policies in place that are designed to promote competition and restrict monopoly practices. As with antidumping regulations, competition policies can limit the prices firms can charge for their products.

Here is an interesting question. Why are some consumers willing to pay US$300 for a tennis racquet, while others will only pay US$100 for a racquet that seems very similar in terms of performance? What do you think justifies the US$200 price difference?

7.5 Promotion Strategy

The next element in the marketing mix is Promotion, i.e. communication strategy. Promotion includes TV, radio, print, online advertising, personal selling, direct mail, public relations, coupons, billboards – this not an exhaustive list! A vital question: which of such methods is best used to communicate with the target market you are interested in? A second vital question: what are the limits to standardized messages and promotion methods? Once again, we come up against the issue of differences between different types of consumer. When you add in country differences, then you begin to see the limits to mass media, branding and standardized messages.

International communication occurs whenever a firm uses its marketing message to sell its products in another country. However, international communication isn't always easy. All too many things can get in the way of the message. Let us look at just three important examples:

Noise levels. This refers to the volume of other messages competing for a potential consumer's attention. The USA, for example, has a higher level of promotional noise than many other developed economies. As a generalization only, noise tends to be higher in developed countries like the USA, Singapore, and Germany than in emerging markets.

Cultural barriers. The effectiveness of a firm's international communication can be jeopardized by cultural barriers – it can be difficult to communicate messages across cultures. A message that means one thing in one country may mean something quite different in another. Firms need to develop cross-cultural literacy, and use local input when developing marketing messages. Such barriers can prevent a firm from using a successful advertising campaign across countries. Proctor & Gamble found, for example, that its advertisement depicting a woman taking a bath and using Camay soap that worked well in Europe flopped in Japan, because in the advertisement, the woman's husband walks in and hints at sexual overtures. In Japan, it is considered bad manners for a man to intrude on his wife. What works well in one country might not work in another… Firms can get around some of these problems by developing cross-cultural literacy, hiring a local advertising agency, and using a local sales force where possible. Proctor & Gamble found that it had to take a very localized approach to selling Tampax tampons in some markets.

Source and country-of-origin effects. Source effects occur when the receiver of the message evaluates the message on the basis of status or image of the sender. You can counter negative source effects by de-emphasizing their foreign origins. A *country-of-origin effect* refers to the extent to which the place of manufacturing influences a customer's product evaluations. BP, for example, changed its name from British Petroleum after it made a big push into the US so that customers would not think about the fact that one of the biggest gasoline companies in the USA is from Britain. Where a product is made can also be a factor in people's willingness to buy it. You would probably rather buy stereo equipment that is made in Japan or in Denmark than in Brazil for example.

When a firm chooses its communication strategy, it has to decide between a **push strategy** that emphasizes personal selling, and a **pull strategy** that uses mass media advertising. Which strategy is best? The choice between strategies depends on:

- **Product type and consumer sophistication** – a pull strategy works well for firms in consumer goods selling to a large market segment. A push strategy works well for industrial products.
- **Channel length** – a pull strategy works better with longer distribution channels.
- **Media availability** – a pull strategy relies on access to advertising media. A push strategy may be better when media is not easily available.

A little more about each of these: how does product type and consumer sophistication affect the choice between a push strategy and a pull strategy? Usually, firms in consumer goods industries that are trying to sell to a large segment of the market choose a pull strategy because it is cheaper than trying to use direct selling. In contrast, firms that are selling industrial products will generally opt for a push strategy because direct selling lets the firm educate customers about the product. Keep in mind that in those poor nations where literacy levels are very low, direct selling may be the best option even for products that would be mass marketed in other countries. The multinational Unilever found this to be true when marketing to the rural poor in India. Its subsidiary Hindustan Unilever established a physical presence with advertisements for its detergents, soap, etc. at village wells and weekly rural markets. It also has a rural distribution network involving more than 100 factories, 7,500 distributors, and over three million retail stores, some little more than stalls. The distribution channel has thousands of wholesalers and retailers to reach India's some 500,000 plus hard-to-access villages.

What is the link between channel length and communications strategy? Typically, when channels are long, direct selling can be a very expensive proposition. Using a pull strategy with mass advertising to create consumer demand may be a better alternative. Imagine having to convince each intermediary in a long Japanese channel to carry your product…

Sometimes, firms find that they do not have a real choice between a push strategy and a pull strategy. A pull strategy relies on advertising media like TV, newspapers, magazines, and so on. If these aren't readily available, then a pull strategy won't work, and firms will have to use a push strategy. So, a push strategy will be best when the firm is selling industrial products or complex new products, when distribution channels are short, and when few print or electronic media are available, while a pull strategy will make sense for consumer products, when distribution channels are long, and when there are sufficient print and electronic media available to carry the marketing message.

Standardized advertising makes sense when:

- It has significant economic advantages.
- Creative talent is scarce and one large effort to develop a campaign will be more successful than numerous smaller efforts.
- Brand names are global.

Standardized advertising does not make sense when:

- Cultural differences among nations are significant.
- Advertising regulations limit standardized advertising.

Some firms, then, will standardize parts of a campaign to capture the benefits of global standardization, but customize others to respond to local cultural and legal environments.

7.6 Place – Distribution Strategy

Place refers to where a product or service is provided. These days, of course, this does not have to be a physical location, but could be virtually, over the internet, e.g. software and movie downloads. How a firm delivers its product to the consumer is a critical element of the marketing mix. Firms can sell directly to consumers, to retailers, or to wholesalers, regardless of where the product is produced. Distribution strategy refers to the means the firm chooses for delivering the product to the consumer. How a product is delivered depends on the firm's market entry strategy. For example, firms that manufacturer the product locally can sell directly to the consumer, to the retailer, or to the wholesaler. Firms that manufacture outside the country have the same options plus the option of selling to an import agent.

In international business, there are at least four main differences in distribution systems you need to bear in mind. Let us look at each of these beginning with retail concentration.

- *Retail Concentration* – a country's distribution system can be very concentrated where a few retailers supply most of the market, or very fragmented where there are many retailers, none of which has a significant share of the market. In a concentrated retail system, a few retailers supply most of the market – this is common in developed countries. In a fragmented retail system there are many retailers, no one of which has a major share of the market – very common in developing countries. The United Kingdom is an example of a country with a concentrated retail system. In the UK, people go to large stores and shopping malls. In contrast, Japan has a more fragmented system where stores serve the local neighbourhood. Usually, we think of greater retail concentration as being associated with developed countries because people have cars to drive to the stores, own large refrigerators to store food in, and many two-income households. However, we are seeing some concentration in developing countries. In 2007, Wal-Mart for example, was doing a booming business in Mexico.

Distribution in a very fragmented market can be a real challenge for companies; Unilever, for example, has resorted to distributing its products by bike and cars in some parts of China.

- **Channel Length** – the number of intermediaries between the producer and the consumer. A short channel (when the producer sells directly to the consumer) is common with concentrated systems. A long channel (when the producer sells through an import agent, a wholesaler, and a retailer) is common with fragmented retail systems. Japan is often associated with long channels. It is not uncommon to have two or three wholesalers between the firm and the retail outlet. Countries like Germany and the USA tend to have much shorter channels.

- **Channel Exclusivity.** How difficult is it for outsiders to access? Sometimes, companies have a hard time breaking into new markets because they cannot access the distribution system. Sometimes, channels are exclusive because retailers like to carry well-established brands rather than take a chance on something new. You have probably seen examples of this at your local grocery store. Japan is a country that often comes to mind when we talk about channel exclusivity. Relationships between retailers, wholesalers and manufacturers in Japan often go back decades, and in some industries it can be virtually impossible for foreign companies to break in.

- **Channel Quality.** Finally, when we talk about distribution, we need to consider channel quality or the expertise, competencies, and skills of established retailers in a country, and their ability to sell and support a foreign company's products. In general, channel quality in developed countries is better than in emerging or developing economies, but even in developed countries problems can prompt companies to develop their own channels. Apple for example, has in recent years opened its own retail stores in countries like the UK to sell its products. The company believes that product knowledge is essential to its success, and feels that relying on an outside firm could be detrimental to its sales.

How should a firm choose a distribution strategy? The company needs to consider the relative costs and benefits of each alternative based on the four factors: retail concentration, channel length, channel exclusivity, and channel quality. When the retail sector is very fragmented, a long channel can be beneficial because this economizes on selling costs and can offer access to exclusive channels. Keep in mind, that the longer the channel, the higher the cost is likely to be because each intermediary will add its own mark-up. So, yes, if price is critical to sales, firms should opt for a shorter channel. A long channel might make sense if the retail sector is very fragmented. In addition, if there are concerns about channel quality, firms should handle distribution on their own, like Apple does.

7.7 Research and Development (R&D) Strategy

In 7.2 above, we talked about basing the firm's product development or diversification strategy around product innovation. How does the globalization of the world economy affect how new products are developed? First, remember that when we are talking about R&D, we are talking about the new product ideas that come from the interactions of scientific research, demand conditions, and competitive conditions. You can probably think of many successful innovations that you use everyday like iPods, 3M sticky note pads, and internet routers. Today, competition is as much about technological innovation as anything else. The pace of technological change is faster than ever and product life cycles are often very short. New innovations can make existing products obsolete, but at the same time, open the door to a host of new opportunities.

Where should a firm locate its R&D? New product development tends to occur more often in countries where more money is spent on basic and applied R&D, where demand for new products in strong, where consumers are affluent, and where competition is intense. You probably recognize that all of these conditions are present in the USA. Indeed, for most of the time after the Second World War, the USA was the leader in new product development, and therefore the location of R&D centres (see chapter 1). However, over the last twenty years or so, things have been changing. The USA is still a leader, but companies from Asia and Europe have also become strong players. Japan for example, is the leader for video games, and Europe is at the head of the pack when it comes to wireless telecommunications. So, today, rather than simply relegating R&D to the USA, successful firms see new product development opportunities in multiple locations.

Just because a firm has a new product with lots of new features does not mean it will automatically be a commercial success. In fact, studies show that only 10 to 20 percent of new products ever have commercial success. Commercialization of new technologies is very costly, and can mean that a firm has to produce multiple versions of a product to meet the needs of individual markets. To increase the chances of a successful product, companies have to integrate product R&D with their marketing, production, and materials management departments. By doing this, firms can be sure that new products meet customer needs, and that all value creation activities are performed efficiently.

Since new product development has a high failure rate, new product development efforts should involve close coordination between R&D, marketing, and production. Integration will ensure that:

- Customer needs drive product development.
- New products are designed for ease of manufacture.
- Development costs are kept in check.
- Time to market is minimized.

Some firms achieve this type of integration by developing cross-functional teams that are led by heavyweight project managers who have significant status in the firm. To be effective, teams should also have members from all of the critical functional areas, situated so that members can be together, have clear goals, and an effective conflict resolution process.

To successfully commercialize new technologies, firms may need to develop different versions for different countries, so a firm may need R&D centres in North America, Asia, and Europe that are closely linked by formal and informal integrating mechanisms with marketing operations in each country in their regions, and with the various manufacturing facilities. Firms that want to build successful global R&D capabilities need to be sure that R&D, marketing, and production are integrated. Hewlett Packard for example, has four R&D centres, one in the USA, one in England, one in Israel, and one in Japan. Similarly, Microsoft has R&D sites in Washington, California, Tokyo, and Cambridge, UK.

7.8 Conclusion

Marketing - seeing the business through the customers' eyes - is highly relevant to international business given the diversity in business environments and markets around the globe. Marketing gives a business the necessary granularity to move from a business strategy to a marketing strategy, and home in on the market segments that the business really needs to develop. The marketing mix is a way of disaggregating further what needs to be done, once the attributes of each market segment have been identified. The chapter took you through product, price, promotion and place strategies and showed you how they must be shaped to specific country conditions. The chapter also brought understanding of the main issues, making R&D important, and making its foreign location both attractive and challenging, a theme pursued further in chapter 9.

In the next chapter we continue the process of linking international strategy with more operational areas, by establishing the ways in which structure must follow strategy. More than this, however, there needs to be alignment not just between business strategy and organization structure, but also with something we call organization architecture – the processes, people, culture, incentives, and control mechanisms of the organization. So let's move to chapter 8.

'Every company has two organizational structures: The formal one is written on the charts; the other is the everyday relationship of the men and women in the organization'

Harold S. Geneen

'The organizational architecture is really that a centipede walks on hundred legs and one or two don't count. So if I lose one or two legs, the process will go on, the organization will go on, the growth will go on'

Mukesh Ambani

'A little knowledge that acts is worth infinitely more than much knowledge that is idle'

Khalil Gibran

'A good decision is based on knowledge and not on numbers'

Plato

CHAPTER 8
Structuring and Integrating the International Business

8.1 Introduction

By organization structure we mean three things. First the formal division of the organization into sub-units such as product divisions, national operations or functions, e.g. human resources, information technology, and marketing. Secondly, we mean the location of decision-making responsibilities within that structure. Decision-making may be centralized, decentralized, or federal – that is with some decisions centralized, others decentralized. Thirdly, structure refers to the establishment of integrating mechanisms to coordinate the activities of sub-units. These may be formal integrating mechanisms, for example the organization structure itself, including reporting lines and role assignment, cross-functional teams, pan-regional committees. Formal integrating mechanisms also include control systems, incentive systems, processes, and culture. Control systems are the metrics used to measure the performance of sub-units and make judgements about how well managers run those sub-units. Incentives are the devices used to reward appropriate managerial and employee behaviour. Processes are the manner in which decisions are made and work is performed within the organization. We met culture before in chapter 7! Organization culture refers to the norms and value systems that employees of an organization sometimes refer to as 'the rules of the game' or 'the way things are done around here'. Culture clearly has an informal unmanageable element, as does knowledge. Many commentators these days make a strong case for knowledge and the way it is managed being a prime integrating mechanism in any business.

In this chapter we discuss first the advantages of centralized versus decentralized structures. We then revisit chapter 4 and the issue of strategic alignment to give an overview of how the desired strategy must shape choice of structure. We then describe four types of organization structure commonly used in internationalizing firms, and when they are most suitably deployed. We point out that in the modern global environment most organizations tend to mix and match, and use variants and parts to customize these structure types in order to support strategy in specific circumstance. Moreover, the bigger the global commitment of the firm, the more coordination problems arise, thus requiring the development of integrating mechanisms, including the skilled management of knowledge. Managers must also be alive constantly to the need to fit environment to strategy to structure and other components of what we call organization architecture – control systems, incentive systems, processes, organizational culture, and people.

8.2 Centralized or Decentralized Structure?

It is important to locate decision-making in the most effective place in an organization. It is not always best to have all the decisions made by a few senior managers at the top of an organization, not least because they rarely have all the information and knowledge needed to make properly informed decisions about remote events and locations. This becomes a real issue when firms are internationalizing, or are already spread around many locations and activities across the globe.

In this context there are a number of arguments for centralization:

- It can facilitate coordination across countries and activities. For example a firm with a manufacturing site in South Korea might have assembly factories in other countries. Centralized decision-making allows these sets of activities and the related logistics to be coordinated more closely.

- Centralization can ensure decisions are consistent with overall organizational objectives. Decentralization can lead to what is called goal displacement as each sub-unit has the power and inclination to pursue its own interests and sub-goals, which may clash with what is optimal for the whole firm.

- Centralization of decision-making and resources can give top management the capability to introduce necessary major organizational changes on an international basis.

- Centralization can avoid duplication of similar activities, thus gaining scale and resources for that activity, e.g. centralizing R&D or production in one or two locations around the globe instead of letting every region carry out R&D.

At the same time decentralized decision-making, or a degree of it, can be a better choice in some circumstances:

- Top management can become overburdened when decision-making is centralized, and this can lead to poor decisions. Routine issues can be delegated to lower level managers, thus allowing senior managers to focus on critical decisions.

- Motivational research suggests that people are more committed, and work harder in their jobs, where they have a greater degree of discretion, control, and freedom in their work.

- Decentralization can increase control. If you establish autonomous, self-contained units within an organization, you can then hold the sub-unit managers accountable for sub-unit performance. The more decision-making powers and resources a sub-unit manager has, the less he/she can blame others or offer excuses for poor performance.

- Decentralization can produce better decisions. Here decisions are made by managers who are closer to the issues, who typically have better quality (including informal) information than those higher up the hierarchy, and who are usually more knowledgeable in the relevant branch of operations.

- Decentralization can offer greater flexibility and responsiveness. Cumbersome decision-making processes can be avoided and well-informed decisions made quickly, with only exceptional issues/decisions needing to be assessed by top management.

8.3 Revisiting International Business Strategy

Recall in chapter 4 how we defined four kinds of multinational strategy:

- **_International (home replication) strategy_**, which stresses the advantages of replication internationally of home country-based competencies, (e.g. brand, distribution network), products, and services. Here pressures for global integration, and for local responsiveness in the foreign markets are low.

- **_Localization (multi-domestic) strategy_**, which considers each country or region as a stand-alone local market worthy in itself of significant adaptation and attention. This responds to Ghemawat's Adaptation Requirements in strategy described in chapter 4.

- **_Global standardization strategy_**, which seeks to develop and distribute standardized products/services worldwide to reap the benefits of economies of scale and shared product development. This is Ghemawat's Aggregation goal described also in Chapter 4.

- **_Transnational strategy_**, which aims to capture the 'best of both worlds' by endeavouring to be both cost efficient (Aggregation focus) and locally responsive (Adaptation focus).

Now let us look at the strategy-structure 'fit' challenge on a broader view. There has always been a debate in the business strategy literature as to whether strategy shapes structure or structure shapes what strategies are possible. But the more fundamental point is that strategy and structure really must be very closely aligned!

Each international strategy is shaped by pressures to globally integrate or be locally responsive, and how each strategy then fits with a particular type of structure. Thus, as an overview of what follows:

- A home replication strategy fits with an **_international division_** structure.

- A localization strategy fits with a **_geographic area_** structure.

- A global standardization strategy fits with a **_global product division_** structure.

- A transnational strategy fits with a **_global matrix_** structure.

We will now look at each of these four fundamental types of structure in detail, picking up variants and the reasons for these, along the way.

8.4 The International Division Structure

This is typically set up when firms initially expand abroad, often when engaging in a home replication strategy. They can encounter a number of problems:

- Foreign subsidiary managers in the international division are not given sufficient voice relative to the heads of domestic divisions.

- International division activities lack synergies because they are not coordinated with the rest of the firm that focuses anyway on, and prioritizes, domestic activities and results. There is a 'silo effect', i.e. the international division is not integrated in important ways with the rest of the firm.

- Firms often phase out this structure after initial market entry, and limited expansion, so it may be regarded as temporary and gain little commitment from even its own managers.

An example of this structure at US-based Cardinal Health is shown in Figure 8.1 below.

Figure 8.1
International Division Structure at Cardinal Health (USA)

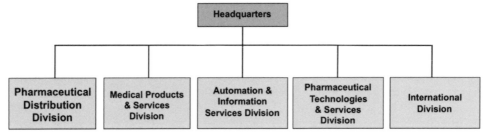

8.5 Geographic Area Structure

Here the MNE is organised according to specific geographic areas. An area may be a country if the market is big enough, or a group of countries. Typically, each area tends to be a self-contained, largely autonomous entity, with its own set of activities, e.g. marketing, R&D, finance, HR, and production. Because such a structure facilitates local responsiveness, it is the more suitable structure for a localization strategy. One example is Mittal Steel, a Europe-based, Indian-owned steel company. This has its headquarters in London, UK. In 2007 it had country managers in charge of Poland, Germany, USA, Mexico, and Canada. These were responsible for production, sales, and finance in these countries, on a stand-alone basis. But note that after a merger with Arcelor in 2007, the company moved to a mixed geographic/product division structure to deal with increased size and global market spread.

The problem with this structure is that it encourages fragmentation of the organization into highly autonomous entities. This can have several consequences. One is that the power base built up in an area can be difficult to control and may resist change when the firm as a whole needs a more suitable structure. Secondly, it can be difficult to transfer core competencies and skills between areas to realize location and experience curve economies more widely in the firm. Thus the structure will be a major barrier to undertaking, and reaping the gains associated with, a global standardization strategy. Figure 8.2 shows the structure of Avon. Headquartered in New York, USA (see www.avoncompany.com), Avon, in 2004, was managed through five geographic areas worldwide.

Figure 8.2
Geographic Area Structure

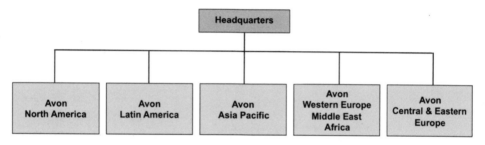

Source: Adapted from www.avoncompany.com. Avon is headquartered in New York, Avon Products is the company behind numerous "Avon Ladies".

8.6 Global Product Division Structure

Firms that have a diversity of products and lines of business domestically, typically adopt a product division structure when they move to operating globally on a large scale. An example is shown in Figure 8.3, which is of the European Aeronautic Defence and Space Company. This is headquartered in Munich, Germany and Paris, France, and is the largest European defence contractor and maker of commercial aircraft (e.g. the airbus).

At EADS each division is largely self-contained and autonomous, with full responsibility for its own value creation activities. The headquarters (HQ) is responsible for the overall strategic development and financial control of the firm.

The belief inherent in using this structure is that the value-creating activities of each product division should be coordinated by that division worldwide. The idea being that the product divisions are too different from one another in goals, means, and products being sold, to merit trying to coordinate activities and effort across the divisions. The product divisional structure often evolves as a response to the coordination difficulties experienced with the international division and worldwide geographic area structures. There is also the argument that with this structure, each division can develop enough scale and core competencies in its product area to achieve economies of scale, location economies, and economies from experience curve effects. For example it facilitates the transfer of core competencies across different global locations within the division, and also simultaneous worldwide launch of new products. This means the structure is good at supporting a global standardization strategy. However, in this structure, power tends to reside with product division managers so a problem often experienced is the lack of voice and power of country managers, resulting in a lack of local responsiveness, and consequent performance challenges.

Figure 8.3
Global Product Division Structure at European Aeronautic Defense and Space Company (EADS)

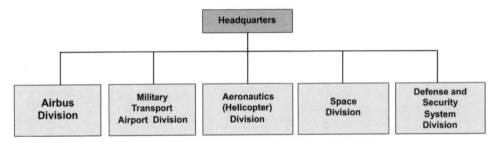

8.7 Global Matrix Structure

The global matrix structure is an attempt to minimize the limitations of the worldwide area and the worldwide product divisional structure. It is designed to support a transnational strategy where a firm is finding that, to survive in its industry, it has to simultaneously focus on realizing location and experience curve economies, delivering local responsiveness and enabling the internal transfer of core competencies and knowledge worldwide. The classic matrix structure is shown in Figure 8.4. You will see that it has both product divisions and geographic areas represented. The philosophy is of dual decision-making, with a product division and geographic area having equal responsibility for operating decisions. Thus in Figure 8.4 Area 2 and Product Division B management will determine jointly the product offerings, marketing strategy, staffing, resourcing, and business strategy for B products sold in Area A. One corollary is that an individual manager will belong to two hierarchies – an area hierarchy and a product division hierarchy and so have two bosses. This can create tensions in loyalties and prioritizing time amongst managers.

However, historically matrix structures exhibit still other problems including:

- Can be bureaucratic, clumsy and slow – they develop their own internal bureaucracies, including more levels of management and many meetings to coordinate activities between the two hierarchies.

- Can result in conflicts and power struggles between areas and product divisions due to joint responsibility, diverging interests and viewpoints.

- Can result in finger-pointing between parties when something goes wrong, because it is often difficult to establish accountability in this structure. One result might be that headquarters can start to lose control over its own organization.

Three things needed for good matrix management would seem to be:

- Clarity of the firm's basic objectives.

- Continuity in the firm's commitment to these over time.

- Consistency in how the various divisions work together.

Figure 8.4
Global Matrix Structure

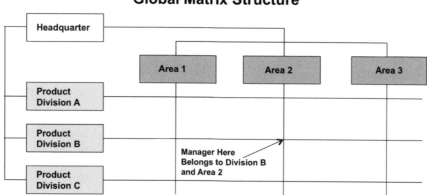

8.8 Evolution and the Need for a Contingency Approach

Firms that continue to expand into international markets and grow in size will tend to expand from an international division structure to:

EITHER a worldwide product divisional structure – adopted by firms that are quite diversified:

- Allows for worldwide coordination of value creation activities of each product division.

- Helps realize location and experience curve economies.

- Facilitates the transfer of core competencies.

- Does not allow for local responsiveness.

OR a worldwide area structure – favoured by firms with low degree of diversification and a domestic structure based on function:

- Divides the world into autonomous geographic areas.

- Decentralizes operational authority.

- Facilitates local responsiveness.

- Can result in a fragmentation of the organization.

- Is consistent with a localization strategy.

Research work by Stopford and Wells in 1972 developed the useful Stopford-Wells framework (see an adapted version in Figure 8.5). This shows the likely evolution of structure towards the global matrix grid, as a firm's foreign product diversity increases along with its foreign sales as a percentage of total sales.

Figure 8.5
How Organizational Structure Changes Over Time

Since this theory was developed, the international business world has changed dramatically in terms of dynamism, size, new players, and competitiveness. The four generic organizational forms described in this chapter are rarely found without contingent variations. Flatter hierarchical organizational forms, which are also strongly networked, are popular today. Coordination and integration mechanisms are also key to the functioning of globally operating firms. As an example of a firm's response to the modern environment, consider the relatively new organization of global player Nestlé. Its corporate headquarters directly controls centralized functions, global product groups, R&D, and five regional organizations.

- Centralized functions – finance and control, information systems, logistics, e-commerce, HQ, corporate affairs.

- Global product groups – each product group is responsible for its own strategy, business development, mergers and acquisitions, and market entry.

- R&D – this function covers and is located in 13 countries.

- Regional organizations – there are five that report direct to HQ. Each region has a number of countries reporting to it with each country manager responsible for sales in that country.

This example tells us that no organizational form is ever the last word in organization structure and new forms emerge as needs and requirements change. National and local traditional forces (i.e. local context) still influence the way in which modern subsidiaries are organized. Contingency theory can be usefully applied to MNE organizations nowadays. Contingency means that different organizations are designed to fit different specific circumstances.a

In practice MNEs have to search continually for better ways of accessing and utilizing all their scarce resources within the firm. Modern MNE organizational structures now must enable optimization of integration mechanisms in order to operate effectively.

8.9 Integrating Mechanisms and the Role of Knowledge Management

When firms pursue global standardization and transnational strategies they develop additional complexity, and coordination problems become ever greater and more important to deal with. MNEs typically have a profusion of sub-units each with their own orientations, ways of working, and goals. For UK-based Unilever this created, at one time in its history, real problems across many years in introducing new products into Europe. The need to resolve disputes between its many national and product divisions extended the time inordinately for introducing new products. This denied Unilever first-mover advantage vital to building a strong market position.

Formal mechanisms used to integrate sub-units include simple direct contact between unit managers and developing specific liaison or lynchpin roles to coordinate and communicate between units. Additionally forming cross-unit temporary teams to take on specific project systems of common interest, and needing resources from the different sub-units, e.g. the development and introduction of a new product and/or the implementation of a new global accounting information system. The greater the need for coordination, the more complex the formal integrating mechanisms need to be. As we have seen, when the need for integration is very high, firms may adopt a matrix structure, in which *all* managerial roles are viewed as integrating roles.

All these solutions have limitations, and need to be supported by informal integrating mechanisms. As a result you will find most MNEs experimenting with or operating knowledge networks supported by an organization culture that values teamwork and cross-unit cooperation.

Knowledge management refers to the structures, processes and systems that develop, leverage, and transfer knowledge. Knowledge is a broader concept including not just factual information but also the know-how and know-why imbedded in individuals and the firm. Knowledge has two dimensions. Explicit knowledge is codifiable, in other words can be written down, stored, and transferred with little loss of richness of message. As we shall see information systems based on information and communications technologies (chapter 10) are widely used in international business, and are very good for storing, transferring, and leveraging explicit knowledge. But tacit knowledge is not codifiable; it is personal, built through doing and experience, and its acquisition and transfer requires hands-on practice.

The knowledge management challenge, then, for international businesses is to organize formal systems and processes that deal with explicit knowledge (e.g. databases, intellectual property, expert systems) and also create learning mechanisms by which tacit knowledge can be shared, transferred, and leveraged (e.g. knowledge networks, use of social media). Both integration strategies can be greatly enhanced by the use of information and communications technologies in the globally operating firm. One means is a knowledge network. All the Big Four consulting companies (PricewaterhouseCoopers, Deloitte Touche Tohmatsu, Ernst & Young, and KPMG) and all global firms that need to share knowledge across sub-units, or within sub-units, have such global networks, allowing informal contacts between managers and knowledge specialists as need arises. Another means of sharing knowledge is through *communities of practice*, established between groups of people doing similar or related work in order to share and create knowledge. This enables people to experiment and innovate informally on the job. When such communities are IT enabled, they operate as virtual communities of practice. The Big Four also endeavour to codify – that is collect, store and make available, as much explicit knowledge as possible so as to create a collective memory system that can be leveraged when similar issues and challenges need to be dealt with. This is a common large firm strategy. As one example, car firms like Toyota, Honda, and Ford routinely collect and store design blueprints for all car components ranging from wing mirrors through to engine parts. These can then be used selectively, in future designs to avoid reinvention and speed product development.

Organizations sometimes experience difficulties in getting sub-units to share knowledge because knowledge frequently gives power to a person or sub-unit. To counter this, firms try to develop a strong sharing, cooperative culture to support the development of processes and structures and modes of knowledge, development, and communication. It is also important to put in incentives that support such a culture and the behaviours it implies.

8.10 Fitting Strategy, Structure and Organization Architecture

Organization structure is part of a larger set of factors that we will call, following Hill, (2011) *organizational architecture*. Organizational architecture is summarized in Figure 8.6, and is the totality of a firm's organization including:

Organizational structure:

- The formal division of the organization into sub-units.

- The location of decision-making responsibilities within that structure – centralized versus decentralized.

- The establishment of integrating mechanisms to coordinate the activities of sub-units including cross-functional teams or pan-regional committees.

Control systems and incentives:

- The control metrics used to measure performance of sub-units, managers, and employees. The main control systems are personal controls, bureaucratic controls, output controls, and cultural controls (where an employee buys into the norms and value systems of the firm).

- The incentive devices used to reward sub-unit, managerial, and employee behaviour. For example, targets linked to profitability can be used to measure sub-unit performance. Employees might be rewarded for exceeding those targets, e.g. given a share of profits achieved beyond targets.

Processes:

- The manner in which decisions are made and work is performed within the organization. Processes can be found at many different levels of the organization. For example, there are processes for formulating strategy, allocating resources, handling customer enquiries, improving product quality, and evaluating employee performance. It is important to distinguish the core processes on which the mission and competitive advantage of the firm depends, and the support processes that are necessary and enabling but do not differentiate the firm's products/services in the market place. The constant demand in firms is to render processes more efficient and effective. Historically the American General Electric MNE developed a number of processes that contributed to its international success, for example, its Six Sigma process for quality improvement, and its process for digitalization of business, using corporate intranets and the internet to automate activities and reduce costs. In firms with many international locations processes typically cross not only organizational boundaries, but also national boundaries. The need to take an end-to-end view of the process is critical for success and this needs integrating mechanisms and cross-organization cooperation. As an example, to design a new software product may require an MNE to use R&D personnel in California, a production workforce in Taiwan, and marketing people located in Europe, Asia, and North and South America.

Organizational culture:

- The norms and value systems that are shared among the employees of an organization. To integrate activity when operating worldwide, some firms try to have strong cultures. For example, Accenture summarizes its culture as 'High performance. Delivered.' Shared cultures stressing cooperation can help in rendering effective informal integrating mechanisms such as knowledge networks. Note that strong cultures are not always supportive of, and may even inhibit, strong international performance. Culture is covered in more detail in chapter 3.

People:

- The employees and the strategy used to recruit, compensate, and retain those individuals and the type of people they are in terms of their skills, values, and orientation. (This component is covered in detail in chapter 11).

Figure 8.6
Organizational Architecture?

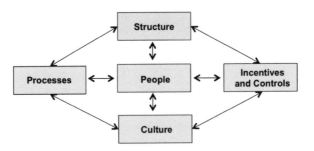

Superior enterprise profitability requires three things to happen: the different elements of a firm's organization architecture must be internally consistent, the organization architecture must *fit* the firm's strategy, and the strategy and architecture of the firm must fit with competitive conditions prevailing in the firm's markets.

We are dealing primarily with structure in this chapter and the other four components of organization architecture are dealt with in more detail in other chapters, especially chapter 11. For present purposes it is important for you to understand the fact that environment, strategy and structure must fit together, but there must also be close fit between the five components of organization architecture for superior international performance to be the outcome.

8.11 Conclusion

In this chapter we established the relationship between multinational strategy, structure, and evolution. The chapter described and assessed when to employ four organizational structures commonly used in international business, namely the international division, geographic area, global product division, and global matrix structures. We discussed what an international business must change in its organization structure to better match its strategy and select a more optimal path. We also introduced the concept of organization architecture, and the importance of fit for firm performance, and recognised the role of knowledge management as an integrating mechanism, and the knowledge implications of different strategies and structures.

The role of an organization structure is to enable strategy. They do this largely by providing stability, certainty, and control. In practice structures have many limitations, not least because they are rarely a perfect fit with strategy in the first place. But, secondly, strategic choices and environmental conditions tend to move faster than structures can adapt, leaving them usually sub-optimal. Therefore, it is important that structure is supported by formal and informal integrating mechanisms including how knowledge networks and how knowledge is organised and managed. Also crucial is aligning environment with strategy, and with what we call organization architecture, which consists of the interrelated components of structure, controls and incentives, processes, culture, and people. This chapter is further endorsement of the need to take a contingency approach when analysing a real life organization's attempts to fit environment, strategy, and organization to achieve superior performance.

*'If you deprive yourself of outsourcing and your competitors do
not, you're putting yourself out of business'*

Lee Kuan Yew

*'Firms fail because they outsource problems, and see
outsourcing as about spending less, rather than a different
way of managing. By all means do what you are best at
and outsource the rest. But 'the best' must include a core
competence in global sourcing'*

L. Willcocks

CHAPTER 9
Global Sourcing of Production and Services

9.1 Introduction

Where should a firm locate its production activities? In today's global world, the answer to this question could be 'anywhere'. Consider this example of a worldwide global sourcing chain. In 2010 BMW employed 70,000 factory personnel at 23 sites in 13 countries to manufacture its vehicles. Workers at the Munich plant built the BMW 3 Series and supplied engines and key body components to other BMW factories abroad. In the USA, BMW had a plant in South Carolina, which made over 500 vehicles daily for the world market. In Northeast China, BMW made cars in a joint venture with Brilliance China Automotive Holdings Ltd. In India, BMW had a manufacturing presence to serve the needs of the rapidly growing South Asia market. BMW must configure sourcing at the best locations worldwide in order to minimize costs (e.g. by producing in China), access skilled personnel (by producing in Germany), and remain close to key markets (by producing in China, India and the USA).

These were BMW's answers to the questions we ask in this chapter. Should all production be located in a single market, or is there a reason to locate different activities in different places? What is the long-term strategic role of foreign production sites? What factors might cause a firm to change its strategy? Should a firm outsource production/services, or handle activities in-house? How can production and logistics be conducted internationally to lower the costs of value creation, and also to add value by better serving customer needs? What factors determine location attractiveness?

In this chapter *global sourcing* is defined as procurement of products or services from suppliers or company-owned subsidiaries located abroad for consumption in the home country or a third country. *Outsourcing* refers to the procurement of selected value-adding activities, including production of intermediate goods or finished products or services, from independent suppliers. Outsourcing, as such, is the handing over to third-party management of selected activities for required outcomes. Firms outsource because generally they are not superior at performing *all* primary and support activities. Most value-adding activities - from manufacturing to marketing to after-sales service - are candidates for outsourcing. Managers must decide between *internalization* and *externalization* – whether each value-adding activity should be conducted in-house or by an independent supplier.

The drivers of global sourcing include:

- Technological advances, including instant internet connectivity and broadband availability.
- Availability of Just-in-time (JIT) and Electronic Data Interface (EDI) logistic systems.
- Declining communication and transportation costs.
- Widespread access to vast information including growing connectivity between suppliers and the customers that they serve.
- Entrepreneurship and rapid economic transformation in emerging markets.

9.2 Locating Production

Production refers to activities involved in creating a product. *Logistics* refers to the procurement and physical transmission of material through the supply chain from the supplier to the customer (see also chapter 7 and Place). The production and logistics functions of a firm have two main strategic objectives. First, to lower costs, and second, to eliminate defective products from the supply chain and the manufacturing process. These two objectives are interrelated, so for example, a firm that improves quality control will also reduce the cost of value creation.

Firms want to locate production so that they are able to accommodate demands for local responsiveness and respond quickly to shifts in customer demand. As one example, several global automakers - like Hyundai - have been shifting production to India to take advantage of the country's low cost labour force. There are at least four major factors that might affect the choice of production location:

Country factors. There are many country factors that influence the decision of where to produce, and we will discuss these in more detail below. For a location to even be a possibility, skilled labour and supporting industries must be available. Remember chapter 6? Regulations on foreign direct investment (FDI) and trade can significantly affect the attractiveness of a country as a production location. In addition, expectations about the future value of a currency can also influence the decision of where to produce. Transportation costs are another factor to consider. For example, China has proved to be a successful production location for the Dutch firm, Phillips NV. In fact, Phillips wants eventually to use China as a global supply base partly because of transportation factors. Philips, the Dutch consumer electronics, lighting, semiconductor, and medical equipment conglomerate, has been operating factories in China since 1985. By 2002, the company had invested US$2.5 billion in China and operated 23 factories there. Initially, Philips believed that it would sell a large portion of its output to the local Chinese market. However, the company quickly discovered that the low wages that make China such an attractive production location also meant that the market for its products was smaller than anticipated. Philips' solution was to export most of its output to the United States and elsewhere.

Fixed costs. Sometimes, the fixed costs of setting up a manufacturing plant are so high that a firm needs to serve the world market from very few locations or even from a single location. It costs more than a billion dollars to set up a semi-conductor plant for example, so a semi-conductor producer is unlikely to establish multiple plants. But the opposite is also true. If fixed costs are low, multiple locations might make sense. How does minimum efficient scale affect the choice of production location? The larger the minimum efficient scale of a plant, the more likely a firm will centralize production in a single location or produce in just a few locations.

Technological factors. How do new technologies influence the decision on where to locate production? Chapter 4 told you that to achieve economies of scale and the costs savings associated with them, firms need to mass produce standardized products. We typically think that firms that produce a greater variety of products have shorter production runs. However, these traditional practices are changing. Today, flexible manufacturing - also called lean production - has been changing the way companies produce, allowing them to challenge the traditional rules of production. These new technologies are designed to reduce set up times for complex equipment, increase the utilization of individual machines through better scheduling, and improve quality control at all stages of the manufacturing process. Remember how in chapter 5 technological advances had made possible the simultaneous pursuit of cost and differentiation strategies – something that Porter derided as a 'stuck in the middle' failing strategy, which it might well have been in the 1980s when he was writing

Why is flexible manufacturing so important? Flexible manufacturing allows companies to produce a wide variety of products at a unit cost that would normally be associated with mass production of a standardized product. Mass customization implies that a firm can customize its product line to meet the needs of different customers without additional costs. Another common flexible manufacturing technology involves flexible machine cells. This type of technology groups various types of machinery, a common materials handler, and a centralized cell controller. Firms that use flexible manufacturing technologies have a competitive advantage over those that do not because they can customize their products to meet the needs of different national markets.

Product factors. Here there are at least two important factors to consider:

- ***The product's value-to-weight ratio.*** If the value-to-weight ratio is high like it might be with a pharmaceutical product, then it makes sense to produce the product in a single location and export it to other parts of the world. For example, it does not cost as much to ship prescription painkillers as it costs to ship a car, so centralized production makes sense. In contrast, when the value-to-weight ratio is low, e.g. with cement (remember CEMEX?), paint, or a car (remember Toyota?), there is more pressure to manufacture the product in multiple locations around the world.

- ***The product's level of standardization.*** When there are few differences in consumer tastes and preferences, the need to be locally responsive is reduced, and centralized manufacturing makes sense. So, for example, a firm might produce calculators or video game consoles at a single location because they can be produced in bulk.

Multiple or Few Locations?

Firms should concentrate production in a few locations when they have substantial fixed costs, when the minimum efficient scale of production is high, and when flexible manufacturing is an option. Establishing multiple production locations can make sense when both fixed costs and minimum efficient scale of production are relatively low, and when flexible manufacturing is a poor alternative. Figure 9.1 provides a summary.

Figure 9.1
Locating Production Facilities

	Concentrated Production Favored	Decentralized Production Favored
Country Factors		
Differences in political economy	Substantial	Few
Differences in culture	Substantial	Few
Differences in factor costs	Substantial	Few
Trade barriers	Few	Substantial
Locations externalities	Important in industry	Not important in industry
Exchange rates	Stable	Volatile
Technological Factors		
Fixed costs	High	Low
Minimum efficient scale	High	Low
Flexible manufacturing technology	Available	Not available
Product Factors		
Value-to-weight ratio	High	Low
Serves universal needs	Yes	No

But note that the strategic advantage of foreign factories can change over time. A foreign factory established to make a standard product to serve a local market, or to take advantage of low cost inputs, can evolve into a facility with advanced design capabilities. Hewlett Packard, for example, located its production in Singapore to take advantage of low costs there, but today, the facility is an important centre for designing and assembling portable inkjet printers. As government regulations change, or as countries upgrade their factors of production, the strategic advantage of a particular location can change. Think about your own country and the changes there – foreign factories arriving or leaving, in the last five to seven years. So, foreign factories may not be low cost manufacturing facilities, but can become vital components in the firm's strategy. For example, carmaker Hyundai added R&D to its operations in India, making the location an even more important component in its overall strategy. Remember also from chapter 4, that an important component of transnational strategy is the notion of global learning, i.e. the idea that valuable knowledge does not just reside at a firm's domestic operations, it can also be found in a firm's foreign subsidiaries.

9.3 Make-or-Buy Decisions

Should an international business make or buy the component parts to go into their final product? The decision of whether to perform an activity in-house or outsource it to another firm, called the *make-or-buy decision*, is an important factor in many firms' manufacturing (and also their service) strategies. Toyota for example, actually produces less than 30 percent of the value of its cars, the rest being outsourced to other companies. Nike and Reebok actually outsource nearly all production activities. Firms typically internalize those value-chain activities considered a part of their *core competence* (see chapter 5), or which involve the use of proprietary knowledge and trade secrets that they want to control. Make-or-buy decisions are much more complex when they involve international markets than when they involve domestic markets. The make-or-buy decision-making process can be presented as a useful diagram (see Figure 9.2, adapted from Peng and Meyer, 2011).

Figure 9.2
Make or Buy Decision-making

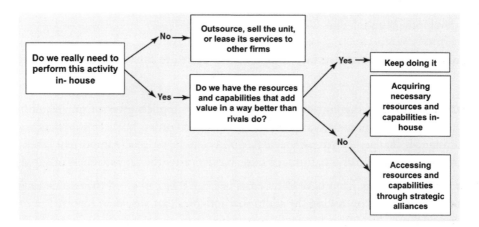

Making components in-house (or vertical integration as it is also called) has several advantages including:

- *Lowers costs.* If a firm is already the most efficient producer of certain products, it makes little sense to outsource to a less efficient producer. The firm can lower costs by continuing to manufacture the product in-house. Boeing the aircraft manufacturer, for example, keeps large systems integration activities in-house because it is more efficient at this activity than any other firm.

- *Facilitates investments in specialized assets.* When a firm has to invest in specialized assets, or assets whose value is contingent upon a particular relationship persisting, internal production makes sense. So, if Nissan develops a new fuel injection system that it believes will be an important competitive advantage, but that requires specialized assets, Nissan will probably choose to produce the system in-house. Because the system is unique to Nissan vehicles, it is not worth an outside supplier making the investments that would be needed. From Nissan's perspective, it would be strategically undesirable to use an outside supplier who would have to make the special investments, because Nissan would be more or less tied to that supplier, and unable take advantage of changes in the supplier market.

- *Protects proprietary technology.* A firm that outsources something that contains proprietary information runs the risk of losing control over that information. Boeing for example, manufactures its own cockpits so as not to give away proprietary information to competitors.

- *Facilitates the scheduling of adjacent processes.* Firms that manufacture in-house also have more control over the planning, coordination, and scheduling of adjacent processes. For firms with just-in-time inventory systems, this can be a real advantage.

Of course the initial decision may lead to other rationales. Take for example Hewlett Packard. The company initially used its new Singapore plant as a low cost location to manufacture electronic components. Later, entire products were produced in Singapore. Later still, the Singapore plant was involved not only in production but also product design. Today, the plant is an important part of Hewlett Packard's global network responsible for manufacturing and also product development and design.

Why should a firm outsource or buy components? Here are some major reasons given by firms:

- *Strategic flexibility.* Buying parts from independent suppliers gives a firm greater flexibility. By buying parts from outside suppliers firms can switch orders between suppliers as circumstances change. Having strategic flexibility can be especially important when exchange rate movements, political situations, or trade barriers alter the attractiveness of suppliers.

- *Cost.* By outsourcing, firms have lower costs because they can avoid the challenges involved in coordinating and controlling the additional activities that would be involved in making the components. Firms can also lower costs when they avoid the lack of incentive that often comes with using internal suppliers. Because internal suppliers have a captive customer, they often do not share the same drive to improve quality and lower prices that independent suppliers have. In addition, it can be difficult to decide how to set transfer prices when products are made in-house. A number of factors, e.g. changes in exchange rates, the ignorance of headquarters about local conditions, can affect how prices should be set. Because of the complexity, internal suppliers located in other countries might choose the easy path of simply passing on cost increases rather than trying to find ways to reduce them.

- *Order capture.* This helps the firm capture orders from international customers. Boeing was able to get a large order from Air India for example, while at the same time agreed to shift some subcontracting work to Indian suppliers.

9.4 Offshoring Global Services and Production

Offshoring is a natural extension of global sourcing, and refers to the relocation of a business process, a business/IT service, or entire manufacturing facility to a foreign country. This can be done on a *captive* offshoring basis, i.e. using a fully or partly-owned subsidiary, or by offshore *outsourcing*. It is important not to assume that offshoring is the same as outsourcing, so look at Figure 9.3 to clarify the different types of sourcing.

Figure 9. 3
Offshoring and Outsourcing

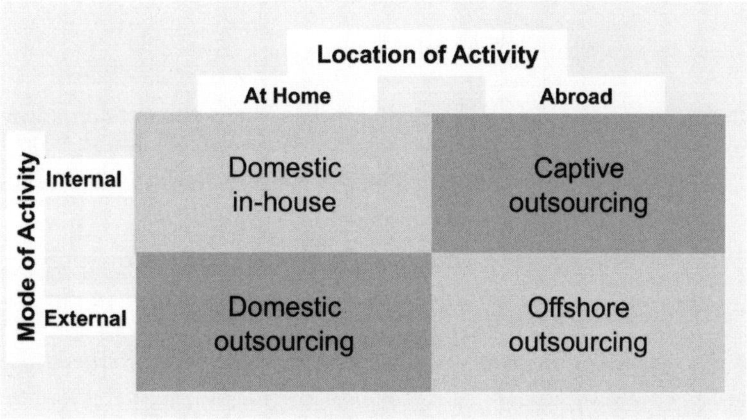

	Location of Activity	
	At Home	**Abroad**
Internal	Domestic in-house	Captive outsourcing
External	Domestic outsourcing	Offshore outsourcing

MNEs are particularly active in shifting production facilities or business processes to foreign countries to enhance their competitive advantages. Offshoring is especially common in the service sector, e.g. banking, software code writing, legal services, and customer-service activities. As just one example, large legal hubs have emerged in India that provide services such as drafting contracts and patent applications, conducting research and negotiations, as well as performing paralegal work on behalf of Western clients. With lawyers in North America and Europe costing US$300 an hour or more, Indian firms (in 2012) could cut legal bills by 75 percent.

When is offshoring problematic? The following are suggestive only, but offer an opportunity to think through offshoring decisions seriously:

Service with customer interaction. In many services sectors the service cannot be separated from its place of consumption. For example, personal contact is vital at the customer end of virtually all value chains. People normally do not travel abroad to see a doctor, dentist, lawyer, or accountant (though this is changing! – see medical care industry developments in India, for example). Consequently, many service jobs will never be offshored. Not surprisingly, therefore, by 2008, less than 15 percent of all service jobs had moved from advanced economies to emerging markets.

Strategic goals. Cost-cutting by offshoring is often a distraction from more beneficial, long-term goals such as enhancing the quality of offerings, improving overall productivity, and freeing up knowledge workers and other core resources that can be redeployed to improve long-term performance.

Stakeholder resistance. Global sourcing tends to invite opposition from employees and other organizational stakeholders. Disaffected middle managers can undermine projects. Poorly planned sourcing projects can create unnecessary tension and harm employee morale. Firms should be vigilant about striking the right balance between the organizational activities that it retains, and those that are sourced from outside.

Challenges. These are multiple, and the following are indicative only:

- A common reason for global sourcing failure is that, when outsourcing, buyers and suppliers tend not to spend enough time upfront to get to know each other well. They rush into a deal before clarifying partner expectations, which can give rise to misunderstandings and inferior results.

- There may be a lot of exposure to exchange rate fluctuations.

- Partner selection, qualification, and monitoring costs may be prohibitively high.

- The increased complexity of managing a worldwide network of production/service locations and partner, and a global supply chain may be too great for internal resources to manage.

- Potential vulnerability to opportunistic behaviour or actions in bad faith by outsourcing suppliers.

- Constrained ability to safeguard intellectual assets.

Much has been written about how offshore outsourcing can be managed effectively and we will look at this in more detail in chapter 10. Meanwhile here are some ideas:

- The parties need to exchange information, transfer knowledge, troubleshoot, coordinate, and monitor.

- Management should collaborate closely with suppliers in co-development and co-design activities. This also enables the focal firm to tap into a stream of ideas for new products, processes, technologies, and improvements.

- Efforts to build strong relationships help create a 'moral contract' between the focal firm and the supplier, which is often more effective than a formal legal contract.

- Escalate commitments by making partner-specific investments (such as sharing knowledge with the supplier) allowing for ongoing review, learning, and adjustment.

- Share costs and revenues by building a stake for the supplier so that, in case of failure to conform to expectations, the supplier also suffers costs or foregoes revenues.

- Maintain flexibility in selecting partners by keeping options open to find alternative partners.

- Hold the partner at bay by withholding access to IP and key assets, in order to safeguard the firm's interests for the long term. If conflicts with the supplier become an ongoing problem, one option for the firm is to acquire full or partial ownership of the supplier.

9.5 Deciding on Location Attractiveness

Selecting a location is one of the major challenges when making offshoring and outsourcing decisions. In Table 9.1 we provide a summary of the 20 major factors that must be considered. The Table is based on Oshri, Kotlarsky and Willcocks (2012). We will look at each of these factors briefly, but you must read the chapter as Essential reading for this component of the subject area.

Table 9.1 Willcocks et al Model for Assessing Country Attractiveness

Cost	Labour costs (average wages for skilled workers and managers)
	Infrastructure costs (unit costs for telecom networks, internet access and power, and office rent)
	Corporate taxes (tax breaks and regulations and other incentives for local investment)
Skills	Skill pool (the size of the labour pool with required skills). Required skills may include technical and business knowledge, management skills, languages, and the ability to learn new concepts and innovate. The scalability of labour resources in the long term (i.e. the ability to supply sufficient labour resources to meet growing demand) is a major issue to consider when choosing a sourcing destination. An indication of the scalability of labour resources in a country is the annual growth in the number of graduates with desired skills. Countries that offer scalability of labour resources are also more likely to keep wages relatively low due to the constant supply of new graduates.
	Vendor landscape (the size of the local sector providing IT services and other business functions). For clients looking to outsource IT or business processes, it is imperative to evaluate the vendor's landscape in terms of the general skills set (or capabilities) and competencies of vendors.

Business and living environment	Governance support (policy on foreign investment, labour laws, bureaucratic and regulatory burden, level of corruption)
	Business environment (compatibility with prevailing business culture and ethics)
	Living environment (overall quality of life, prevalence of HIV infection, serious crime per capita)
	Accessibility (travel time, flight frequency, and time difference)
Quality of infrastructure	Telecommunication and IT (network downtime, speed of service restoration, and connectivity)
	Real estate (both the availability and quality)
	Transportation (scale and quality of road and rail networks)
	Power (reliability of power supply)
Risk profile	Security issues (risks to personal security and property-related issues such as fraud, crime, and terrorism)
	Disruptive events (including the risk of a labour uprising, political unrest, and natural disasters)
	Regulatory risks (the stability, fairness, and efficiency of the legal framework)
	Macroeconomic risks (such as cost inflation, currency fluctuation, and capital freedom)
	Intellectual property risk (strength of the data and IP protection regime)
Market potential	Attractiveness of the local market (the current gross domestic product and its growth rate)
	Access to nearby markets (in both the host country and adjacent region)

Factor 1: Costs. Companies considering outsourcing services, IT, or business processes typically compare a range of costs, including labour costs (average wages for skilled workers and managers), infrastructure costs (unit costs for telecom networks, internet access and power, office rent), and corporate taxes (tax breaks and regulations and other incentives for local investment) across potential outsourcing locations. In addition, they are now also looking at value-added dimensions for how they might benefit over time. Oshri et al. (2012) compare 14 non-BRIC countries (BRIC countries are Brazil, Russia, India, and China; non-BRIC countries have smaller populations and only emerging outsourcing service sectors). Note the great variations in types of costs and also how dynamic these costs can be.

Factor 2: Skills. This factor encompasses the skill pool (the size of labour pool with required skills) and the vendor landscape (the size of the local sector providing IT services and other business functions). Required skills may include technical and business knowledge, management skills, languages, and the ability to learn new concepts and to innovate.

The scalability of labour resources in the long term (i.e. the ability to supply sufficient labour resources to handle growing demand) is a major issue to consider while deciding on a sourcing destination. Clients looking to outsource IT or business processes must evaluate the vendor landscape in terms of the skills set (or capabilities) and competencies of vendors. In this regard, clients should assess each vendor's ability to respond to the customer's ongoing needs (a delivery competency), radically improve service in terms of quality and cost (a transformation competency), and be willing and able to align its business model to the values, goals, and needs of the customer (a relational competency).

Factor 3: Business and Living Environment. This factor considers government support (policy on foreign investment, labour laws, bureaucratic and regulatory burden, level of corruption), the business environment (compatibility with prevailing business culture and ethics), the living environment (overall quality of life, prevalence of HIV infection, serious crime per capita), and accessibility (travel time, flight frequency, time difference).

Factor 4: Quality of Infrastructure. Quality of infrastructure includes telecommunication and IT (network downtime, speed of service restoration, connectivity), real estate (availability and quality), transportation (scale and quality of road and rail network), and power (reliability of power supply).

Factor 5: Risk Profile. This factor assesses security issues (risks to personal security and property-related issues such as fraud, crime, and terrorism), disruptive events (risk of labour uprising, political unrest, natural disasters), regulatory risks (stability, fairness, efficiency of legal framework), macroeconomic risks (cost inflation, currency fluctuation, and capital freedom), and intellectual property (IP) risk (strength of data and IP protection regime). Risk is a critical factor so we will spend a bit more space on the topic here.

Central and Eastern European countries, in particular those that have recently joined the European Union, have been considered by Western partners as safer to live in and visit than countries in the Middle East, Africa, and some countries in Asia and the Americas. The Czech Republic, for example, is considered one of the most stable post-communist countries. Furthermore, CEE countries have suffered less from natural disasters than countries in Asia and the Americas. For example, the flooding in Prague in 2002 caused minor damage compared to the damage caused to Thailand and its population following the 2004 earthquake in the Indian Ocean that hit Thailand through a series of devastating tsunamis.

Terrorist attacks also affect the attractiveness of a country for trade to the business community. There are risk issues as well concerning piracy, IP rights protection, and copyright laws that affect country attractiveness for trade and outsourcing.

Political risk has a significant impact on a country's attractiveness. Political unrest and government change in Egypt in early 2011 is an example of how the attractive image of Egypt as an offshoring destination has changed momentarily as Western companies based in Egypt started pulling out work from the country following the unfolding crisis and Egypt's internet and mobile network shutdown on January 28th 2011. It is doubtful that Egypt will be able to quickly recover from the tarnished reputation as an attractive offshoring destination following these events.

Factor 6: Market Potential. Market potential can be assessed based on the attractiveness of the local market (current gross domestic product and gross domestic product growth rate) and access to nearby markets (in the host country and adjacent regions). This may take one or more forms:

- Whether the local market is attractive for setting up a captive operation (client consideration) or delivery centre (vendor consideration) that would use local labour, infrastructure, and resources.

- Whether the local market is populated with sophisticated local service suppliers (client and vendor consideration).

- Whether local or nearby market have demand for outsourcing services (vendor consideration for setting up a service centre).

Finally, those who are comparing potential sourcing destinations must consider the influence of certain ***cities*** on such a decision. The rationale for this is that costs, availability of skills, and infrastructure may vary significantly across cities within the same country. Even factors such as the environment, risk profile, and market potential can present varying results when examined in each city of the same country. The Global Services Tholons Report (Vashistha and Khan, 2008) argues that comparing countries is superficial because "no two cities of a country would be at the same level of skills maturity or offer the same cost advantage". For example, some cities graduate more engineers, others more accountants. Therefore, sourcing decisions can be more accurate if these assess the attractiveness of potential locations such as cities rather than countries.

One approach to assessing the attractiveness of cities for outsourcing is that proposed by Farrell (2006), in which the scale and quality of workforce, business catalyst, cost, infrastructure, risk profile, and quality of life are amongst the more critical factors. Vashistha and Ravago (2010) have compared a large number of cities and came up with a list of the top ten global services outsourcing cities: six are in India, and the others are Manila and Cebu City in the Philippines, Dublin in Ireland, and Shanghai in China. They also found that amongst emerging global outsourcing destinations, Kraków in Poland, Beijing in China, Buenos Aires in Argentina, Cairo in Egypt, and São Paolo in Brazil were the top five on this list. Of course this list will be very dynamic, and needs to be revisited on almost a yearly basis. You can read more on this subject, and the location criteria to use, in Oshri et al. (2012) chapter 3.

9.6 Nearshoring and Beyond – The Services Scene

Nearshoring is an activity in which a client outsources work to a supplier located in a foreign low-wage country and yet the vendor is close in distance and in terms of time zone differences. Recall Ghemawat and CAGE in chapter 4! Compared to offshore outsourcing, the benefits of nearshoring include lower travel costs, fewer time zone differences, and closer cultural compatibility. Canada, for example, is a significant nearshore destination for US clients. Indeed, some analysts argue that US clients can have lower costs when nearshoring work to Canada as compared with the strategy to offshore-outsource to India. But this might have changed in recent years with the weakening of the US against the Canadian dollar!

In their study of nearshoring, Carmel and Abbott (2007) argue that distance still matters and point to customers choosing the nearshore option to gain benefit from one or more of the following constructs of proximity: geographical, temporal, cultural, linguistic, economic, political, and historical linkages. Their study identifies three major global nearshore clusters based around clients in North America, Western Europe, and a smaller cluster in East Asia.

Nearshoring represents a major way in which non-BRIC countries can compete with India for market share. The top Indian firms now offer a variety of location choices to their clients, which mitigates some of the currency costs incurred in uncertain markets. For example, India-based TCS can offer its British clients services that are "farshore" (India), nearshore (Budapest, Hungary), and onshore from their offices in London, Nottingham, or elsewhere. Another Indian firm, Infosys, has "proximity development centres" and like other Indian firms has also refined its internal processes in mitigating time zone difficulties.

Willcocks and Lacity (2012) argue that, in addition to the continuing nearshoring trend, there is what can be called a "bestshoring" trend. The concept of bestshoring can be explained through the example of the outsourcing contract between TCS and ABN AMRO (Oshri et al., 2012). In this contract, TCS provides IT services to the bank from offshore locations (Mumbai and São Paulo), from nearshore locations (Budapest and Luxembourg), and from an onshore location (Amsterdam). The client and the vendor assess the most appropriate location to provide services based on some of the criteria outlined above (e.g. availability of skills, language, cost). Our research suggests that clients and suppliers are increasingly moving to such an arrangement for either insourced or outsourced IT and business services.

Will nearshoring dominate offshoring strategy in the coming years? Nearshoring will be only one component within the bestshoring strategy. According to Willcocks and Lacity (2012), locations in CEE and Mediterranean Africa will be attractive to Western European and Gulf States clients; those in Asia Pacific to China, India, and Japan; and those in Central and South America to North America. Shared language, culture, or history will continue to influence purchasing decisions. Clearly the BRIC countries themselves are increasingly interested in non-BRIC services and locations.

9.7 Conclusion

In this chapter we have introduced the variants of sourcing covering both production and services. We pointed out the benefits and challenges of global sourcing for the firm and under what circumstances an offshore 'make' production decision is advantageous. This connects up with the issue of foreign direct investment covered in chapter 6. We also provided the rationale for why, under certain circumstances, firms will offshore outsource production. Through the lens of the make-or-buy decision we also looked at global sourcing of services and trends and rationales for different sourcing decisions. This looks forward to chapter 13, which will consider IT and business process outsourcing decisions and management in more detail.

We then provided a key 20 factors model that codifies the major variables a firm needs to consider when deciding on where to locate production or services. Again this links up with an earlier-location-theme we addressed in chapter 6. The chapter also pointed out the importance of analyzing not just country but city location attractiveness, and argued that this needed to be done regularly, given the dynamics of political economy worldwide. Finally we returned to the theme of whether distance still matters, and examined the trends towards nearshoring, and concluded that nearshoring was part of a much bigger trend towards what might be called 'bestshoring' production and services in the constant search for the combination of in-house, captive offshore, domestic and offshore outsourcing that will optimize global performance of the firm. The next chapter looks at global information systems management, an important part of which, these days, concerns global IT sourcing decisions and management.

'Twenty-five years of studies show there is this amplifier effect with IT. A good management is made much better by the application of IT; a bad management is made dramatically worse'

L. Willcocks, 2003

'The trigger point is the articulation of a business issue or opportunity which, if successfully addressed, would radically advance... business vision and strategy. If there is no new idea associated with IT investment, then the most that can be expected is that some existing business idea will operate a little more efficiently as old technology is replaced by new'

David Feeny

'The real problem is not whether machines think, but whether people do'

B. F. Skinner

CHAPTER 10
Global Information Systems Management

10.1 Introduction

Historically organizations operating abroad have tended to act local. They have customized products and services, and the information technologies (IT) underpinning their production and sale, for local consumption based on local culture, language, and regulatory climate. This has not always worked, or internationalization of the firm has moved on, requiring new recipes for success. Over the last 20 years, and particularly in the last 10, organizations have been adapting to the flattening world discussed in chapter 1. On the extreme version of this, IT is the fundamental enabler, and the world can be regarded as a single market. Increasingly organizations can be found standardizing their IT platforms to match more standardized strategies and operations globally. At the same time, as we have seen throughout the book, localization is also important – the issue being how much is required in particular circumstances.

While we can find many examples of flat-world globalized organizations, the reality is that, as chapter 4 makes clear, many businesses competing in foreign markets are not acting as truly globalized organizations. Instead, they have set out on a globalizing journey. In this journey, they must apply business environmental analysis to understand drivers and challenges (see chapters 2, 3, and 4). They need to arrive at business strategy (chapters 4 and 5) for the global context and sector(s) they are operating in. They need to establish an organization structure that fits strategy (see chapter 8), and organize their management and business processes (see chapters 8-11). And critically, they need to create the technology platform and strategy that fits and supports strategic direction. This is summarized in Figure 10.1.

The IT centralization-decentralization challenge facing senior managers is reflected in this statement from a senior executive in an energy multinational:

'We are standardizing as much as possible of our back-office, using shared services and outsourcing. Our history is a lot of diversity, and it's developed over the years to an unacceptable level of global inefficiency. But we also worry about going too much the other way, and losing local sensitivity and nuance. Getting the balance right is a real challenge. It's all too easy to get locked in to projects and solutions that just go too far in the other direction'.

Figure 10.1
International Information Systems Architecture

So how do you follow a path that allows for local discretion, and possible innovation, while delivering efficiencies in local and global operations? Recall chapter 4. Such a company is thus challenged with managing its information and technology resources in a way that maximizes both business flexibility and business standardization. Business flexibility is the ability to tailor products, services, and business processes to local markets to create customer value. Business standardization is the equal need to find common ways of gaining business process efficiencies across the company to reduce working capital, and to leverage human knowledge across business and product units for organizational learning (Kettinger et al., 2010).

In this chapter we focus on managing global information systems. This is a vast subject! So while the chapter gives an overview and a guide to understanding global systems management, we will focus primarily on three critical challenges for globalizing businesses. These are business-IT alignment, IT enterprise architecture, and IT sourcing decision-making.

10.2 Business and IT Alignment – From Strategy to Operations

IT represents the convergence of electronics, computing information and media technologies and capabilities. IT consists of **equipment** – hardware, software, tools; **techniques** – methods, procedures, skills and routines; and **people** ('liveware'). In the modern business context, IT supports **a business information system** – a relatively organized combination of technologies, people, knowledge, data, and information utilized for business purpose.

We define alignment as the process by which those responsible for managing information technology (IT) and stakeholders from the rest of a firm work together to achieve long-term business value. As you look through the cases in this chapter, you will see that the alignment of technology capability with global business purpose is a never-ending struggle for just about all businesses. Business environments are dynamic, business purposes constantly change in the face of competition and consumer demand, and technologies advance rapidly. Business users worldwide are demanding and increasingly IT literate. The senior IT manager, or CIO (Chief Information Officer), not only has to manage the firm's legacy systems, but decide when to introduce, and how to integrate the new technologies constantly arriving from suppliers. For example, Luftman et al. (2012) found the top five technology applications on the CIOs' radar in 2012 were business intelligence, Enterprise Resource Planning systems, cloud computing, mobile and wireless, and customer relationship management. There are also make-versus-buy decisions. For example, do you develop a global accounting system in-house, or buy a package, and customize it where you can? Consider W.R. Grace, a world leader in specialised chemical and construction products. W.R Grace consolidated its general ledger system successfully using an SAP General Ledger application. But even using a package can become a major global implementation challenge. IT outsourcing can be a partial solution, but IT service suppliers also need attention – they need to be located within overall business and IT strategy, selected, controlled, and managed.

Yes, managing global information systems presents major challenges. Luftman et al. (2012) provides useful evidence on the top ten challenges experienced across the world. Note there are, as you would expect, regional differences, but globally the top ten IT issues in rank order are:

- IT and business alignment.
- Business agility and speed to market.
- Business process management and business process re-engineering.
- Business productivity and cost reduction.
- IT reliability and efficiency.
- IT strategic planning.
- Security and privacy.
- Enterprise architecture and infrastructure capability.

How to deal with these challenges? The answer is alignment with the business from the strategy level all the way through to organization development, and delivery. Willcocks et al. (2003) is useful here in pulling together from many sources 18 practices that define best practice in information systems management. These are organized into four practice areas:

Providing Direction – strategy formulation and the strategic use of IT.

1. A clear ***business*** strategy is needed.

2. Develop sub-strategies. Strategy for IT is subdivided into four sub-strategies:

   - IS (demand side, business applications, business information requirements).

   - IT (supply side, technology platform).

   - Information and Technology Governance strategy (IT/IS leadership, how IT is managed, roles and responsibilities, how the IT function is structured).

   - IT market sourcing strategy.

These are the four tasks of the IT function. The first ***business*** (IS) task is to elicit and deliver on business requirements. The second ***technical*** (IT) task is to define the architecture of the technology platform that will be used over time to support the business applications. The third ***governance*** task is to define the governance - rules and responsibilities - and coordination mechanisms for managing the organization's IT/IS activities. The fourth ***sourcing*** task involves understanding and selectively using internal resources and external IT services.

3. Navigate through the four domains of IT. Willcocks et al. (2012) suggest these are:

   - IT hype – where the potential of IT is over-marketed.

   - IT Capability – often described as technology applications in search of business solutions.

   - Useful IT – everyone can make a case for investing in IT, but all too much of IT may be merely useful and not value for money.

   - Strategic IT – the relatively few applications that give disproportionate business value for the firm.

4. Ensure that the IT's agenda is not led by the specific interests of the IT group or of particular user groups or organization units but is business-led – meaning that the agenda delivers on business purpose.

5. Put in planning processes that identify business needs and align them with IT capabilities present and future.

6. Put in measurement processes that keep IT performance under review and on-track.

Establishing the IT Organization – structure, staffing and capabilities.

7. Evolving the maturity of the IT function from a simple technically competent IT service organization to one that is strategic partner with the business that can manage and make use of strategic IT, to one that is capable of business innovation with IT in collaboration with the business and external IT service organizations.

8. Putting in an IT organization structure that reflects that of the firm as a whole (see chapter 8). The choices are between centralized, decentralized or federal.

Managing IT Development and Project Management

9. Keep project management as an in-house core capability.

10. Only outsource mature tasks that are well understood, easily monitored, and for which a detailed contract can be written (see also below).

11. Use multi-functional groups for business innovation tasks where the means are uncertain, and the objectives cannot be well defined.

12. Adopt prototyping and timebox approaches to projects. Break them down into smaller projects that can be accomplished by building a working system model and be delivered in a short deadline – usually under six months.

Delivering On-Going Operations and Infrastructure

13. Retain nine core IT capabilities to keep control of your IT destiny. Willcocks et al. (2003) list these as IT/IT governance, business systems thinking, relationship building, designing technical architecture, making technology work, informed buying, contract facilitation, and contract monitoring.

14. Staff these capabilities with a small group of high performers who have distinctive skills, motivations, and behaviours.

15. Put in place the capabilities for running and delivering a sourcing strategy *before* undertaking large-scale outsourcing projects. We will deal with IT outsourcing in more detail below.

16. Keep in-house non-core IT activities where they are cheaper and/or better done in-house, i.e. where you cannot find an IT service company as efficient or competent as your own IT people.

17. Ensure IT people are business focused and put *business imperatives* before their understandable fascination with technology.

18. Infrastructure is seen as more than an architecture plus technology platform. It is seen as a complex mix of technology, skills, processes, and suppliers, and treated as part of the overall organization design, and foundation of global strategic flexibility. We will come to this in the next section!

10.3 Managing Global Enterprise IT Architecture

The globalizing firm must be thoroughly competent at the IS management practices described above if it is to leverage effectively its enterprise IT architecture. At the core of a globalizing organization's information capabilities is its enterprise IT architecture, defined as the organizing logic for applications, data, and infrastructure technologies, as captured in a set of policies and technical choices, intended to enable the firm's business strategy (Ross, 2003). For Kettinger et al. (2010) enterprise IT architecture comprises:

- *Enterprise systems (ESs)* that manage the information and knowledge related to the core global business processes, such as order fulfilment, materials and service acquisition, customer acquisition and retention, manufacturing, and distribution. ESs span functional and organizational boundaries.

- *IT infrastructure*, consisting of the information, people, and IT practices required for planning and operating the hardware, software, and networks supporting the ESs. Sometimes infrastructure has been referred to as 'all IT except the applications'.

IT enterprise architecture is critical for the globalizing firm. We are going to find out why by using the excellent article by Kettinger et al. (2010) to clarify types of enterprise IT architecture and how they fit with the international business strategies we discussed in chapter 4.

For a globalizing enterprise, the IT architecture can foster the needed business flexibility and business standardization required to compete globally. By embedding the core business processes in the firm's IT infrastructure, enterprise IT architecture can facilitate business standardization and global centralization of information management decision rights. Additionally, embedding customizable locally developed modules in the enterprise IT architecture provides local business units with greater capability to pick and choose architecture components, thus fostering local business flexibility. We know from chapter 4 that global competitiveness increasingly requires optimization of both business flexibility and business standardization. Bartlett and Ghoshal (1998) focused on the interplay between these goals and identified four alternative approaches to operating globally. Bear in mind that their typology is slightly different from the one we use in this book:

- The *Multinational approach* seeks to establish and maximize business flexibility around the world, managing a portfolio of multiple distinct business units (BUs).

- The *International approach* introduces business standardization for adapting and transferring parent company knowledge to foreign markets while maintaining business flexibility, often in terms of regional infrastructure support.

- The *Transnational approach* further leverages regionalization of processes to create business standardization in the core business processes, and establishes BUs as strategic partners that must exchange knowledge and capabilities across the entire company.

- The *Global approach* treats the world market as an integrated whole, maximizing business standardization while maintaining needed business flexibility for competing globally.

These approaches do not indicate a rigid stage model where companies start out as multinationals and gradually evolve to the global approach. In some situations where a company's customer value proposition and capability to deliver is similar worldwide, a company can move directly to the global approach. This is rare. Instead, companies typically must choose one of the other three approaches that best fits their immediate needs and capabilities, and then gradually evolve from that approach towards the global approach. As Kettinger et al. (2010) state: *'in the end, standardization is not the goal of globalizing but the means to an end: a sustainable, learning, growth-oriented company capable of flexibly outperforming competitors at local, regional, and global business levels'.*

The enterprise IT architecture designs discussed below seek to balance the right mix of business flexibility and business standardization in the context of globalization. For example, the enterprise IT architecture for the multinational approach tends to be relatively higher on flexibility and lower on standardization while that for the global approach tends to be relatively lower on flexibility and higher on standardization.

10.4 Enterprise IT Architecture for the 'Multinational' Approach

The enterprise IT architecture for the multinational approach provides flexible ESs and IT infrastructure country by country and business unit by business unit. This sounds like the localization strategy we described in chapter 3! In many ways, the enterprise IT architecture for the multinational approach is a throwback to the pre-IT, high-coordination-cost era when the only way to meet local needs was to decentralize information management decision rights to local managers. Since the introduction of IT, initial efforts have often been made to establish a modicum of control through matrix structures that ask for higher levels of financial accountability, however, well-established local cultures and operating modes can make it difficult to easily introduce greater standardization. Kettinger et al. (2010) suggest the following strengths and weaknesses.

This highly decentralized architecture favours local optimization over cost-efficiencies and organization-wide learning. Local unit managers define and execute management strategies for their businesses and develop their own IT practices and information behaviours and values. Local deployment of IT resources for delivering applications tailored to each BU's unique needs is often viewed by senior management as providing the required business flexibility to deliver maximum value to the customer and growing the business locally.

However, as we saw in chapter 8 and organization structures, the emphasis on business flexibility leads to duplicate ES implementations across BUs. This lack of regional or global standardization of IT infrastructure services can lead to substantially higher operating costs across the company.

10.5 Enterprise IT Architecture for the 'International' Approach

The defining characteristics of the enterprise IT architecture for the international approach are regionally-based shared services for IT infrastructure with flexible country-driven customization of enterprise systems (ESs). The enterprise IT architecture for the international approach attempts to leverage parent-company IT infrastructure resources to gain costs efficiencies within local BUs while still fostering what Kettinger et al. (2010) call 'sense-and-respond' capabilities at the local level. This fits with the international approach described in chapter 7.

The impetus for moving from the multinational to the international approach often comes from corporate leaders who view BU IT costs as unmanaged and unnecessarily high. Headquarters typically appoints senior IT managers at the corporate and/or regional level to oversee IT infrastructure decisions: developing networking standards, limiting technology choices across the company, and reducing IT infrastructure costs. Also, the corporate office often introduces standards for information sharing and access, although much of the transactional data is still embedded in the local systems of each BU.

With the international approach, regional IT directors typically report to headquarters, but they are rarely able to compel, but must rather persuade, local BU managers to adhere to decisions with which they disagree.

Shared IT infrastructure services of the enterprise IT architecture for the international approach offer multiple advantages. These include:

- Smaller markets and/or underdeveloped regions gain the ability to share a more robust IT infrastructure than the local economy and knowledge/skill base would allow.

- Some companies manage to reduce the overall costs of IT operations by consolidating data centres and economizing on networks.

- Companies are better able to build awareness about best practices that can be shared and voluntarily adopted by local BUs (Kettinger et al., 2010).

However Kettinger et al. (2010) note a number of weaknesses. The development of IT standards and policies is driven by committees of BU managers and corporate staff, which involve long decision cycles. While cost benefits emerge from having a regionally standardized IT infrastructure, similar savings are typically not realized with standardized ESs unless they include back-office applications. Common systems often lack ownership and buy-in at the local level. Local resistance to such systems may be increased because of local managers' 'not invented here' attitude or because they see them as being imposed by Corporate HQ. Because the use of shared services is optional, incompatibility and duplication of systems can still increase operating costs. Data is still embedded in local applications, limiting best-practice sharing and organizational learning.

The move to shared IT infrastructure services while maintaining business flexibility offers an organization moving to the international approach the potential to achieve cost efficiencies and information sharing beyond those with the multinational approach. Here is a case of a successful move, researched by Kettinger et al. (2010).

In 2001, the sales and trading business of Citigroup's Central & Eastern Europe, Middle East & Africa (CEEMEA) region covered 31 countries, with customers including corporations, governments, institutions, and individuals. Country business units within the CEEMEA region were managed in a decentralized way. Differences in geographies, histories, languages, religions, and economic and political systems were reasons put forward by local business managers for maintaining the multinational approach. As a result, countries ran their own IT infrastructures and ESs, rarely sharing performance results or best practices. No integrated risk management monitoring existed across the CEEMEA region due to the fragmentation of systems.

Citigroup's CEEMEA regional office based in London, UK, convinced the many country managers that the availability of a jointly designed, consolidated IT infrastructure platform would benefit both local and corporate information needs. This platform would enable operational efficiency, leveraged product expertise, and pooled local market knowledge. Over a four-year period, CEEMEA invested in a robust regional intranet platform linking the regional hub in London and the dispersed countries.

While the London hub initiated the IT infrastructure standardization and information sharing across countries, the diversity of the region's country-based financial regulations and cultures required specific changes in information use driven by local country employees. The transition initiative was recognized as a bottom-up effort to improve information capabilities at the country and regional levels. From 2002 to 2005, after the common IT infrastructure was in place, Citigroup CEEMEA implemented a single regional IT platform with standardized back-office shared services (e.g. financial reporting, risk and credit management, trading flow) to increase operational efficiency across the region.

10.6 Enterprise IT Architecture for the 'Transnational' Approach

By now you will have come to the conclusion that what Kettinger et al. (2010) are calling a transnational strategy is more or less the transnational strategy of our chapter 8 Try to bear this in mind in what follows. The goal of the enterprise IT architecture for the transnational approach is a corporate-wide, standard global IT infrastructure with a transnational business application environment. With Kettinger et al.'s transnational approach, the organization finds ways to exploit and accelerate the convergence of local preferences by educating heterogeneous local market segments about common value propositions and by developing products that can be sold and serviced regionally or worldwide. In addition to IT infrastructure standards, ES front-office and back-office process standards are established.

To succeed with the transnational approach, policy decisions often involve negotiations between global product managers pushing for increased business standardization, and local managers advocating the ability to modify products and services to deliver maximum value to local market segments. In essence, ES decisions are handled through a managed consensus. Open debate is encouraged up to a point, after which a top-down decision is made and local/regional BU managers are expected to implement corporate directives. Ultimately, corporate IT resources are redirected to build a standardized IT infrastructure, and information-sharing tied to the firm's core processes becomes mandatory.

Kettinger et al. (2010) offer CHEP as a firm moving from an international to a transnational approach. CHEP, a leading US-based provider of pallet and plastic container pooling and tracking services, operates in approximately 40 countries. The regional nature of the business initially conditioned the setup of CHEP's operations – characterized by independent regions having individually tailored systems and poor information sharing worldwide. But customers began to complain about CHEP's inefficient administrative systems, service, and information when doing inter-regional business, while the company itself became aware of the high costs of duplicating systems across regions. In response, CHEP reviewed its existing international approach and decided to standardize the IT infrastructure as well as the internal functional systems globally to reduce costs and increase reliability. In turn, highly distinctive business systems necessary for competitive advantage or adapting to regional variation (such as customer integration) were to be maintained and further enhanced. While CHEP's approach to information and IT was global, the implementation was managed at a regional level, allowing for regional differences.

10.7 Enterprise IT Architecture for the 'Global' Approach

This represents what we called in chapter 8 the 'global standardization strategy'. When customers' product and service value propositions do not vary significantly worldwide, and the mechanisms required to deliver that value are similar, the globalizing firm tends to seek a global corporate-driven IT strategy across all business units. The enterprise IT architecture for the global approach fosters information capabilities that are globally scaled and developed at the organization's centre. With this architecture, companies establish strong top-down cultures and carefully measure customer satisfaction to ensure success. While managers in companies adopting the global approach recognize they must sell to local markets, they seek, as much as possible, to design and manage the enterprise processes and IT architecture in a standardized manner globally. The standardization of information embedded in ESs and the IT infrastructure enables organizational learning at the global level. A company following the global approach might seek to roll out a product, say, in the US market and three months later in the Chinese market. To achieve this requires consistent and accurate information for global decision-making.

Kettinger et al. (2010) note a number of strengths with this approach. Tighter alignment is possible between business strategy and the IT deployed worldwide. Speed and effectiveness of doing business globally is facilitated by the worldwide IT infrastructure: common business systems and modularized solutions that work well with the enterprise's rationalized data model but that can be customized for local information presentation and use. Front- and back-office information-sharing throughout the enterprise allows the organization to learn and implement best practices worldwide. Finally, systems are implemented only once rather than in every region or country, saving substantial money and time.

However, while this sounds seductive, recall our senior manager's earlier concern about balance. Global standardization can be problematic if business conditions or markets change very rapidly and the global business model is not capable of being reconfigured to accommodate the change. A company adopting the global approach must be particularly skilful in sensing new business trends and have strong lines of communication with local operations. In the pre-IT era, such an approach would not have been possible; however, with global networks and reconfigurable ERP solutions reducing coordination costs, this weakness may largely be avoided with the right enterprise IT architecture design and information management. Local customers may reject homogenized regional or global product and service delivery and reassert their traditional preferences, creating openings for competitors willing to meet those unique needs.

To bring a number of aspects together - business strategy, structure, and IT - it is useful to revisit CEMEX, whom we mentioned in chapter 4. Here we draw upon Lasserre and Picoto (2007) and Kettinger et al. (2010). Recall that through its global acquisitions, CEMEX has grown over the last two decades from a local Mexican cement producer to become the world's largest building materials supplier and third-largest cement producer. At first, CEMEX was supportive of local business unit investment in IT to improve performance and share best practices. While that approach spurred local innovation, it also led to duplication of applications, processes, and projects across the company. In 2000, the CEO saw an urgent need not only to reduce IT costs, but also to make the IT organization more agile to improve customer satisfaction and speed up post-merger integration. In response, the company launched a US$200 million programme called "The CEMEX Way". This amounted to a global approach.

According to Kettinger et al. (2010), The CEMEX Way had three main components: process and systems standardization, a new governance model, and e-enabled processes. To support permanent standardization, eight oversight e-groups were made responsible for the effectiveness of the company's core processes. The e-groups comprised business experts as well as HR and IT representatives. Their mandate was to define where standardization made sense and what had to be improved before standardizing. The groups used a single set of methodologies and tools to document and consolidate best practices for each process to form a knowledge database.

In 2005, the company acquired the UK-based multinational firm RMC, expanding CEMEX's geographic reach and creating new opportunities for economies of scale. Despite the cultural differences between RMC and CEMEX, The CEMEX Way proved to be a successful integration approach. The company reported more than US$200 million dollars in synergy savings in 2006 with expected savings of US$380 million dollars in 2007 (Lasserre and Picoto, 2007). Processes became simpler and more efficient; knowledge sharing and control were improved. Shared services reduced application and system duplication. An open corporate information structure improved CEMEX's flexibility and agility. The alignment of processes, HR, and IT facilitated quick adaptation. All of this was achieved while IT spending was reduced from 5 to 2 percent of sales (Kettinger et al., 2010).

CEMEX has continued to grow through mergers and acquisitions, and new acquisitions are integrated with less time and less effort. CEMEX has developed its own way of acquiring. It sends integration experts to the new acquisition to transfer CEMEX's global knowledge, culture, and practices. Adopted ideas learned from merged firms are rolled out globally, not just locally. In this way, CEMEX continues to foster coordination and collaboration in global innovation. As a result of The CEMEX Way, IT evolved from a business services enabler to a business transformation agent (Kettinger et al., 2007). The development of an information-oriented workforce culture has been instrumental in CEMEX's efforts to globalize with high business flexibility and standardization. At CEMEX, performance and appraisal criteria are set up to support the information-centric culture. Overall, the good information management practices enable transparency throughout the organization, resulting in self-regulating behaviour.

10.8 Enterprise IT Architecture and Globalization: Key Success Factors

So how can companies turn the apparent business paradox of achieving business flexibility and business standardization at the same time into a business advantage? Kettinger et al. (2010) offer nine key success factors for the globalizing journey. These success factors will ensure that a company achieves alignment with its business strategy expressed as the right balance between business flexibility and business standardization:

- Vision for the Journey and Destination.
- Scoping the Transition.
- Mobilizing the Management Team.
- Implementing Dedicated Change Management Programmes.
- Developing an Information-Oriented Culture.
- Shifting the Balance of Power.
- Developing a Global Mindset.
- Sharing Best Practices.
- Shifting Profit and Loss Responsibilities and Reporting Lines.

10.9 Global IT Sourcing Decisions and Risks

You have covered a lot of this subject already. In Chapter 9 you learned about make-or-buy decisions; offshoring global services and production; and deciding on location attractiveness. In section 13.2 (above) you learned about IT sourcing strategy, the retained capabilities needed and how to manage the role of outsourcing in IT development, IT projects, IT operations and infrastructure. Here we will focus specifically on three issues – making the IT sourcing decision, outsourcing and offshoring risks, and how to manage across the outsourcing lifecycle.

According to Willcocks and Lacity (2012), by 2012 the IT and Business Services outsourcing market was over US$450 billion in annual revenues. Of this, about 65 billion represented the offshore outsourcing market. IT outsourcing was set to increase at 5 to 8 percent annually over the next five years, while business process outsourcing was set to expand by 8 to 12 percent annually. However we talk here of global IT *sourcing* because outsourcing is by no means always the best option, and does incur a range of risks. Good management mitigates these risks. The range of options is shown in Table 10.1.

Table 10.1: Sourcing Options

Sourcing Options	Description
In-house provision; insourcing	A sourcing option in which the organization owns the IT assets and employs its own IT staff
Staff augmentation; Contract labour,	A sourcing option in which an organization buys in low- to mid-level labour to supplement in-house capabilities; the client manages the people, usually at the client site
Management Consulting	A sourcing option in which an organization buys in high-level expertise to supplement in-house capabilities
Shared Services	A sourcing option in which an organization centralizes and standardizes IT delivery
Traditional Outsourcing; Fee-for-service outsourcing; Exchange-based Outsourcing;	A sourcing option in which a client pays a fee to a provider in exchange for the management and delivery of specified IT services. The client is in charge of specifying needs and the provider is in charge of managing the resources to deliver those needs
Cloud Computing; Netsourcing; Application Service Provision	With this utility model, clients pay a usage-based fee to providers in exchange for services being delivered over a network, typically the internet
Joint Ventures; Strategic Partnerships	A specific type of contract entered into by two or more parties in which each agrees to furnish a part of the capital and labour for a business enterprise

There are a number of sourcing options available. Using the scope of outsourcing as a criterion (i.e. the degree to which a process is managed internally or by a third party) Willcocks et al. (2011) distinguishes three models:

- *Total outsourcing*, which refers to transferring more than 80 percent of a function's operating budget to external providers.

- *Total in-house sourcing*, which refers to retaining the management and provision of more than 80 percent of the function's operating budget within the organisation.

- *Selective outsourcing*, which refers to sourcing selected functions to external parties while managing 20 to 80 percent of the function's operating budget internally.

When outsourcing, organizations also have to decide about the number of providers to engage. Selective multi-sourcing has the advantages of choosing best-of-breed providers, mitigating the risks of relying too much on one provider, and helping clients adapt in changing environments. Multi-sourcing has several disadvantages, including increased transaction costs as organizations manage more providers, interdependencies and interfaces. The major advantages of bundled services from a single provider include simplified procurement, simplified governance, fewer transaction costs, and economies of scale and scope. But bundled services increase switching costs and the risks of relying on one provider.

How to make strategic sourcing decisions about IT? Willcocks et al. (2011) suggest a process to evaluate which activities are good candidates for outsourcing and which are not. They suggest that business activities should be assessed in terms of their contribution to business operations, as well as in terms of their contribution to competitive positioning – see Figure 10.2:

Figure 10.2
Strategic IT Sourcing: By Business Activity

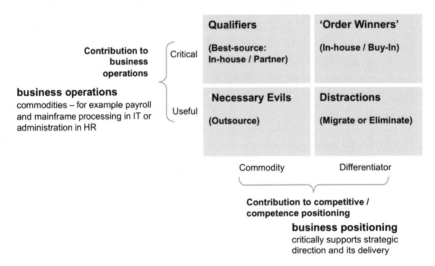

- *Order winners* are activities that contribute greatly to the company's business operations and its competitive positioning. These activities in essence constitute the basis of the firm's differentiation relative to its competitors and should be kept in-house. For example, such activities for Dell, the computer multinational, include those that maintain and enhance the speed of operations and its focus on core business.

- *Qualifiers* are activities that are critical for business operations yet do not contribute to the company's competitive positioning in a major way. These activities should be 'best' sourced, which could include the involvement of a third party if it meets the right cost and quality criteria and has strong partnering capability. For example, aircraft maintenance systems are a minimum requirement for airlines to compete in the industry, but they do not constitute an important differentiator between airlines.

- *Useful commodities or Necessary evils* are activities that do not contribute significantly to the company's business or its competitive positioning. These activities constitute good candidates for outsourcing. For example, in the case of Dell in the early 2000s, such activities included administration, inventory, and payroll tasks. Most IT outsourcing is of this type, e.g desktop maintenance, data centres, payroll, accounting systems. Typically the safest activities are discrete, mature and stable.

- *Distractions* are failing attempts to differentiate a company from its competitors. These activities should be eliminated or migrated to another quadrant. For example, Dell in 1989 opened retail outlets, but it soon discovered that its major distinctive competence was the direct model of selling.

Having identified activities that are **outsourcing candidates**, Willcocks et al. (2011) suggest another matrix to evaluate whether the market can service the requirement. If the market is not cheap, capable, or mature enough, then the organization will need to seek a largely in-house solution. Figure 13.3 captures the major elements for consideration and plots the cost efficiencies and capabilities the market can offer against carrying out the activity internally.

Figure 10.3
Strategic IT Sourcing: By Market Comparison

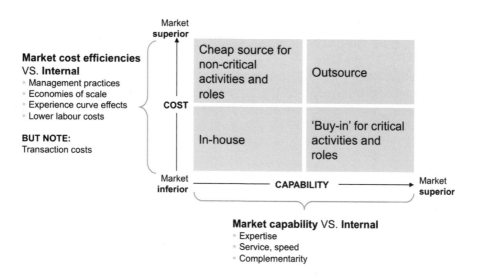

Where the market can carry out a task cheaper and better, then outsourcing is the obvious decision, but only for **qualifiers** and **necessary evils**. As an example, Federal Express provides customer delivery for Dell. Where the market (i.e. Federal Express in this case) offers an inferior cost and capability, then in-house sourcing would be the better alternative. Where the market offers a better-cost deal, then this should be taken, but only for non-key activities (necessary evils). Where the market offers superior capability but at a premium price above what the in-house cost might be, there may still be good reasons for buying in or close partnering with the third party, not least to leverage and learn from their expertise, and apply it to **qualifying** and even **order-winning** tasks.

1. In summary, what factors **do** make an IT activity a less risky outsourcing candidate? These are the main business, economic, and technical reasons:

2. Useful/critical commodities vs. critical differentiators.

3. Discrete IT activities vs. IT integrated into complex processes.

4. Stable mature IT activities vs. new technologies, development/innovation tasks.

5. Market cheaper and/or better vs. in-house costly and/or inferior capabilities.

6. IT/business processes re-engineered vs. outsourcing IT problems/messes.

10.10 Managing Across the Outsourcing Lifecycle

Finally, IT outsourcing risk also occurs when managers, having signed the contract, do not manage across the outsourcing lifecycle to deliver the results. Cullen et al. (2005) provide details of the necessary management activities over nine phases of the outsourcing lifecycle. The evidence is that to be effective outsourcing requires a comprehensive approach. I will distill the major lessons and principles organized as a health check of key questions and answers, based on Willcocks (2011) and Willcocks and Lacity (2012).

Check 1 – Risk Management
Key issue: 'What are the risks and how do we manage them?'

The top five risks that actually materialise in outsourcing arrangements are consistently: hidden costs of contract, credibility of vendor claims, irreversibility of contract, lack of expertise in managing outsourcing, and loss of control over IT/operations. One could write a book just on the number one risk experienced by clients, namely hidden costs. Favourite sources engendering this risk include:

- Signing incomplete contracts.

- Ambiguities and loopholes in the contract reinterpreted less favourably later, in different circumstances.

- Underestimating the costs of management – usually between 4 to 8 percent of contract value (more if offshoring), or failing.

- Over-reliance by all parties on poor measurement of internal cost/service baseline.

- Not allowing the supplier a reasonable margin.

Some examples. In signing an incomplete contract a health care organization subsequently had to pay higher prices for add-on services that materialised over a five- year contract. Actual costs came in at 200 percent of those appearing in the original cost-saving agreement. A bank agreed to pay for the transfer of all software licence agreements, until it realised the cost was going to exceed the planned cost savings over the five-year datacentre deal. On slim margins, the supplier refused to change the terms, and the parties beat each other up over the contract for its duration. Poor contracts can make for poor relations! A major engineering company entered a strategic relationship with a global supplier to transform its IT function, but within three years they were in serious dispute over US$40 million of invoicing, because the client had not handed over good cost/service data, and the supplier had not checked this carefully enough in the initial rush to transition and deliver service.

Clients also need to look at the risks of pressing suppliers hard on cost reductions. A 'winner's curse' can occur where a supplier wins the contract but stands to make no money from the deal. We find that suppliers sign such deals about a fifth of the time, thinking they can make up the margin on add-on services, working smarter, or counting the value of having a prestige client, a reference site, or a bridgehead to future contracts. Sometimes they just oversell or do not calculate well. The problem is that in three quarters of 'winner's curse' cases the actions of the supplier in, for example, cutting its costs, reducing staff quality and headcount, and minimizing technology investment, translates into degradation of service, dispute, and poor client experiences.

Outsourcing – handing some activity, asset, or people over to third party management – is inherently risky. It therefore falls upon the client to weigh carefully and mitigate the risks typically incurred. And the risk approach should always be energised by the thought that the client always remains ultimately accountable for risk, despite all too frequent attempts we see to pass these on to the supplier. Risks can be mitigated by the practices we sketch in answer to the next seven questions.

Check 2 – Learning Curve

Key issue: 'Where are we on the learning curve?'

Organizations typically pass through four phases en route to outsourcing management maturity. In the first, *Hype* and *Fear*, they either believe supplier claims too easily, or only believe the negative publicity. Believing the hype can lead to instant long-term, sometimes large-scale, commitments that are not properly understood or resourced. Fear can lead to an increasingly complacent and sub-optimal internal back-office function. In practice most organizations, at least with their IT, have passed into and through the second Cost Focus phase. Here by experiential learning, making mistakes, and focusing primarily on a cost reduction agenda, the organization feels its way into the fundamental principles that need to be observed to make use of the services market. The effective organizations here tend to be what we describe as 'smart in their ignorance'. They recognise risks and their own incapabilities. Historically we have seen organizations at this stage outsource less than 30 percent of the relevant back-office, use several suppliers for services they are best at, outsource stable, mature activities, usually on three to five year contracts. In phase three, clients are better able to manage and leverage relationships with suppliers, richer practices emerge, and a concern to focus on quality and more strategic objectives. We find relatively few clients are in a fourth value-added phase, even with their IT. Here strategic sourcing and mature capabilities enable a focus on value-added and collaborative innovation with suppliers.

It is important to assess where you are on the learning curve. Clients should not commit beyond their ability to manage the objectives, supplier portfolio, and activities outsourced. The mistakes organizations make in phases one and two are invariably due to inexperience. These include:

- Outsourcing areas and problems they do not understand.

- Having unrealistic, multiple objectives, and expectations.

- Focusing on cutting costs, not managing differently.

- Not building a five-year overall sourcing strategy.

- Signing long-term contracts for short-term reasons.

- Expecting too much from suppliers, and not enough from themselves.

These sorts of practices need to be turned around. In practice it takes several generations of outsourcing for a client organization to move slowly up the learning curve. We have also found that organizations are not particularly good at transferring learning from their ITO experiences, to their newer, BPO and offshore contracts. But the phase four organizations we have studied (for example StatoilHydro, KPN, Spring Global Mail) can respond very positively to all eight health check questions and also exhibit very strong collaborative and innovation capability when working with their suppliers.

Check 3 – Sourcing Strategy

Key issue: 'How do we select the right sourcing options and craft strategy for the next five years?'

Clients that leverage outsourcing successfully do their homework in **Architecting** and **Engage** phases before contracts are signed. They investigate the market and their own capabilities, they target potential outsourcing candidate areas, develop a sourcing strategy, and design a detailed process to implement this. They then embark on careful selection and negotiation, and ensure that contracts can operate as default guarantors if relationships and management prove defective. Organizations that skimp on this homework tend to find that they are always in catch-up mode. Their higher goals and the promise to themselves to become business and strategy focused are lost through pressure of events, firefighting, and operational matters.

To arrive at a sourcing strategy, a client needs to use business and market logic. We saw this at work above in Figures 10.2 and 10.3. In practice, mature organizations tend to have a portfolio of suppliers; they multi-source, but are always seeking to reduce supplier numbers to the minimum compatible with retaining competitiveness, best-in-class service, and optimal governance. This will involve going through a detailed process of configuring the sourcing approach to cover service scope, supplier grouping, financial scale, pricing framework, duration of contracts, resource ownership, and commercial relationship. As your eyes glaze over, keep remembering: the homework matters!

Check 4 – Retained Core Capabilities

Key issue: 'What in-house capabilities do we need to build governance and management?'

Our work on cloud and the future of business re-affirms the continuing relevance of the call for clients to retain four tasks in-house. The four tasks remain core to the function whether it is, for example, IT, human resources, procurement, accounting, finance, estate management, or call centres being outsourced. The four tasks are eliciting and delivering on business requirements, ensuring technical/process capability, managing external supply, and governance. In our model client organizations need to retain nine capabilities to achieve these four tasks. We posit a much smaller, high performance team whose capabilities need to be built over time, as an organization moves up the learning curve, and is able, increasingly, to take on larger scale outsourcing, that has more strategic business impacts.

Initially a client will need to build its technical service delivery capability through developing, for example, in the IT function, the roles of CIO, contract facilitator, technical architect, and technical fixer. With reliable service in place it can move towards a more business-focussed agenda, requiring the CIO to become more a business partner, and relationship builders, business systems thinkers, and contract monitors to manage more outsourcing. Amongst the most mature clients we see them leveraging suppliers effectively and managing large-scale outsourcing, by also having informed buying and vendor development capability, with sometimes the old CIO role splitting into two roles – business innovator, and chief technology officer.

We regularly find firms that outsource give away too much of their technical capability. A major bank did precisely this, and four years into one of the world's biggest ten-year deals, had also too few people with the wrong skills sets, in terms of relating to the business, and managing external supply. It took two years to rebuild the IT function and take back control of its IT destiny in time to contribute to a major business transformation.

Outsourcing will require different skills from those traditionally found in the IT function. Existing staff may have some of these, or can be upskilled through training. You may also have to buy in some key staff. The task then, is to retain such people by paying them the market rate, and offering them interesting and challenging, value-adding work. None of this is easy, but the alternative to an invest-to-save approach on human resources is, we have found, to run into endless problems without the resourceful in-house staff to deal with them. Retained capabilities continues to be the single most neglected area in outsourcing, and insidiously threatening to the long-term health of any deal. The promise of cloud services brings its own dangers here. Beware of the anorexic retained organization.

Check 5 – Type of Relationship

Key issue: 'Do we need a power-based or trust-based relationship?'

Experienced practitioners will tell you that the relationship and mutual trust were absolutely key in all their successful outsourcing arrangements. However, there is no such thing as an instant relationship, and trust is built over time, through performance. Where does this leave us? A contract-based relationship is a starting point. Here ensuring an exhaustive, complete contract, detailed metrics for performance, meaningful penalties and escalation procedures, ensuring the client has alternative potential service avenues, and is not over-dependent on a single supplier for critical work – such practices can give the client a good initial default position to operate from. But staying locked into a coercive, short gain, 'getting more for less' philosophy can achieve only limited objectives. It can also be poor signalling to the supplier, with adverse consequences for supplier commitment and behaviour. Invariably the client has to be on a journey with the supplier to a more partnering, trust-based relationship if they are to deliver on bigger objectives.

In examples that we have researched, initial trust is based on belief in the goodwill, competence, and willingness to conform to each other's expectations, and in the fairness of the contractual arrangements. Long-term trust, however, is built through behaviour (performance and fairness) over time. Clients trust suppliers who deliver the services promised, suppliers trust client relationship managers who facilitate the supplier's success within the organization, while mutual trust comes from resolving conflicts fairly (and swiftly), through flexibility, open communications, and knowledge-sharing to mutual advantage.

Check 6 – Supplier Capabilities
Key issue: 'What service supplier capabilities do we require?'

A common mistake on suppliers is, firstly, to believe that everything written in the marketing brochure will be available to the client, and relevant to the client, and, secondly, to get blinded by the supplier's listing of resources, instead of how these will get translated into the *capabilities* you need. What you need from the supplier depends on your outsourcing objectives. Most commonly, clients want a better service at a lower cost, or with an improving cost base. Check out the supplier's *delivery* competency, in particular their capabilities in regard to domain expertise, business management, governance, leadership, programme management, sourcing, and behaviour management. If you want *transformation* of the back-office then additionally look for capabilities in process re-engineering, technology exploitation, and customer development. If you are looking for long-term business development supported by your outsourcing supplier then your supplier needs a strong *relationship* competency. Look for capabilities in planning and contracting, organization design, customer development, governance, leadership, and programme management.

It is incumbent on the client to establish through due diligence that the supplier does indeed have the capabilities required. Check out the track record in previous deals, do site visits and workshops, and listen to independent voices, including previous clients. The client also needs to check the detail of who is going to staff up these capabilities, and receive guarantees on the quality and tenure of those human resources. There is a danger in getting the A team that wins the bid and beds down the initial transition, and the B or even C team for the remaining three of five years of the contract. As one CIO told us *'I see myself in competition with all its other clients for the supplier's prime attention and resources.'* The astute client, then, will need to work out ways in which the supplier can go the extra mile. Attractive aspects that can be leveraged include: the prestige of the client, the size of the contract, the potential for additional work, the profit margin offered, the opportunity for the supplier to enter new markets, or for knowledge transfer to the supplier.

Check 7 – Lifecycle Management

Key issue: How do we negotiate and manage across the outsourcing lifecycle?'

Outsourcing cannot be treated as a fire-and-forget missile. A deal has to be managed across its lifecycle through, according to our research, some 54 major activities distributed across nine phases. The trouble begins when the ink on the contract is dry, because any lack of due diligence at the architecting stage (scoping, evaluation, negotiation, and implementation planning) reveals itself when 'the rubber hits the road' as you and the supplier transition services and staff.

Organizations on the optimal path manage the pre-contract phases very carefully, use detailed cost-service baselines against which to assess supplier bids, vet suppliers diligently, and do not throw away the deal's promise through over-legalistic or over-ambitious, adversarial, negotiating tactics. For transition they establish the precedents for operational performance by, for example, establishing the post-contract management infrastructure and processes, ensuring implementation of consolidation, rationalization and standardization, validating baseline service scope, costs, levels and responsibilities, and managing service requests beyond baseline. In the middle phase clients move their energy and focus to achieving added value above and beyond operational performance. In the mature phase they assess and plan for strategic sourcing options and business continuity well ahead of contract renewal or termination.

Check 8 – Benchmarking for Service

Key issue: 'How do we benchmark, monitor, and make the back-office a true service operation?'

The trick - everyone will tell you - is to measure what is meaningful. In recent years this has meant a leaning amongst clients (it is hardly a major shift so far) towards more business focused rather than technical measures. With increasing maturity on both sides, the technical measures will come to be left to suppliers. Also more use of scorecards, to consolidate the relatively few but key metrics that drive service and direction. Effective scorecards: (1) are administratively feasible, (2) measure what they purport to measure, and (3) drive the right behaviours. Service is a much over-used word in outsourcing. What it should refer to is not what the supplier does, not what the supplier provides, but what the customer experiences. The big four metrics to focus on are (a) quantity – how many, in what time, (b) performance – quantity versus target, (c) value – does it make business sense, and (d) quality – did the customer like it?

Dealing with these eight questions gets a client organization on to a global rightsourcing agenda. Successful outsourcing experiences tend to share certain attributes. There is selective outsourcing, with real clarity about what cannot be outsourced. Detailed contracts, most usually three to five years in length, are arrived at that preserve the business intent of the deal. Sourcing decisions are made jointly by business and IT executives. Internal and external bids are invited to establish competition. A limited number of suppliers are chosen to keep management feasible, maintain competition, while ensuring suppliers do not tread on each other's toes. The objectives focus more on fair market price and good service than cost reductions alone. There is an escalating rather than an instant long-term commitment to large-scale outsourcing. Contracts are about aligning incentives and win-win as far as possible, rather than 'us versus them'. Client management stays engaged, rather than stepping aside. This is not the only way to outsource, but for most organizations it is the low risk approach.

10.11 Conclusion

There is a lot in this chapter. The reason is that most international business writers acknowledge the importance of IT in the global as well as the domestic context (just look at Thomas Friedman in chapter 1) but, unlike him, do not really understand in detail how it works and how it can be managed. As a result, global information systems management is a surprisingly understudied area in international business studies. In fact the thorough treatment of IT in international business textbooks is most noticeable by its absence!

In this chapter, we saw yet again the crucial importance in global business management of aligning international business strategy with what underpins strategy – in this case IT platforms, applications, and people. The first part of the chapter looked at IT management – such areas as governance regimes, processes, organization, and capabilities. In the second part we looked at the criticality of enterprise IT architecture for successfully operating internationally in the contemporary world. We saw how IT architecture needs to be aligned with business strategy and structure, and the challenges in achieving this. In the third part we looked at global IT sourcing, and especially the rise of outsourcing and how to make sourcing decisions, mitigate risks and manage across the lifecycle of any outsourcing arrangements. Hopefully you will be left with the understanding that outsourcing is best seen not as a way of handing off problems – though many do use it for that! Instead outsourcing should be seen as part of a larger global sourcing decision, and as an opportunity to achieve strategic focus and build core capabilities. This means learning another way of managing that can leverage the capabilities of service suppliers to achieve global competitive advantage for the firm.

You will have gathered from this chapter, if you did not realise it before, that IT is to a surprising extent as much about management and people as it is about technology. Which leads us to our next chapter on international human resources management.

'In looking for people to hire, you look for three qualities: integrity, intelligence, and energy. And if they don't have the first, the other two will kill you'

Warren Buffett

'Generally people say it costs companies three times as much as a normal employee to have someone working in expatriate capacity'

Chris Brewster

'To lead people, walk beside them... As for the best leaders, the people do not notice their existence. The next best, the people honour and praise. The next, the people fear; and the next, the people hate... When the best leader's work is done the people say, 'We did it ourselves!''

Lao Tzu

CHAPTER 11
International Dimensions of Human Resources Management

11.1. Introduction

Human resource management (HRM) refers to the activities an organization carries out to utilize its human resources effectively. It includes activities like determining the overall human resource strategy, how a firm should be staffed, how managers will be evaluated, how management development will be achieved, what compensation packages will look like, and how the firm will manage its relationship with labour. These activities typically include those shown in Figure 11.1.

In this chapter we cannot cover all these issues in depth, and we have dealt with a number of other relevant issues – workforce diversity, corporate social responsibility, and managing culture in earlier chapters. However, we will look at the international dimensions of the following major areas:

- Determining the firm's human resource strategy.
- Staffing.
- Performance evaluation.
- Training and management development.
- Compensation.
- Labour relations.

As companies have become more dependent on foreign markets both as a source of revenues and as a source of low cost labour and materials, international human resource strategy has become increasingly important for firms. Human resource management tends to be more complex in international companies as compared to domestic companies because of differences in labour markets, culture, legal systems, economic systems, and the many other factors we met in chapters 2 and 3.

Figure 11.1
Human Resources Management

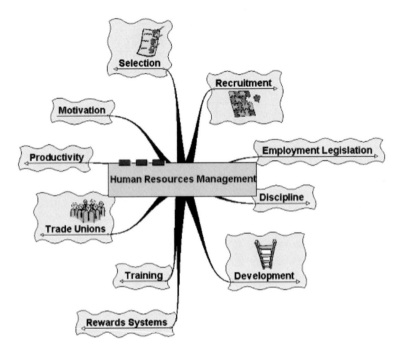

What is the link between international business strategy and IHRM? Remember that a firm's strategy (see chapter 4) is implemented through its structure and organization (see chapter 8), and if the right structure and organization are not there, the strategy will not work. But firms also need to ensure there is a fit between their international business strategy and human resources practices. This gives rise to international human resource management (IHRM), that is, the process of selecting, training, developing, and compensating personnel in overseas positions. IHRM strategy must fit with and support the international strategy (chapter 4) and structure (chapter 8) chosen by the firm. For example, a firm pursuing a localization strategy needs to be sure that local managers are involved in decision-making. Similarly, a firm with a transnational strategy needs to have the means to transfer and disseminate information throughout the firm. What staffing policies would support this objective? Through optimal use of a diverse workforce, IHRM can help the firm reduce the costs of value creation and add value by better serving international customer needs. IHRM must also determine when to use expatriate managers – citizens of one country working abroad. Questions like who should be sent on foreign assignments, how they should be compensated, how they should be trained, how they should be reoriented when they return home.

Clearly the area of IHRM offers major challenges not least because, as we shall see, MNEs necessarily have diverse workforces and a mix of cultures that need managing. In this chapter we focus on how key areas can be managed.

11.2 Types of Staffing Policy

A firm's staffing policy involves the selection of employees who fit the needs of a specific job, and who will be effective at promoting the firm's corporate culture – the firm's norms and value system. A strong corporate culture can help the firm implement its strategy. Therefore General Electric, for example, hires people who not only have the skills necessary for a particular job, but who also have behavioural styles, beliefs, and value systems that fit with the company's corporate culture. Peng and Meyer (2011) point to three main approaches to staffing policy within international businesses:

1. *Ethnocentric approach.* Firms with an ethnocentric approach to staffing fill key management positions with parent country nationals. In the past, this approach was very popular. Companies like Proctor & Gamble, Phillips, and Matsushita for example, all had ethnocentric approaches to staffing. Why follow an ethnocentric approach to staffing? It makes sense for firms with an international strategy. Firms that pursue an ethnocentric policy believe that there is a lack of qualified individuals in the host country to fill senior management positions. They also see it as the best way to maintain a unified corporate culture. Many Japanese companies transfer managers to foreign operations for this reason. Transferring core competencies to a foreign operation via parent country nationals can create value, and many Japanese companies do this via managers from the parent company. But it limits advancement opportunities for host country nationals and can lead to 'cultural myopia' where a firm doesn't really understand host country cultural differences and what they mean. If local managers do not see room for advancement, they will be less motivated.

2. *Polycentric approach.* Firms that follow a polycentric approach to staffing recruit host country nationals to manage subsidiaries in their own countries, while parent country nationals fill key slots at headquarters. An advantage of this approach is that it avoids the cultural myopia mentioned above as a problem with the ethnocentric approach. This, of course, is especially beneficial to a company following a localization strategy (see Chapter 4). A polycentric approach can also be less expensive to implement because it avoids the cost of expatriate managers. However, a key drawback of the polycentric approach is that it creates a gap between the home country and host country operations. This gap can make it difficult to transfer core competencies, or achieve experience curve or location economies. Firms that follow a polycentric approach often have a hard time shifting to new strategies. Unilever, the UK-based MNE, found this out when it tried to shift to a transnational strategy. The company's subsidiaries had been operating more or less autonomously and resisted pressure to give up that sovereignty. Another drawback with a polycentric staffing policy is that host country nationals, because they only have limited opportunities to gain experience outside their own countries, have difficulty progressing beyond senior positions within their own subsidiary.

3. ***Geocentric approach.*** Between the extremes of the ethnocentric approach and the polycentric approach is the geocentric approach where the best people, regardless of their nationality, are sought for key jobs throughout the organization. This is consistent with building a strong, unifying culture and informal management network. It makes sense for firms pursuing a global or transnational strategy. It enables the firm to make the best use of its human resources. It builds a cadre of international executives who feel at home working in a number of different cultures and these managers can be the first step to building a strong corporate culture. A geocentric staffing policy can also help firms reduce cultural myopia and be more responsive to local markets. Keep in mind though, that a firm might not be able to pursue this strategy if immigration policies limit their ability to hire certain individuals. In the USA and Switzerland for example, extensive documentation is needed to hire a foreigner rather than a local citizen. Also a geocentric strategy can be costly and difficult because of the training and relocation costs involved.

A summary comparison of these three approaches appears in Figure 11.2.

Figure 11.2
Comparison of Staffing Approaches

Comparison of Staffing Approaches

Staffing Approach	Strategic Appropriateness	Advantages	Disadvantages
Ethnocentric	International	Overcomes lack of qualified managers in host nation Unified culture Helps transfer core competencies	Produces resentment in host country Can lead to cultural myopia
Polycentric	Localization	Alleviates cultural myopia Inexpensive to implement	Limits career mobility Isolates headquarters from foreign subsidiaries
Geocentric	Global standardization and transnational	Uses human resources efficiently Helps build strong culture and informal management networks	National immigration policies may limit implementation Expensive

11.3 Expatriates: Recruitment and Selection

Firms that decide to use expatriate managers, or citizens of one country who are working in another country need to think about how they can help the managers be successful. Why? Because the expatriate failure rate is high. Good recruitment and selection procedures can reduce the risk of failure.

Issues with Expatriates

Expatriate failure, or the premature return of an expatriate, is common. Studies over the years, like Tung (1982) and Lee (2007) have shown that between 16 and 40 percent of American expatriates on assignment in other developed countries come home early. About 70 percent fail to complete their assignments in developing countries. The cost of failure is high – it can cost between US$0.25 million and US$1 million per employee.

The main reasons for US expatriate failure are:

- The inability of an expatriate's spouse to adapt.
- The manager's inability to adjust.
- Other family-related reasons.
- The manager's personal or emotional maturity.
- The manager's inability to cope with larger overseas responsibilities.

The reason for European expatriate failure is:

- The inability of the manager's spouse to adjust.

The main reasons for Japanese expatriate failure are:

- The inability to cope with larger overseas responsibility.
- Difficulties with the new environment.
- Personal or emotional problems.
- A lack of technical competence.
- The inability of spouse to adjust.

Firms can reduce expatriate failure through improved selection procedures. Mendenhall and Oddou (1985) identified four dimensions that predict expatriate success, self-orientation, others-orientation, perceptual ability, and cultural toughness:

1. *Self-orientation* – the expatriate's self-esteem, self-confidence, and mental well-being.

2. *Others-orientation* – the ability to interact effectively with host-country nationals.

3. *Perceptual ability* – the ability to understand why people of other countries behave the way they do.

4. *Cultural toughness* – how well an expatriate adjusts to a particular posting tends to be related to the country of assignment.

Some experts also believe that a global mindset, involving cognitive complexity and cosmopolitan outlook, is the fundamental attribute of a global manager. This mindset is often acquired early in life from a bicultural family, living in a foreign country, or learning a foreign language as a regular part family life. AstraZeneca, one of the world's largest pharmaceutical companies, and IBM, one of the world's major IT and services companies are just two examples of firms that promote the notion of a global mindset by encouraging its managers to accept foreign postings and to be comfortable working with people from different countries and cultures. A global mindset is considered by many firms to be the fundamental attribute of a global manager.

Expatriates who have high self-esteem, self-confidence, and mental well-being are most likely to succeed in foreign assignments. Countries that are perceived to be more similar to an expatriate's home country are usually easier to adapt to. Many Americans, for example, find it relatively easy to adapt to working in Britain, but not to working in India.

11.4 Expatriate Training and Development

After selecting a manager for a position, training and development programmes should be implemented. Training focuses upon preparing the manager for a specific job. Management development is concerned with developing the skills of the manager over his or her career with the firm. This gives the manager a skill set and reinforces organizational culture. Historically, most firms focus more on training than on management development, but recently there has been a realization that management development can be an essential component in a firm's overall strategy.

Training

Recall that the inability of both the manager, and the manager's spouse to adjust to the new environment were among the most common reasons for expatriate failure. Cultural training, language training, and practical training can all help reduce this type of failure. Yet, some studies found that only about a third of managers sent on longer term foreign assignments received this type of training. Cultural training is designed to develop an appreciation for the host country culture that should help the manager deal with host country nationals. Considering that spouses and other family members also have difficulty adapting to new cultures, the entire family should receive cultural training prior to going on an assignment.

Given that English is the world language of business, is it important to get local language training? Relying exclusively on English limits a manager's ability to interact with host country nationals. Knowing even a little of the local language can help a manager build rapport with local employees. Practical training helps the manager and his/her family ease into the daily life of the new country. Having a support network of other expatriates can help with this process. But, studies show only about 30% of managers sent on one- to five-year expatriate assignments received training before their departure. One can begin to see why there is a high rate of expatriate failure, perhaps.

Training should include preparing and developing expatriate managers for re-entry (repatriation) into their home country organization. Once a manager has successfully completed a foreign assignment, a new set of challenges begins. The repatriation process can be just as difficult as going on the assignment in the first place. Sometimes, managers who have had lots of responsibility and autonomy while on assignment will return to find that they have no clear position waiting for them, or a position that doesn't really utilize the new skills they've developed. The home office job lacks the high degree of authority and responsibility that expatriates had in their overseas job. They may feel that the company does not value international experience, or they may no longer be well-known among people at headquarters. Their old job may have been eliminated or drastically changed. Technological advances at headquarters may have rendered their existing skills and knowledge obsolete.

One study showed that between 60 and 70 percent of repatriated employees had no idea what their position would be when they returned home. Firms have to prepare expatriates for their re-entry into their home country. Firms that do not have a programme in place that re-integrates employees into the home country organization may not be able to capitalize on the knowledge the expatriate gained while on assignment.

Monsanto as a global provider of agricultural products, and is an example of a firm that has developed a repatriation programme designed to avoid these problems. With 20,000 employees it usually has 100 middle managers abroad. They and their families all undergo a rigorous selection process and cross-cultural training. Each manager has an agreement about how the posting fits with business objectives, and the job opportunities on returning home. On returning home they are debriefed and also showcase their experiences to fellow managers in formal information exchanges. Monsanto also pays attention to returning families, and facilitates sessions to deal with the sorts of problems highlighted above.

Management Development

In contrast to management training, recall that management development focuses on increasing the overall skill levels of managers through management education and the rotation of managers through various positions in the firm. The goal is to develop managers with experience in a variety of areas. As one example amongst many, Ericsson, the Swedish telecommunications firm, transfers people back and forth between headquarters and subsidiaries as part of its management development programme. Management development can be used as a strategic tool to build a strong, unifying culture, and an informal management network. Both of these support a transnational or global standardization strategy. Management development programmes increase the overall skill levels of managers through ongoing management education, and rotations of managers through jobs within the firm to give them varied experiences. Management development can be a strategic tool to build a strong unifying culture and informal management network, both of which are supportive of a transnational and global strategy.

11.5 Performance Appraisal

Peng and Meyer (2011) define performance appraisal as the evaluation of employee performance for promotion, retention, or termination purposes. It is important not to confuse an employee on what a performance appraisal is! In some organizations the phrase is used to refer to appraisal solely for development purposes. Such an appraisal process must be separated from an appraisal for promotion, retention or termination purposes! Who should conduct the appraisal? What should it be based on? The performance of the subsidiary or the firm as a whole? Usually, two groups evaluate expatriate managers, host country managers and home country managers. However, biases creep in. Home country managers tend to rely on hard data when they evaluate expatriates. If a home country manager does not really know what is going on in the subsidiary, the manager may just look at numbers like profitability or market share, which may not give a good picture of what the subsidiary has actually accomplished. Think for example of how a simple change in exchange rates might affect a business unit's profit.

Host country managers can be biased toward their own frame of reference. Cultural differences for example, may affect how they interpret a manager's style, and could result in a negative evaluation. Problems with the evaluation process are so bad that a number of studies over the years show that a majority of managers surveyed often think that a foreign assignment could be either detrimental or immaterial to a manager's career. Evaluating expatriates can be especially complex. How can a firm do a better job with performance appraisal?

Many managers believe that more weight should be given to an on-site manager's appraisal than to an off-site manager's appraisal. In addition, including a former expatriate who has worked in the same location in the process could minimize bias. Finally, if an on-site manager is responsible for evaluation, the home office should be consulted prior to completing a termination evaluation.

11.6 Compensation

Another area of human resources that generates a lot of discussion is compensation. How much should a manager be paid? Should an American working in China be paid the same amount as his/her Chinese colleague in a similar position, or should he/she be paid what he/she earns at home in a similar position? A top US HR executive made an average of US$525,923 in the 2005-2006 period, compared to US$237,697 in Japan, and US$158,146 in Taiwan. Similar differences exist across all senior management jobs like CEO, CFO, CIO, for example. Is that fair? The question is: should pay be equalized across countries? Many firms have recently moved toward a compensation structure that is based on global standards. This is especially important in firms with a geocentric staffing policy, as suggested by Figure 11.3.

As one example, in 2003 McDonald's revamped its compensation and performance appraisal systems to create a system that is perceived by employees as being more equitable across borders. To achieve this, McDonald's instituted performance and compensation guidelines, yet left room for local managers to customize the program. However, many firms still set pay according to the prevailing standards in each country, though there has been a definite move in the last ten years towards more firms developing consistent global compensation structures, at least for their senior managers.

How, then, do firms pay expatriates? There seem to be two main approaches. The first is the going rate approach. This pays expatriates the going rate for comparable positions in a host country. Thus when Chinese firm Lenovo sends Chinese expatriates to New York, it pays them the going rate for comparable positions in New York. This has the merit of simplicity, and is attractive where the going-rate in the host country - the USA in this case - is higher than in China. But the going rate differs from country to country. For example, if the average US CEO in 2010 had a total compensation package of over US$2 million a year, the average British CEO receives less than US$1 million, the Japanese CEO US$500,000 and the Chinese CEO US$200,000. Repatriation from New York to Beijing could be difficult under the going rate approach!

Figure 11. 3
Compensation Approaches

Type of Company	Payment
Ethnocentric	How much home-country expatriates should be paid.
Polycentric	Pay can and should be country-specific.
Geocentric/Transnational	May have to pay its international cadre of managers the same.

Most international firms use a balance sheet approach to compensation. This method equalizes purchasing power across countries so that employees have the same standard of living as they had at home, plus a financial incentive for accepting the foreign assignment – see Figure 11.4.

On the left side of Figure 11.4 you can see how the salary is spent in the home country. This spending pattern in the home country is protected when the employee moves abroad as his company picks up the additional costs on taxes, housing, goods, and services (Figure 11.4, third column). The good news for the expatriate is that there is also typically a premium and incentives for moving abroad, also paid by the company. The advantages of this approach are that the expatriate has equity between assignments, and the approach facilitates repatriation. But the approach is costly, complex to administer, and creates big disparities between expatriate managers and their local peers in the host country. As you can see the overall package can be substantial, and this explains why there is a trend for not sending expatriates abroad unless there is a strong need for specialist skills, and even then the trend is towards as-needed trips rather than long postings. The further trend is towards developing a cadre of internationally mobile executives and phasing out special premiums and incentive payments altogether, and only dealing with cost-of-living issues when designing international pay packages.

Figure 11.4 Cost of expatriate managers

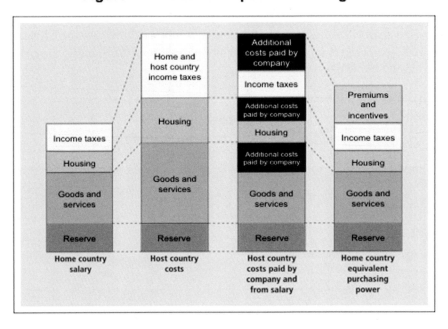

Expatriate compensation packages are usually made up of a base salary, a foreign service premium, various allowances, tax differentials, and benefits:

Base salary: expatriate base salaries are generally set in a similar range as the base salaries for similar positions in the home country.

Premium: expatriates are usually paid some sort of premium for taking on the foreign assignment ranging from 10 to 30 percent of the base salary.

Allowances: in addition, to the base pay and foreign service premium, expatriates usually also receive some allowances. There are four types of allowance – hardship, housing, cost-of-living, and education:

- *Hardship allowances are usually paid when the location of the assignment is particularly challenging and deficient by home country standards.*
- *Housing allowances are given so that the expatriate can have a similar standard of housing as he/she would have in the home country.*
- *Cost-of-living allowances are designed to equalize differences in living costs across countries.*
- *Education allowances ensure that children receive adequate schooling.*

Tax is also an issue. So that expatriates do not have to pay taxes in both the home country and the host country, firms will usually agree to pay host country taxes if the countries involved do not have a reciprocal tax treaty (see Figure 11.4). Finally, benefits packages are usually paid to make sure the expatriate has similar medical and pension benefits as he/she would get if he/she worked at home.

11.7 Labour Relations

In addition to dealing with the challenges of staffing foreign operations at the management level, firms must also deal with the local labour force. The key issue here is the degree to which organized labour is able to limit the choices available to international companies. Sometimes, labour unions can actually limit a firm's ability to follow a transnational or global standardization strategy. US motor giant GM, for example, at one stage was unable to consolidate its operations in the most efficient manner because labour unions objected to the proposed changes. What concerns organized labour?

1. A main concern for labour is that the MNE can essentially counter union bargaining power by threatening to move production to another country. Ford, for example, at one stage threatened to move production elsewhere in Europe when British workers were particular active in expressing their dissatisfaction.

2. Labour also worries that MNEs will only bring low-skilled tasks to foreign operations, and keep the high skilled tasks at home. By doing this, it is easier for a company to switch production to another country.

3. Another concern for labour is that MNEs will try to impose unfamiliar labour practices imported from other countries. Many Japanese companies have tried to bring their labour practices to foreign markets. In the USA for example, Japanese auto plants are not unionized.

Organized labour has responded to the increased bargaining power of multinational corporations by trying to establish their own international organizations; lobbying for national legislation to restrict multinationals; trying to achieve regulation of multinationals through international organizations such as the United Nations. So far, these efforts have had only limited success.

How do companies approach labour relations? In the past, companies usually delegated labour relations to individual subsidiaries. More recently, companies have been shifting to a centralized approach with the goal of increasing their bargaining power. Firms are realizing that how work is organized in a facility can be important to the firm's competitive advantage. You might think for example, of the advantages Japanese companies have as a result of their approach to labour. Many firms are centralizing labour relations to enhance the bargaining power of the multinational relative to organized labour. However, it is also true that the way in which work is organized within a plant can be a major source of competitive advantage so it is important for management to have a good relationship with labour.

A firm's management of labour relations is also very reliant on country specific factors and traditions. For example, labour unions have traditionally been strong in Germany. Unions set the pay scale for around 90 percent of the country's workers, with wages determined by job classifications. Union membership is voluntary, but there is only one union in each major industry. In Japan, union–management relationships are extremely cooperative; social custom dictates non-confrontational behaviour. In some northern European countries there are traditions of what is called industrial democracy: the legally mandated right of employees to participate in significant management decisions. Forms of industrial democracy include ***Codetermination*** – a legal system that requires workers and their managers to discuss major strategic decisions before companies implement the decisions. Also ***Work councils*** – groups that consist of both worker and manager representatives who are charged with dealing with matters such as improving company performance, working conditions, and job security.

In Germany, industrial democracy and codetermination are both very strong, especially in the steel and auto industries. In Denmark, industrial democracy gives workers the right to participate in management on both a direct and an indirect basis. Japan's use of industrial democracy concepts are not tied to political philosophy, as in Europe, but more oriented toward Japanese culture and the belief in group harmony.

11.8 Conclusion

International human resource management throws up distinctive challenges, and this chapter has chosen to focus on three major ones: IHRM policy types, the management of expatriates, and comparative labour relations. We detailed three policy approaches - ethnocentric, polycentric, and geocentric - their advantages and disadvantages, and when they are best used. We then assessed the challenges experienced by expatriate employees and concluded that a range of policies were required across recruitment and selection, training and development (not least to assist repatriation), performance appraisal, and compensation packages. Finally we brought attention to typical labour relations issues in the international arena.

Human resources is a difficult area to manage in domestic settings, but the challenges are even more complex when the firm is operating internationally. There is not just the question of policy on appointments – which we dealt with in this chapter. Nor is it just the issue of managing expatriates, or collaborating with organized labour. The problems are complex because the workforce goes to the heart of the business organization. It carries the culture of the organization, much of its codified knowledge and all of its tacit knowing, and as such people are integral to the formulation and performance of most organizational capabilities discussed in chapter 5. If this were not enough, then IHRM introduces the cultural and social diversity we detailed in chapter ??, as well as the need to deal with formal political, legal and economic institutions, and issues of corporate social responsibility we looked at in earlier chapters. Consider also that essentially management is achieving work through others. When these others are spread around the globe, have different attitudes, skills, motivations and behaviours, you begin to realise what I hope this book has made increasingly clear. Frederick Herzberg once said that every job should be a learning experience. Global business management provides such work, and is a challenging, fascinating, fast moving place to be.

A Guide to Further Reading

General

There are many texts on international business. The following have certain strengths, not least, all of them are quite detailed and give strong coverage of the area.

Rugman, A. and Collinson, S., 2012. *International Business*. 6th ed. London: FT Prentice Hall. This is a more advanced text, which I have used on Postgraduate MSc and MBA courses. It is particularly strong on regional analysis and detail.

Peng, M. and Meyer, K., 2011. *International Business*. New York: South Western, Cengage Learning. This is a book I have used on undergraduate courses. It is written more from a European perspective, but global in coverage, which is particularly good on putting forward an institution-based perspective on international business.

Hill, C., 2013. *International Business: Competing in The Global Marketplace*. 9th ed. New York: McGraw Hill. I have used this on third year undergraduate courses. This is a comprehensive text written from a more North American perspective, but global in coverage, which is particularly good at working in economic perspectives on the issues.

There are weekly and daily sources that cover global developments and business and management topics. Amongst these the following are very informative, and have regional versions, and/or regular special supplements.

- *The Economist* – which has weekly news and regular relevant special studies.
- *The Financial Times* – daily world commentary. Also has a backlog and regular regional and theme special issues.
- *The Wall Street Journal* – detailed daily world commentary.

The main journals for additional articles on globalization, business strategy, management and digital business are:

Academy of Management Executive, Academy of Management Review, Strategic Management Journal, Long Range Planning, Journal of Management Studies, Journal of International Business Studies, Journal of Management, Journal of Information Technology, Management Information Systems

Quarterly Executive, Journal of Strategic Information Systems, Organization Science, Management International Review, Harvard Business Review, Sloan Management Review and *California Management Review.*

Globalization and International Trade

Ghemawat, P., 2001. Distance Still Matters: The Hard Reality of Global Expansion. *Harvard Business Review*, December.

Nag, R., Hambrick, D. et al., 2007. What is Strategic Management Really? *Strategic Management Journal*, 28, pp.935-955.

Rugman, A. and Hodgetts, R. (2001) The End of Global Strategy. *European Management Journal*, 19, pp.333-343.

Peng, M. and Pleggenkuhle-Miles E., 2009. Current Debates in Global Strategy. *International Journal of Management Reviews*, 11(1),pp51-68.

Hill, C., 2013. *International Business: Competing in The Global Marketplace*. 9th ed. New York: McGraw Hill. Chapter 5

Case: Chowdary, N., Vivek, M. and Gonela, S., 2010. CEMEX's Cost of 'Globalised' Growth: The Cash Crunch? *European Case Clearing House*. Ref 310-016-1.

Ghemawat, P., 2007. *Redefining Global Strategy*. Boston: Harvard Business School Press.

Dickens, G., 2011. *Global Shift. Mapping the Changing Contours of the Global Economy*. 6th ed. London: Sage.

Hall, P. and Soskice, D., eds., 2001. *Varieties of capitalism*. Oxford: Oxford University Press.

Hafsi, T. and Thomas, H., 2005. The Field of Strategy. *European Management Journal*, 23, pp.507-519.

Yin, E. and Choi, C., 2005. The Globalization Myth. *Management International Research*. 45, pp.103-120.

Rivoli, P., 2005. *The Travels of a T-Shirt in the Global Economy*. Hokoben: Wiley.

Walter, A. and Sen, G., 2009. *Analysing the Global Political Economy*. Princeton: Princeton University Press.

Friedman, T., 2006. *The World Is Flat*. New York: Penguin.

Case: Lasserre, P. and Picoto, J., 2007. CEMEX: Cemex international strategy. *European Case Clearing House*. 06/2007, Ref-5451, 307-233-1.

International Business Strategy

Teece, D., Pisano, G. and Shuen, A., 1997. Dynamic Capabilities and Strategic Management.

Strategic Management Journal, 18, pp.509-533.

Porter, M., 1996. What Is Strategy? *Harvard Business Review*, 74(6), pp.61-78.

Peng, M., Wang, D. and Jiang, Y., 2008. An Institution-based view of International Business Strategy. *Journal of International Business*, 39, pp.920-936.

Teaching case: Khayat, N., 2010. Globalisation of Komatsu: Digging Out of Trouble. *European Case Clearing House*, Ref 310178-1.

Teaching case: Qumar, S., 2011. Alarm Ringing: Nokia in 2010. *European Case Clearing House*, Ref 3110541.

Case: Qumar, S., 2010. Toyota: The Once in a Century Challenge. *European Case Clearing House*, Ref 3100351.

Peng, M., 2001. The Resource Based View and International Business. *Journal of Management*, 27, pp.803-829.

Decker, C. and Mellewigt, T., 2007. Thirty Years After Michael E. Porter. *Academy of Management Perspectives*, 21, pp.41-55.

Barney, J., 2001. Is the Resource Based View a Useful Perspective For Strategic Management Research? *Academy of Management Review*, 26, pp.41-56.

Peteraf, M., 2003. The Foundation of Competitive Advantage: a resource-based view. *Strategic Management Journal*, 14, pp.179-191.

Spulber, D., 2007. *Competitive Strategy*. Cambridge: Cambridge University Press.

Segal-Horn, S. and Faulkner, D., 2010. *Understanding Global Strategy*. USA: Southwestern.

Case: Nell, P. et al., 2009. Pfizer and the challenges of the global pharmaceutical industry. *European Case Clearing House*, Ref 3100011.

Becoming International: Entry and Evolution

Cantwell, J. et al., 2010. An evolutionary approach to understanding international business activity. *Journal of International Business*, 41, pp.567-586.

Chen, S., 2010. A general TCE model of international business institutions: Market failure and reciprocity. *Journal of International Business*, 41, pp.935-949.

Hennart, J., 2010. Down with MNE-centric theories! Market entry and expansion as the bundling of MNE and local assets. *Journal of International Business*, 40, pp.1432-1454.

Teaching case: Chen, W. and Wu, K., 2009. Baidu and Google: Face Off in The Forbidden City. *European Case Clearing House*, Ref 309-090-1.

Rothaermal, F., Kotha, S. et al., 2006. International Market Entry by US Internet Firms. *Journal of Management*, 32, pp.56-82.

Hoffmann, W., 2007. Strategies For Managing A Portfolio of Alliances. *Strategic Management Journal*, 28, pp.827-856.

Khanna, T. and Palepu, K., 2006. Emerging Giants: Building World Class Companies In Developing Countries, *Harvard Business Review*, October, pp.60-69.

Dyer, J., 1997. Effective Interfirm Collaboration. *Strategic Management Journal*,18, pp.543-556.

McDougall, P. and Oviatt, B., 2000. International Entrepreneurship. *Academy of Management Journal*, 43, pp.902-906.

Dunning, J. and Lundan, S., 2008. *Multinational Enterprises and the Global Economy.* Cheltenham, UK: Edward Elgar Publishing.

Rugman, A. and Brewer, T., 2003. *The Oxford Handbook of International Business*. Oxford: Oxford University Press.

Teaching case: Lehmberg, D., 2011. Sharp Corporation: Beyond Japan. *European Case Clearing House,* Ref 9B11MOO7.

Teaching case: Prasad, N., 2010. Brilliance Auto: A Chinese automaker with Global Ambitions. *European Case Clearing House,* Ref 3100771.

Organizational Foundations for the Globalizing Business

Goold, M. and Campbell, A., 2002. Do You Have a Well Designed Organization? *Harvard Business Review*, 80(3), pp.117-124.

Malhotra, N. and Hinings, C., 2010. An organizational model for understanding internationalization processes. *Journal of International Business*, 41, pp.330-349.

Buckley, P. et al., 2009. The internalisation theory of the multinational enterprise: A review of the progress on a 30-year research agenda. *Journal of International Business,* 40, pp.1563-1580.

Teaching case: Leslie, S. and Sorenson J., 2010. Siemens: Building a structure to drive performance and responsibility cases (A) and (B). *European Case Clearing House,* SM181A and SM181B.

Technological Foundations for the Globalizing Business

Porter, M., 2001. Strategy and the Internet. *Harvard Business Review*, March.

Markus, L., 2004. Technochange Management: Using IT to Drive Organizational Change. *Journal of Information Technology*, 19, pp.4-20. Also in Willcocks and Lee (eds), 2008. *Major Currents in Information Systems.* Palgrave. Volume 4 paper 50.

Weill, P. et al., 2002. Building IT Infrastructure for Strategic Agility. *Sloan Management Review*, 44, 1.

Ross, J., 2003. Creating a Strategic Architecture Competency: Learning in Stages. *MISQ Executive*, 2, 1. Also in Willcocks and Lee (eds), 2008. *Major Currents in Information Systems.* Palgrave. Vol. 4, paper 49.

Blomkvist, K. et al., 2010. Quo vadis? The entry into new technologies in advanced foreign subsidiaries of the multinational enterprise. *Journal of International Business,* 41, pp.1525-1549.

Rangan, S. and Sengul, M., 2009. Information technology and transnational integration: theory and evidence on the evolution of the modern multinational enterprise. *Journal of International Business,* 40, pp.1496-1514.

Monteiro, E. and Hepso, V., 2002. Purity and Danger of and Information Infrastructure. *Systemic Practice and Action Research,* 15, 2.

Teaching case: Kumar, K. and Kumar M., 2008. SAP: Establishing A Research Centre in China. Asia Case Research Centre, University of Hong Kong. Ref 05/xxxc.

Burgelman R., Christensen, C. et al., 2009. *Strategic Management of Technology and Innovation.* New York: McGraw Hill.

Anand, N., Gardner, H. et al., 2007. Knowledge-Based Innovation. *Academy of Management Journal,* 50, pp.406-428.

Swanson, E. and Ramiller, N., 2004). Innovating Mindfully With Information Technology. *MIS Quarterly*, 28(4), pp.553-583.

Sorensen, C. and Lund-Snis, U., 2001. Innovation Through Knowledge Codification. *Journal of Information Technology*, 16, pp.83-97.

Lee, H. et al., 2004. Innovation Through Supply Chain Reconfiguration. *MISQ Executive,* 3.

Watts, S. and Henderson, J., 2006. Innovative IT Climates: CIO Perspectives. *Journal of Strategic Information Systems*, 15, pp.125-151.

Trott, P., 2008. *Innovation Management and New Product Development.* New York: Prentice Hall.

Alavi, M. and Leidner, D., 2001. Knowledge Management and Knowledge Management Systems: Conceptual Foundations and Research Issues. *MIS Quarterly*, 25(1), pp.107-136.

Jeyeraj, A. et al., 2006. A Review of the Predictors, Linkages and Biases In IT Innovation Adoption Research. *Journal of Information Technology*, 21, pp.1-23. Also in Willcocks and Lee (eds), 2008. Major Currents in Information Systems. Palgrave. Volume 4 paper 53.

Keil, M. and Mann, J., 2000. Why Software Projects Escalate: An Empirical Analysis of Four Theoretical Models. *MIS Quarterly*, 24(4), pp.631-664.

Ross, J. and Beath, C., 2006. Sustainable IT Outsourcing Success: Let Enterprise Architecture Be Your Guide. *MISQ Executive*, 5,4.

Pollock, N., Williams, R. and D'Adderio, L., 2007. Global Software and its Provenance. *Social Studies of Science*, 37, pp.254-280.

Avgerou, C., 2003. *Global Diversity and Information Systems.* Oxford: Oxford University Press.

Ross, J. and Beath, C., 2005. The Federal Broker Model at Dow Chemical Co.: Building World Class External and Internal Capabilities. *CISR* 355, Center for IS Research: MIT.

Ichijo, K. & Kohlacher, F., 2008. Tapping tacit local knowledge in emerging markets: the Toyota way. *Knowledge Management Research & Practice*, 6, pp.173-186.

Schulze, U. and Leidner, D., 2002. Studying knowledge management in Information systems research: discourses and theoretical assumptions. *MIS Quarterly*, 26(3), pp.213-235.

Watson, H.J., Wixom, B.H., Hoffer, J.A., Anderson-Lehman, R. and Reynolds, A.M., 2006. Real-time business intelligence: Best practices at Continental Airlines. *Information Systems Management*, Winter, 7-18.

Managing Across Boundaries - Contexts, Managements, Cultures

Kirkman, B., Lowe, K. et al., 2006. A Quarter Century of Culture's Consequences. *Journal of International Business Studies*, 37, pp.285-320.

Johnson, J., Lenartowicz, T. et al., 2006. Cross-Cultural Competence in International Business. *Journal of International Business Studies*, 37, pp.525-543.

Ghemawat, P., 2007. *Redefining Global Strategy: Crossing Borders in a World Where Differences Still Matter.* Chapter 2: The Differences Across Countries: CAGE distance framework. Boston: Harvard Business Press.

Johnson, G., Whittington, R. and Scholes, K., 2011. *Exploring Strategy*. London: Prentice Hall. Ch.5.

Tung, R. et al., 2010. Beyond Hofstede and GLOBE: Improving the quality of cross-cultural research. *Journal of International Business,* 41, pp.1259-1274.

Lichtenstein, N., 2010. In the age of Wal-Mart: Precarious work and authoritarian management in the global supply chain. In C. Thornley, S. Jefferys, and B. Appay *Globalization and Precarious Forms of Production and Employment: Challenges for Workers and Unions.* Cheltenham, UK: Edward Elgar Publishing. pp.10-22.

Clegg, S., Carter, C., Kornberger, M., and Schweitzer, J., 2011, International and Collaborative Strategies in *Strategy: Theory and Practice.* Thousand Oaks, CA: Sage. Ch.10, pp.321-358. See also Ch.12.

Hartman, L.P. and Werhane, P.H., 2009. *The Global Corporation: Sustainable, Effective and Ethical Practices (A Case Book)* New York & London: Routledge. Ch.2, "Merck Co., Inc." (A), section 2.2. And "Nike". Ch.6, section 6.2.

Teaching case: Roberts, M., 2010. Lundbeck Korea: Managing an international growth engine. *European case clearing house*, Ref 9B10MO12.

Teaching case: Taj H., F. et al., 2009. Cairn India Ltd: Globalisation versus government intervention. *European Case Clearing House,* Ref 3102561.

Teaching Case: Dwesar, R., 2011. Bharti Airtel: Going Global. *European Case Clearing House,* Ref 3110511.

Leung, K., Bhagat, R. et al., 2005. Culture and International Business. *Journal of International Business Studies,* 36, pp.357-378.

Mintzberg, H., 2009. *Managing.* London: Financial Times.

Hales, C., 1999. Why Do Managers Do What They Do? *British Journal of Management,* 10(4), pp.335-350.

Hooker, J., 2003. *Working Across Cultures.* Stanford: Stanford University Press.

Brewer, P., 2010. Globe practices and values: a case of diminishing marginal utility? *Journal of International Business,* 41, pp.1316-1324.

Sucher, S. et al., 2011. Global diversity and inclusion at Royal Dutch Shell (B) the impact of restructuring. *European Case Clearing House,* Ref 9611051.

Heracleous, L., 2003. Types of inter-organizational networks and the strategic role of directors. *Strategy and Organization: Realizing strategic management,* Cambridge UK: Cambridge University Press. pp.184-210.

Bechky, B., 2003. Sharing meaning across occupational communities: The transformation of understanding on the production floor, *Organization Science* 14, pp.312-330.

Bowker, G. and Star, S.L., 1999. *Sorting Things Out: Classification and its Consequences.* Cambridge MA: MIT Press.

Carlile, P.R., 2004: Transferring, translating, and transforming: An integrative framework for managing knowledge across boundaries, *Organization Science,* 15(5), pp.555-568.

Wenger, E., 1998. *Communities of Practice: Learning, Meaning and Identity.* Cambridge, UK: Cambridge University Press.

Ellingsen, G. and Monteiro, E., 2003: A patchwork planet: Integration and cooperation in hospitals, *Computer Supported Cooperative Work,* 12, pp.71-95.

Vaast, E. and Walsham, G., 2009. Trans-situated learning: Supporting a network of practice with an information infrastructure, *Information Systems Research,* 20(4), pp.547-564.

Levina, N. and Vaast, E., 2005. The emergence of boundary spanning competence in practice: Implications for implementation and use of information systems, *Management Information Systems Quarterly,* 29(2), pp.335-364.

Walsham, G., 2001. *Making a world of difference: IT in a global context.* Chichester: Wiley.

Krishna, S., Sahay, S. and Walsham, G., 2004. Managing cross-cultural issues in global software outsourcing, *Communications of the ACM,* 47(4), pp.62-66.

Hartman, L.P. and Werhane, P.H., 2009. *The Global Corporation: Sustainable, Effective and Ethical Practices (A Case Book).* New York & London: Routledge. Ch.7.

Oborn, E. and Barrett, M., 2010. Boundary object use in cross-cultural software development teams, *Human Relations*, 63(8), pp.1199-1221.

Menipaz, E and Menipaz, A., 2011. *International Business,* Thousand Oaks, CA: Sage. Ch. 3 and 12.

Galan, J.I. and Sanchez-Bueno, M.J., 2009. Strategy and structure in context: Universalism versus institutional effects, *Organization Studies,* 30(6), pp.609-27.

Hitt, M.A., Tihanyi, L., Miller, T. and Connelly, B., 2006. International diversification: Antecedents, outcomes and moderators, *Journal of Management,* 32, pp.831-867.

Morgan, G. and Kristensen, P.H., 2006. The contested space of multi-nationals: Varieties of institutionalism, varieties of capitalism, *Human Relations,* 59, pp.1167-1490.

Johnson, G., Whittington, R. and Scholes, K., 2011. *Exploring Strategy: Text and Cases.* 9th ed. Harlow UK: FT Prentice Hall, Pearson. Ch.5.

Hartman, L.P. and Werhane, P.H., 2009. *The Global Corporation: Sustainable, Effective and Ethical Practices (A Case Book).* New York & London: Routledge.

Global Sourcing and Logistics

Oshri, Kotlarsky, J. and Willcocks, L., 2012. *The Handbook of Global Outsourcing and Offshoring,* 2nd ed. London: Palgrave.

Levy, D., 2005. Offshoring In The New Global Political Economy. *Journal of Management Studies,* 42, pp.685-693.

Willcocks, L., Reynolds, P. and Feeny, D., 2008. Evolving IS Capabilities To Leverage The External IT Services Market. *MISQ Executive,* 6(3), pp.127-145.

Trent, R. and Monczka, R., 2005. Achieving Excellence in Global Sourcing. *Sloan Management Review,* 47, 1.

Gottfredson, M., Puryear, R. and Phillips, S., 2005. Strategic Sourcing. *Harvard Business Review,* February, pp.132-139.

Oshri, I., 2009. Captive Center Strategy: Two Cases. (Available from Leslie Willcocks, free of charge for educational purposes).

Keerthy, B., 2005. Outsourcing Innovation: Opportunities and Challenges. IBSCDC paper available from www.ecch.com.

Liu, R. et al., 2011. Why are different services outsourced to different countries. *Journal of International Business,* 42, pp.558-571.

Teaching case: Larsen, M.M. et al., 2010. The Lego Group: An Outsourcing Journey, *European Case Clearing House,* Ref 9B10M094.

Gregorio, D. et al., 2009. Offshore outsourcing as a source of competitiveness for SMEs. *Journal of International Business*, 40, pp.969-988.

Farrell, D., 2005. Offshoring: Value Creation Through Economic Change. *Journal of Management Studies*, 42, pp.675-683.

Rossetti, C. and Choi, T., 2005. On The Dark Side of Strategic Sourcing. *Academy of Management Executive*, 19(1), pp.46-60.

Cousins, P., Lamming, R. et al., 2010. *Strategic Supply Management: Principles Theory and Practice*. London: Prentice Hall.

Gottfredson, M., Puryear, R. and Phillips, S., 2005. Strategic Sourcing, *Harvard Business Review*, February, pp.132-139.

Parmigiani, A., 2007. Why Do Firms Both Make and Buy? *Strategic Management Journal*, 28, pp.285-311.

Stanko, M., Bohlmann, J. and Calentone, R., 2009. Outsourcing innovation. *Sloan Management Review*, November.

Ross, J., 2006. Enterprise Architecture: Driving Business Benefits From IT. *CISR Working Paper*, Center for IS Research: MIT.

Cousins, P., Lamming, R. et al., 2010. *Strategic Supply Management: Principles Theory and Practice*. London: Prentice Hall.

Carmel, E. and Agarwal, R. The Maturation of Offshore Sourcing of IT Work. In Willcocks and Lee. eds., 2008. *Major Currents in Information Systems*. London: Sage. Vol. 4, paper 57.

Rottman, J. and Lacity, M., 2006. Proven Practices for Effectively Offshoring IT Work. *Sloan Management Review*, 47(3), pp. 56-63.

Managing Across Boundaries - Leadership, HR, Teams, Projects

Stall, G., et al., 2010. Unravelling the effects of cultural diversity in teams. *Journal of International Business*, 41, pp.690-709.

Rodrigues, R. and Guest, D., 2010. Have careers become boundaryless? *Human Relations,* 63(8), pp.1157-1175.

Hartman, L.P. and Werhane, P.H., 2009. *The Global Corporation: Sustainable, Effective and Ethical Practices (A Case Book)*. New York & London: Routledge. Ch.9 "Leadership".

Barrett M. and Oborn E., 2008. Global sourcing in a developing country context: organizing IS resources to develop local knowledge. In Heinzl, A., Hirschheim, R., Winkler, J. and Dibbern, J. eds., 2006. *Information Systems Outsourcing: Enduring themes, new perspectives and global challenges*. 3rd ed. Berlin Heidelberg: Springer.

Sahay, S., Nicolson, B. and Krishna. S., 2003. Managing the knowledge transfer process: the case of Sierra and its Indian subsidiary. *Global IT Outsourcing: Software development across borders.* Cambridge, UK: Cambridge University Press. pp132-154.

Sahay, S., Nicolson, B. and Krishna, S., 2003. Cross-cultural communication challenges: GSAs between Japanese and Indian firms. *Global IT Outsourcing: Software development across borders.* Cambridge: Cambridge University Press. pp.176-202.

Oshri, I., Kotlarsky, J. and Willcocks, L.P., 2009. *The Handbook of Global Outsourcing and Offshoring.* Basingstoke, UK: Palgrave Macmillan. Ch.9, Case study 3 (BAE Systems).

Koster, K., 2010. *International Project Management.* Thousand Oaks, CA: Sage. Ch.6 and 8.

Teaching case: Singh, J., 2011. GE Healthcare A) and B). *European Case Clearing House,* Refs 3110481 and 3110491.

House, R., Hanges, P. et al., 2004. *Culture, Leadership and Organizations.* Thousand Oaks, CA: Sage.

Kotlarsky, J., van Fenema, P.C. and L.P. Willcocks, 2008. Developing a Knowledge-Based Perspective on Coordination: The Case of Global Software Projects. *Information & Management,* 45(2), pp.96-108.

Adler, N. and Gundersen, A., 2008. *International Dimensions of Organizational Behaviour.* Cincinnati: South Western.

Kumar, K. et al., 2009. Offshoring and the global distribution of work. *Journal of International Business,* 40, pp.642-657.

Katsikeas, C., 2009. Developing successful trust-based international exchange relationships. *Journal of International Business,* 40, pp.132, 155.

Heracleous, L., 2003. Types of inter-organizational networks and the strategic role of directors. *Strategy and Organization: Realizing strategic management.* Cambridge, UK: Cambridge University Press. pp.184-210.

Bechky, B., 2003. Sharing meaning across occupational communities: The transformation of understanding on the production floor. *Organization Science* 14, pp.312-330.

Bowker, G. and Star, S.L., 1999. *Sorting Things Out: Classification and its consequences* Cambridge MA: MIT Press.

Carlile, P.R., 2004. Transferring, translating, and transforming: An integrative framework for managing knowledge across boundaries. *Organization Science,* 15(5), pp.555-568.

Wenger, E., 1998. *Communities of Practice: Learning, Meaning and Identity.* Cambridge, UK: Cambridge University Press.

Ellingsen, G. and Monteiro, E., 2003. A patchwork planet: Integration and cooperation in hospitals. *Computer Supported Cooperative Work,* 12, pp.71-95.

Vaast, E. and Walsham, G., 2009. Trans-situated learning: Supporting a network of practice with an information infrastructure. *Information Systems Research.* 20(4), pp.547-564.

Levina, N. and Vaast, E., 2005. The emergence of boundary spanning competence in practice: Implications for implementation and use of information systems. *Management Information Systems Quarterly,* 29(2), pp.335-364.

Walsham, G., 2001. *Making a world of difference: IT in a global context.* Chichester: Wiley.

Krishna, S., Sahay, S. and Walsham, G., 2004. Managing cross-cultural issues in global software outsourcing. *Communications of the ACM,* 47(4), pp.62-66.

Hartman, L.P. and Werhane, P.H., 2009. *The Global Corporation: Sustainable, Effective and Ethical Practices (A Case Book).* New York & London: Routledge. Ch.7.

Regional Business Strategies and International Trade

Rugman, A. and Verbeke, A., 2004. A Perspective On Regional and Global Strategies of Multinational Enterprises. *Journal of International Business Studies*, 35, pp.3-18.

Ghemawat, P., 2007. Managing Differences: The Central Challenge of Global Strategy. *Harvard Business Review,* March, pp.42-55.

Ghemawat, P., 2005. Regional Strategies For Global Leadership. *Harvard Business Review,* December.

Teaching case: Dwesar, R., 2011. Bharti Airtel: Going Global. *European Case Clearing House.* Ref 3110511.

Davies, H. and Ellis, P., 2001. Porter's Competitive Advantage of Nations. *Journal of Management Studies*, 37, pp.1189-1215.

Eisenmann, T., 2006. Internet Companies' Growth Strategies. *Strategic Management Journal,* 27, pp.1183-1204.

Hill, C., 2013. *International Business: Competing in the Global Marketplace.* 9th ed. New York: McGraw Hill. Ch. 2, p.8.

Europe – see Rugman and Collinson (2012); Suder, G. (2008) *Business In Europe,* Los Angeles: Sage.

Cool, K. et al., 2011. AXA and the non-life insurance industry in Europe in 2010. *European Case Clearing House*, Ref 3110241.

China: see Rugman and Collinson, 2012 c Ramamurti, R., 2010. Review of 'Getting China and India Right', *Journal of International Business*, 41, pp.557-60.

Japan: see Rugman and Collinson, 2012. Sharp: Beyond Japan. *European Case Clearing House,* Cranfield.

North America: see Rugman and Collinson, 2012.

Latin America and Emerging Economies: Rugman and Collinson, 2012.

Meyer, K., 2004. Perspectives on multinational Enterprises in Emerging Economies. *Journal of International Business*, 34, pp.259-277.

Khaire, M. et al., 2011. Globant. *European Case Clearing House,* Ref 9811519 (Argentina)

India: Gupta A. and Wang, H., 2008. *Getting China and India Right.* Hoboken: Wiley. *Journal of International Business* (2010) – April special issue on Asia and Global Business; Industrial and Corporate Change (2009) 18(2) special issue on The Internationalization of Indian and Chinese Firms. Vijay, T., 2010. Apple iPhone In India: Emotionally connected versus product-price performance disconnected? *European Case Clearing House,* Ref 3100411.

Korea: Dadwal, T. et al., 2009. Cyworld, South Korea's social networking site's global expansion strategies. *European Case Clearing House,* Ref 3072621.

Middle East: Alcacer J. et al., 2010. Vodafone Qatar: Building a telco in the Gulf. *European Case Clearing House,* Ref 9711414.

References

AMA The Definition of Marketing, 2007, American Marketing Associationg. http://www.marketingpower.com/AboutAMA/Pages/DefinitionofMarketing.aspx. Retrieved 2011-04-04.

Ansoff, H. (1988) *Corporate Strategy*, London: Penguin.

Barney, J. (2001) Is the Resource Based View a Useful Perspective For Strategic Management Research? *Academy of Management Review*, vol. 26, pp. 41-56.

Bartlett, C. A. and Ghoshal, S. (1998) *Managing Across Borders: The Transnational Solution*, Boston: Harvard Business School Press.

Bhagwati, J. (2004) *In Defence of Globalization*, Oxford: Oxford University Press,.

Buckley, P. et al (2009) The internalisation theory of the multinational enterprise: A review of the progress on a 30 year research agenda, *Journal of International Business*, vol. 40, pp. 1563-1580.

Cantwell, J. et al (2010) An evolutionary approach to understanding international business activity, *Journal of International Business*, vol. 41, pp. 567-586.

Carmel, E. and Abbott, D. (2007) Why nearshore means that distance matters, *Communications of the ACM*, vol. 50, no. 10, pp. 40-46.

Chandler, A. (1962) *Strategy and Structure* (p. 13), Cambridge, MA: MIT Press.

Collings, D. and Scullion, H. (2009) **Special issue** on Global Staffing, *International Journal of Human Resources Management*, vol. 20, no. 6, pp. 1249-1450.

Cullen, S. Seddon, P. and Willcocks, L. (2005) Managing The Outsourcing Lifecycle Imperative, *MISQ Executive*, vol. 4, no. 1, pp. 229-24.

Davies, H. and Ellis, P. (2001) Porter's Competitive Advantage of Nations, *Journal of Management Studies*, vol. 37, pp. 1189-1215.

Decker, C. and Mellewigt, T. (2007) Thirty Years After Michael E. Porter, *Academy of Management Perspectives*, vol. 21, pp. 41-55.

Dicken, P. (2007) *Global Shift: Mapping the Changing Contours of the World Economy*, London: Sage.

Dunning, J. and Lundan, S. (2009) *Multinational Enterprises and the Global Economy*, 2nd edition, Cheltenham: Elgar.

Farrell, D. (2006) Smarter Offshoring, *Harvard Business Review*, pp. 85-92.

Fonstad, N. and Subramani, M. (2009) Building Enterprise Alignment: A Case Study, *MISQ Executive*, vol. 8, no. 1, pp. 31-41.

Friedman, M. (1970) The Social Responsibility of Business is to Increase Profits, *The New York Times Magazine*, September 13th.

Friedman, T. (2007) *The World Is Flat*, 3rd edition, New York: Picador.

Ghemawat, P. (2010) Strategy and The Business Landscape. International Edition, 3rd edition, Boston: Pearson. Chapter 7 on Developing A Global Strategy.

Ghemawat, P. (2001) Distance Still Matters: The Hard Reality of Global Expansion, *Harvard Business Review*, December.

Ghemawat, P. (2007) Managing Differences: The Central Challenge of Global Strategy, *Harvard Business Review*, March, pp. 42-55.

Ghemawat, P. (2005) Regional Strategies For Global Leadership. *Harvard Business Review*, December.

Gottfredson, M., Puryear, R. and Phillips, S. (2005) Strategic Sourcing, *Harvard Business Review*, February, pp. 132-139.

Hall, P. and Soskice, D. (eds.) (2001) *Varieties of Capitalism*, Oxford: Oxford University Press.

Hennart, J. (2010) Down with MNE-centric theories! Market entry and expansion as the bundling of MNE and local assets, *Journal of International Business*, vol. 40, pp. 1432-1454.

Hill, C. (2013) *International Business: Competing in The Global Marketplace*, 9th edition, New York: McGraw Hill. ISBN 9780071220835.

Hitt, M. D., Ireland,D. and Hoskisson,R. (2003) *Strategic Management*, 5th edition, p. 9, Cincinnati: Thomson South-Western.

Hoffmann, W. (2007) Strategies For Managing A Portfolio of Alliances, *Strategic Management Journal*, vol. 28, pp. 827-856.

Hofstede, G. (1997) *Cultures and Organizations*, New York: McGraw Hill.

House, P., Hanges, M., Javidan, P. et al (2004) *Culture, Leadership and Organizations*, California: Thousand Oaks.

Huntingdon, S. (1996) *The Clash of Civilizations and the Remaking of World Order*, New York: Simon and Schuster.

Johnson, G., Whittington, R. and Scholes, K. (2012) *Exploring Corporate Strategy*, 9th edition, London: Prentice Hall.

Kettinger, W. et al, (2010) Designing Enterprise IT Architectures to Optimize Flexibility and Standardization in Global Business, *MISQ Executive*, June, vol. 9, no. 2.

Khanna, T. and Palepu, K. (2006) Emerging Giants: Building World Class Companies In Developing Countries, *Harvard Business Review*, October, pp. 60-69.

Keerthy, B. (2005) Outsourcing Innovation: Opportunities and Challenges. IBSCDC Paper available from www.ecch.com

Kovasznai D. and Willcocks, L. (2012) Escalation in Global Outsourcing Projects – The Expertrans-C&C BPO case. *JIT Teaching Cases*, pp. 1-7.

Kumar, K. and Kumar M. (2008) SAP: Establishing A Research Centre in China, *Asia Case Research Centre*, University of Hong Kong, Ref 05/xxxc, (VLE).

Lacity, M. and Willcocks, L. (2012) Sourcing Information Technology Services: A Review of the Evidence, LSE Outsourcing Unit Research Paper, London.

Lee, H. (2007) Factors that influence expatriate failure, *International Journal of Management*, vol. 24, pp. 403-15.

Larsen, et al (2010) The Lego Group: An Outsourcing Journey, *European Case Clearing House*, Ref 9B10M094.

Lasserre, P. and Picoto, J. (2007) CEMEX: Cemex international strategy, *Case Clearing House* – 06/2007-5451, 307-233-1. (VLE)

Laudon, K. and Laudon, J. (2012) *Management Information Systems: Managing The Digital Firm*, 12th edition, London: Pearson. Chapter 15 available on the web at www.pearsonglobaleditions. com/laudon

Levy, D. (2005) Offshoring In The New Global Political Economy, *Journal of Management Studies*, vol. 42, pp. 685-693.

Liu, R. et al (2011) Why are different services outsourced to different countries, *Journal of International Business*, vol. 42, pp. 558-571.

Luftman, J., Zadeh, H., Derkesen, B. et al (2011-12) Key Information Technology and Management Issues: An international study, *Journal of Information Technology*, vol. 26, no. 3, pp. 1-15.

Mendenhall, M. and Oddou, G. (1985) The dimensions of expatriate acculturation: a review, *Academy of Management Review*, vol. 10, pp. 39-47.

Mintzberg, H. (2009) *Managing*, London: Prentice Hall/FT.

North, D. (2005) *Understanding the Process of Economic Change*, Princeton: Princeton University Press.

Ohlin, B. (1933) *Interregional and International Trade*, Cambridge, MA: Harvard University Press.

Oshri, Kotlarksy and Willcocks (2012) *Handbook of Global Outsourcing and Offshoring*, 2nd edition, London: Palgrave. ISBN 9780230293526.

Oster, S. (1994) *Modern Competitive Analysis,* 2nd edition, New York: Oxford University Press, p. 4.

Peng, M. and Pleggenkuhle-Miles E. (2009) Current Debates in Global Strategy. *International Journal of Management Research.*

Peng, M. (2001) The Resource Based View and International Business, *Journal of Management,* vol. 27, pp. 803-829.

Peng, M., Wang, D. and Jiang, Y. (2008) An Institution-based view of International Business Strategy, *Journal of International Business,* vol. 39, pp. 920-936.

Porter, M. (1996) What is strategy? *Harvard Business Review,* Nov-Dec vol. 74(6) pp.61-78.

Peng, M. and Meyer, K. (2011) *International Business,* London: Cengage Learning, South Western. 1408019566

Peng, M. (2009) *Global Strategic Management,* 2nd International Edition, UK: Cengage.

Peteraf, M. (2003) The Foundation of Competitive Advantage: a resource based view, *Strategic Management Journal,* vol. 14, pp. 179-191.

Qumar, S. (2010) Toyota: The Once in a Century Challenge, *European Case Clearing House,* case 310-035-1.

Ronen and Shenkar (1985) Clustering Countries on Attitudinal Dimension, *Academy of Management Review,* vol. 10, pp. 435-454.

Ross, J. (2003) Creating a Strategic IT Architecture Competence: Learning in Stages, *MISQ Executive,* March, vol. 2, no. 1, pp. 31-43.

Rothaermal, F., Kotha, S. et al (2006) International Market Entry by US Internet Firms, *Journal of Management,* vol. 32, pp. 56-82.

Rugman, A. and Collinson, S. (2012) *International Business,* 6th edition, London: FT Prentice Hall. ISBN 9780273716549.

Rugman, A. and Hodgetts, R. (2001) The End of Global Strategy, *European Management Journal,* vol. 19, pp. 333-343.

Sen, A. (1999) *Development As Freedom,* London: Anchor Publishing.

Shpilberg, D., Berez, S., Puryear, R. et al (2007) Avoiding the Alignment Trap in Information Technology, *Sloan Management Review,* Fall, vol. 49, no. 1, pp. 50-58.

Teece, D., Pisano, G. and Shuen, A. (1997) Dynamic Capabilities and Strategic Management, *Strategic Management Journal,* vol. 18, pp. 509-533.

Trent, R. and Monczka, R. (2005) Achieving Excellence in Global Sourcing, *Sloan Management Review,* vol. 47, p. 1.

Trompenaars, F. (1993) *Riding The Waves of Culture: Understanding Cultural Diversity of Business,* London: Nicholas Brealey.

Tung, R. (1982) Selection and Training Procedures of US, European and Japanese Multinationals, *California Management Review,* vol. 25, pp. 57-71.

Vasishtha, A. and Khan, I. (2008) Top 50 emerging global outsourcing cities, http://epam.com

Vasishtha, A. and Ravago, M. (2010) Top 100 – a study of the top outsourcing cities. http://www.globalservicesmedia.com/News/Home/top-100

Vernon, R. (1966) International investments and international trade in product life cycle, QJE, pp.190-207, May.

Vivek and Gonela (2010) Cemex's Cost of Globalised Growth: The Cash Crunch? *European Case Clearing House,* Ref 3100161.

Willcocks, L. (2011) Take the Outsourcing Health Check, *Professional Outsourcing Magazine,* issue 7, pp. 6-12.

Willcocks, l., Petherbridge, P. and Olson, N. (2003) *Making IT Count: Strategy, Delivery, Infrastructure,* Oxford: Butterworth Heinemann. Chapter 2.

Willcocks, L. and Griffiths, C. (2010) The Crucial Role of Middle Management in Outsourcing, *MISQ Executive*, vol. 9, no. 3, pp. 177-193.

Willcocks, L. and Lacity, M. (2012) *The New IT Outsourcing Landscape*, London: Palgrave.

Willcocks, L., Reynolds, P. and Feeny, D. (2008) Evolving IS Capabilities To Leverage The External IT Services Market, *MISQ Executive*, vol. 6, no. 3, pp. 127-145._

Williamson, O. (1985) *The Economic Institutions of Capitalism*, New York: Free Press.

Yin, E. and Choi, C. (2005) The Globalization Myth, *Management International Research,* vol. 45, pp. 103-120.